Philip Phillips

Hallowed Songs

For Prayer and Social Meetings

Philip Phillips

Hallowed Songs

For Prayer and Social Meetings

ISBN/EAN: 9783337181826

Printed in Europe, USA, Canada, Australia, Japan

Cover: Foto ©Thomas Meinert / pixelio.de

More available books at **www.hansebooks.com**

Hallowed Songs.

(NEWLY REVISED.)

BY

PHILIP PHILLIPS.

FOR

PRAYER AND SOCIAL MEETINGS.

Containing Hymns and Tunes, carefully selected from all sources, both old and new, and are of the most spiritual and reviving character, adapted also to

Divine Worship.

Mission churches, and those who are not able to provide the large Hymn and Tune Books, will find in this Collection 300 of the most precious Hymns in the English language, set to appropriate Tunes, making a *neat little Hymn and Tune Book*, for the *Choir* and Congregation, in which *all the people* can be supplied at a very *small expense;* also

Sabbath Schools,

who may use this book, will not only avoid *light, meaningless Hymns and Tunes*, but will also grow up to love and join the Service of Song in the Sanctuary; and old and young will thereby be taught to love and praise God together.

———∞◦∞———

New York, 37 Union Square, Broadway:
PHILIP PHILLIPS.

CINCINNATI, CHICAGO, AND ST. LOUIS:
HITCHCOCK & WALDEN.

PREFACE.

IN revising "Hallowed Songs," it will be seen that I have dropped all duplicated tunes (68 in number), and placed in their stead *new* and *popular tunes*, and have also adopted a shape and size most durable and convenient for use, thereby making the REVISED EDITION a *neat little Hymn and Tune Book* for the *Sanctuary*, *Prayer Meeting*, and *Sabbath School*. New churches, which are constantly being established throughout our great country, will find in this work a fine variety of *choice* Hymns and Tunes, suited to all occasions in religious worship, at a *very small expense*.

PHILIP PHILLIPS.

Revised Edition, entered according to Act of Congress, in the year 1870,
By PHILIP PHILLIPS,
In the Clerk's Office of the District Court of the United States for the Southern District of New York.

PRACTICAL SUGGESTIONS.

Singing in the Prayer-meeting.

After the opening exercises (which usually consist of Singing, Reading the Scriptures, and Prayer), let the singing assume more of an impromptu style, but of a deeply spiritual and prayerful character. Let the verse or Hymn be wisely adapted to whatever phase of Christian experience seems to pervade the meeting at the time, and promptly sung *instantly* at the close of the prayer or remarks.

Be sure never to sing, unless you have something apropos, or feel that the singing will bless some heart.

Should the meeting be dull, sing more frequently, but not too many verses, and never so often as to give the meeting more of a singing than a prayerful aspect.

Every Prayer Room should be well supplied with books—"Hallowed Songs" of the most spiritual and reviving character.

Good spiritual singing, from the heart, will render a Prayer Meeting *attractive, interesting*, and above all, *profitable*.

Singing in the Sanctuary.

The first requisite is to provide books from which all the people may be able to sing intelligently. There should be at least one book for every two worshipers.

Hold stated Singing Meetings for the purpose of rehearsing the Hymns and Tunes for the coming Sabbath, and for general improvement in Singing.

Urge *all* the people to attend these meetings, and let the music be under the direction of the chorister.

By adhering to the above simple suggestions, Congregational Singing can be successfully introduced.

Singing in the Sabbath School.

After a selection is made and order observed, let the Superintendent or Chorister announce some song, having direct reference to the lesson of the day, or circumstances of the occasion.

Then lay every thing else aside, and let all present engage heartily in singing the hymn.

Never sing in Sunday School for amusement merely, but let the songs of praise and salvation be not only instructive, but also full of Gospel. Use more of the substantial and Standard Hymns and Tunes, such as are used in churches, and sing them from the heart, with promptness and lively animation.

The right song, sung with the right spirit, at the right time, will have the right effect.

Classified Index,

GIVING THE FIRST LINES OF A FEW PROMINENT HYMNS UNDER EACH OF THE FOLLOWING SUBJECTS:

Opening and Closing.

	PAGE		PAGE
A charge to keep	272	Out on an ocean	69
And are we yet	284	Oh, for a closer walk	235
Bless us to-night	22	Prayer is the soul's	233
Bright home of	154	Prayer is appointed	241
Come, thou fount	27	Responsive Scripture	312
Come, let us join	234	Shall we gather at	108
From every stormy wind	248	When shall we	66
In mercy, Lord	224	Where do you journey	121
Lord, dismiss us	49	What various hindrances	244
My days are gliding	72		

Faith and Prayer.

	PAGE		PAGE
Am I a soldier of	228	My soul be on	287
Did Christ o'er	278	Oh, for a faith	220
From every stormy	248	Oh, for a heart	221
How pleased and	301	Oh, how happy are they	302
Long my spirit	140	Oh, for a glance	265
Lord, in the morning	225	Softly on the breath	182
My faith looks up	23	Sweet hour of prayer	25

Exhortation and Revivals.

	PAGE		PAGE
Alas! and did	14	Say, sinner, hath a voice	243
Come, come to Jesus	9	Show pity, Lord	250
Come, humble sinner	214	Stay, thou insulted	267
Come, ye sinners	35	There is a fountain	10
Hasten, sinner, to	288	To-day the Saviour	187
Oh, that my load of	251	Why not to-night	8

Humility and Guidance.

	PAGE		PAGE
Consecration hymn	56	Holy Spirit, faithful guide	7
Dear comrade	192	Nearer, my God, to thee	23
Go and tell Jesus	196	Saviour, like a shepherd	28
God has said	162	Sun of my soul	260
Guide me, O thou	74	Silently the shades	283
He leadeth me	178	With me abide	20

Mission and Temperance.

Disciples of Jesus	116	The morning light	52
From Greenland's icy	51	Weep for the fallen	146
From all that dwell	237	What are you going to do	168
Soon may the last glad	255	Working for the	128

Christmas and Thanksgiving.

All hail the power	208	Hark, what means	40
Before Jehovah's awful	240	Here freedom spreads	265
Bless, O my soul, the	238	Hark, the herald angels	294
Come, let us tune	238	Jesus shall reign	241
Christ, the Lord, is	294	Majestic sweetness	211

Anniversary and Rejoicing.

Blest be the tie	284	Jesus, lover of my soul	291
Blest are the sons	285	My country, 'tis of	293
God bless our native	299	Soldiers of Christ	250
How beauteous are	230	Welcome, sweet day	282
I now have found abiding	12		

Jesus' Cross and Crown.

A crown of glory	170	I hear the Saviour say	296
Beautiful cross	42	Jesus, I my cross	39
Go and tell Jesus	196	Jesus is mine	45
Hark, the gospel	156	Must Jesus bear	218
In the cross of Christ	17	Sweetest note in	297
I will sing for	110	When I survey the	261

Bible and Heaven

Blessed Bible, how	153	On the cross where Christ	104
I'm but a stranger	61	There is an hour	58
I will sing you	114	There is a land of	229
I am waiting by the	21	There's a light in	175
My latest sun	174	Think of a home over there	202
No sorrow there	54	Who are these	68

Classified Index.

God, Praise and Duty.

	PAGE		PAGE
All hail the	208	God is the refuge	239
Blow ye the trumpet	30	Jesus shall reign	241
Battling for the Lord	160	Majestic sweetness	211
Congregational Chorus	98	Work, for the night	120
Come, brethren, don't	76		

Infant Class and Solos.

I gave my life for thee	308	Jesus is here	206
I'm trying to climb	124	Let me go	112
I'm working for the	128	Mary Magdalene	57
I'm kneeling at	136	O happy day	79
Jesus loves me	46	Pilgrim's Mission	310
Jesus the water	138	We are out on	194

Affliction and Death.

Asleep in Jesus	262	Oh, for the death	276
Come, ye disconsolate	33	Oh, why should gloomy	215
Did Christ o'er	278	Though trouble assail	63
Earth's stormy night	90	With me abide	20
Just as I am	32	Why should our tears	232
Jesus, let thy	36	When we pass through	83

Entirely New and Very Old Tunes.

All to Christ I owe	206	No sorrow there	54
Bright Home	151	Old Hundred	240
Christ at the Wheel	62	Outside the Gate	130
Christian Union	41	Pilgrim's Mission	310
Cleansing Fountain	10	Resolution	214
Cling to the mighty One	118	Rest for the weary	166
Consecration Hymn	56	Safe within the vail	80
Dalston	301	That blessed Name	306
De Fleury	60	That will be joyful	164
Eltham	82	The Convert	302
Evening Shadows	148	The Further Shore	83
Greenville	49	The old, old Story	141
I'm kneeling at the Door	136	The sweetest Name	297
Joyfully, joyfully	172	Why not to-night	8
Loved ones gone before	44	Who's like Jesus	95
Lovest thou me	290	Will you go	86
Lyons	63	With me abide	20
More like Jesus	97	Woodland	58
Mount Vernon	67	Working for the Master	125

Hallowed Songs, Revised.

GUIDE. 7s.

M. M. Wells.

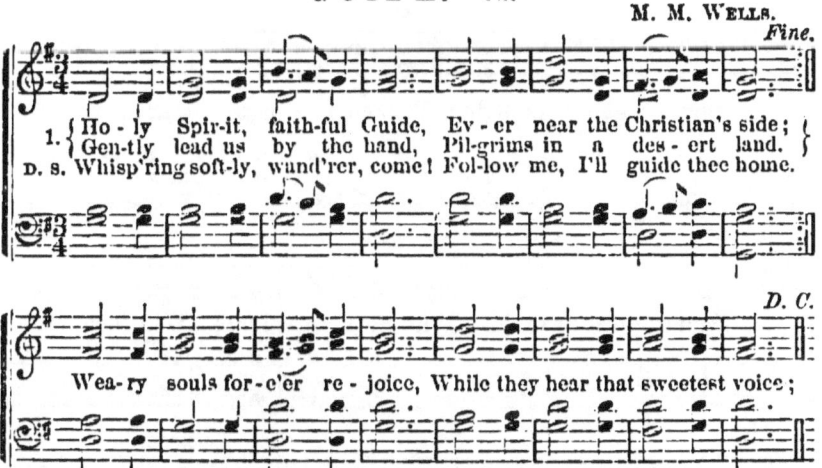

No. 1.   *"He will guide us into all truth."*

2 Ever present, truest friend,
Ever near, thine aid to lend,
Leave us not to doubt and fear,
Groping on in darkness drear,
When the storms are raging sore,
Hearts grow faint and hopes give o'er;
Whisper softly, wanderer, come!
Follow me, I'll guide thee home.

3 When our days of toil shall cease,
Waiting still for sweet release,
Nothing left but heaven and prayer,
Wondering if our names are there;
Wading deep the dismal flood,
Pleading naught but Jesus' blood;
Whisper softly, wanderer, come!
Follow me, I'll guide thee home.

PHILIP PHILLIPS.

1. Oh! do not let the word de - part, And close thine
eyes a-gainst the light; Poor sin-ner, hard - en not thy heart;
p
f
p affetuoso.
Thou wouldst be sav'd— Why not to night? Why not to -
slower.
night? Why not to-night? Thou wouldst be sav'd—Why not to-night?

No. 2.

"Choose ye this day whom ye will serve."

2 To-morrow's sun may never rise
  To bless thy long-deluded sight;
This is the time! oh, then be wise!
  Thou wouldst be saved—Why not to-night?

3 The world has nothing left to give—
  It has no new, no pure delight;
Oh, try the life which Christians live!
  Thou wouldst be saved—Why not to-night?

4 Our God in pity lingers still,
  And wilt thou thus his love requite?
  Renounce at length thy stubborn will,
  Thou wouldst be saved—Why not to-night?

5 Our blessed Lord refuses none
  Who would to him their souls unite;
  Then be the work of grace begun!
  Thou wouldst be saved—Why not to night?

JESUS WAITS FOR THEE.

H. P. MAIN.

1. Come, come to Je-sus! He waits to welcome thee, O Wand'rer! ea-ger-ly; Come, come to Je-sus!

No. 3. *"Ye would not come to me that ye might have life."*

2 Come, come to Jesus!
  He waits to ransom thee,
  O Slave! eternally;
  Come, come to Jesus!

3 Come, come to Jesus!
  He waits to lighten thee,
  O Burdened! graciously;
  Come, come to Jesus!

4 Come, come to Jesus!
  He waits to give to thee,
  O Blind! a vision free;
  Come, come to Jesus!

5 Come, come to Jesus!
  He waits to shelter thee,
  O Weary! blessedly;
  Come, come to Jesus!

6 Come, come to Jesus!
  He waits to carry thee,
  O Lamb! so lovingly;
  Come, come to Jesus!

CLEANSING FOUNTAIN. C. M.

1. There is a fountain filled with blood, Drawn from Imman-uel's veins, And sin-ners plunged beneath that flood, Lose all their guilt-y stains; Lose all their guilt-y stains, Lose all their guilt-y stains; And sin-ners plunged beneath that flood, Lose all their guilt-y stains.

No. 4.

2 The dying thief rejoiced to see
  That fountain in his day;
And there may I, though vile as he,
  Wash all my sins away.

3 E'er since by faith I saw the stream
  Thy flowing wounds supply,

Redeeming love has been my theme,
  And shall be till I die.

4 Then in a nobler, sweeter song
  I'll sing thy power to save,
When this poor, lisping, stammering
  Lies silent in the grave. [tongue

ETERNAL LIFE.

Wouldst thou be saved? no time to lose; A-rise, and run the heavenly road;
Wouldst thou be blest? then, pilgrim, haste To leave destruction's dread abode.

Chorus. O come! (O come!) the Sav-iour calls, "I am the way, the truth, the life;" Come hith-er, bur-dened soul, to me.

No. 5. *"Fight the good fight of faith; lay hold on eternal life."*

Pilgrim.
Oh, tell me how! oh, tell me where!
The way I long have sought to know;
But fear the guilt and sin I bear
Will sink me in the depths of woe. *Cho.*

Evangelist.
God's word will guide thee; dost thou see
A light from yonder distant hill?
On, Pilgrim, on! it shines for thee,
With steady course pursue it still. *Cho.*

Pilgrim.
God's word shall guide me; yes, I see
A light from yonder distant hill;
Oh, tell me, does it shine for me?
Hail, glorious light! I will, I will! *Cho.*

Pilgrim.
Farewell, a long farewell to those
Who seek to stay me as I fly;
My ears against their call I close,
Life, life, eternal life! my cry. *Cho.*

NOTE.—*This song may be sung as a Duet between the Teachers and the School; or when rendered as Solos (in dialogue), the Chorus should be sung from another room, or gallery out of sight, as an echo.*

ABIDING REST.

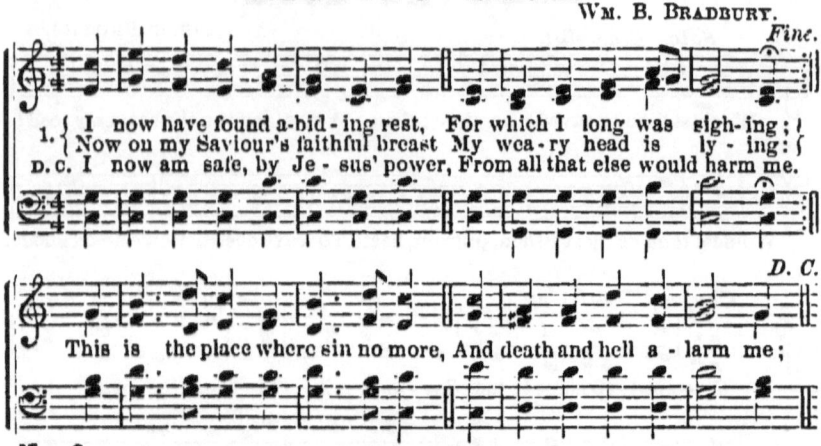

No. 6. *"I write unto you, little children, because your sins are forgiven you for his name's sake."*

2 He whispers me—"I'm wholly thine,
    And thou art mine forever;
Henceforth all fear and doubt resign,
    Confiding in my favor;
Thy every want shall find supply
    From my exhaustless treasure;
I'll fill thy spirit with my joy,
    The pledge of endless pleasure."

3 From Jesus and his love, who now,
    By terrors to divide me,
My great and many sins would show!
    His wounds from vengeance hide me:
My sins are great—I'll not despair,
    Though conscience, too, arraigns me,
Nor doubt my Saviour's watchful care—
    His arms of love sustain me.

4 I thank thee, God's beloved Son,
    Thy boundless grace adoring,
Which brought thee from thy glorious throne,
    Our peace with God restoring;
Oh, make my heart a shrine, where peace
    Shall keep her constant dwelling!
Where grateful praise shall never cease,
    Abroad thy glories telling.

THE RIVER OF LIFE.

PHILIP PHILLIPS.

No. 7. *"And he showed me a pure river of water of life, clear as a crystal, proceeding out of the throne of God and of the Lamb."*

    2 Oh, drink of this river, its full crystal flood
      Refreshes and lightens of sin's weary load;
      Its ripples ne'er mix with the billows of strife,
      This is the "Pure River of Water of Life."

    3 This beautiful river our boast well may be,
      'Tis fresh, overflowing, and better, 'tis free;
      The sin-sick rejoice in this "peace-speaking" tide,
      This river is Jesus, the "once crucified."

ALAS! AND DID MY SAVIOUR BLEED?

S. J. VAIL.

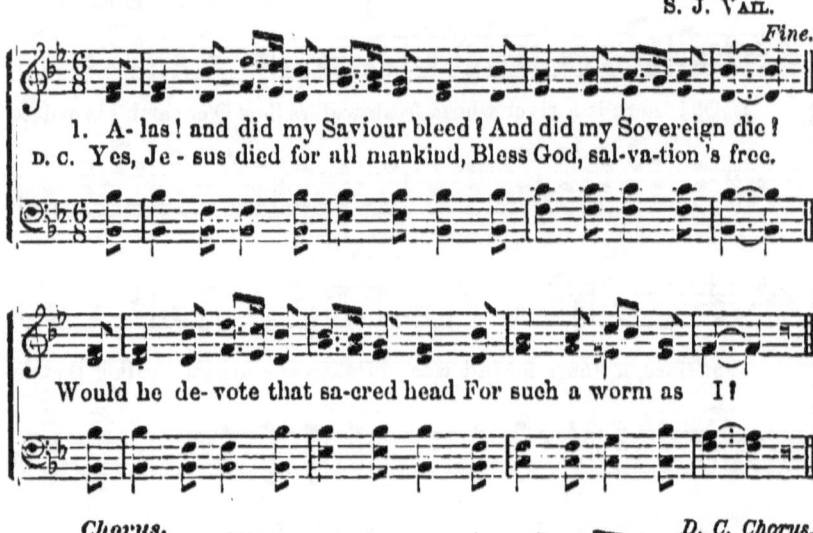

1. A-las! and did my Saviour bleed? And did my Sovereign die?
D. C. Yes, Je-sus died for all mankind, Bless God, sal-va-tion's free.

Would he de-vote that sa-cred head For such a worm as I!

Chorus.   D. C. Chorus.
Je-sus died for you;   Je-sus died for me;

No. 8.

2.
Was it for crimes that I had done,
  He groaned upon the tree?
Amazing pity! grace unknown!
  And love beyond degree.—*Cho.*

3.
Well might the sun in darkness hide,
  And shut his glories in,
When Christ, the mighty Maker, died,
  For man, the creature's sin.—*Cho.*

4.
Thus might I hide my blushing face
  While his dear cross appears;
Dissolve my heart in thankfulness,
  And melt mine eyes to tears.—*Cho.*

5.
But drops of grief can ne'er repay
  The debt of love I owe;
Here, Lord, I give myself away,
  'Tis all that I can do.—*Cho.*

Hallowed Songs, Revised. 15

EVEN ME.
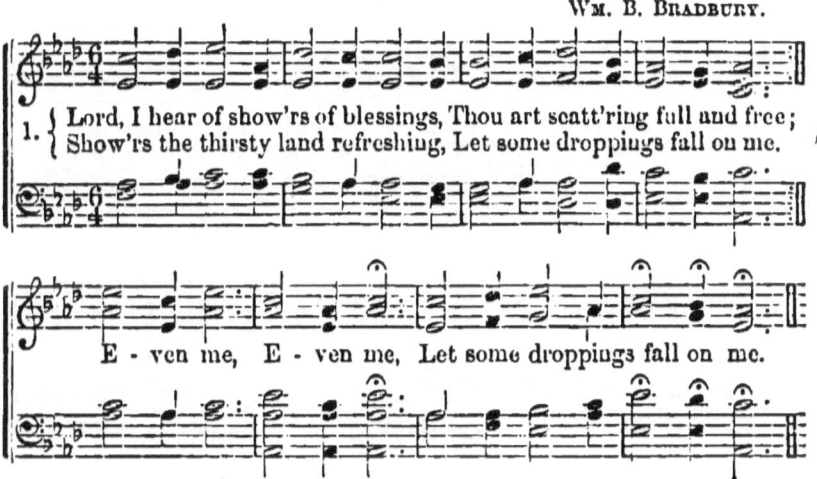

Wm. B. Bradbury.

1. Lord, I hear of show'rs of blessings, Thou art scatt'ring full and free; Show'rs the thirsty land refreshing, Let some droppings fall on me.
E - ven me, E - ven me, Let some droppings fall on me.

No. 9.

2 Pass me not, O God, my Father,
  Sinful though my heart may be;
Thou mightst leave me, but the rather,
  Let thy mercy fall on me—Even me.

3 Pass me not, O gracious Saviour,
  Let me live and cling to thee:
Fain I'm longing for thy favor:
  Whilst thou 'rt calling, call for me—Even me.

4 Pass me not, O mighty Spirit,
  Thou canst make the blind to see:
Witnesses of Jesus' merit,
  Speak the word of power to me.

5 Love of God, so pure and changeless;
  Blood of Christ, so rich and free;
Grace of God, so rich and boundless,
  Magnify it all in me—Even me.

6 Pass me not, thy lost one bringing;
  Bind my heart, O Lord, to thee;
Whilst the streams of life are springing,
  Blessing others, oh, bless me—Even me.

JESUS PAID IT ALL.

WM. B. BRADBURY.

1. Naught of mer-it or of price, Re-mains to jus-tice due;
Je - sus died, and paid it all,— Yes, all the debt I owe.

Chorus.
Je - sus paid it all, ... All the debt I owe,
Je - sus paid it, paid it all,
Je - sus died and paid it all, Yes, all the debt I owe.

No. 10.

2 When he from his lofty throne,
  Stoop'd down to do and die,
 Every thing was fully done;
  "'Tis finished!" was his cry.
 Jesus paid it all, &c.

3 Weary not, O toiling one,
  Whate'er thy conflict be,
 Work for him with cheerful heart,
  Who suffered all for thee.
 Jesus paid it all, &c.

Hallowed Songs, Revised.   17

4 Clinging to the Saviour's cross,
  Look up by simple faith,
  Praise him for the pardoning love
  That saves from endless death.
    Jesus paid it all, &c.

5 Bring a willing sacrifice—
  Thy soul to Jesus' feet;
  Stand in him, in him alone,
  All glorious and complete.
    Jesus paid it all, &c.

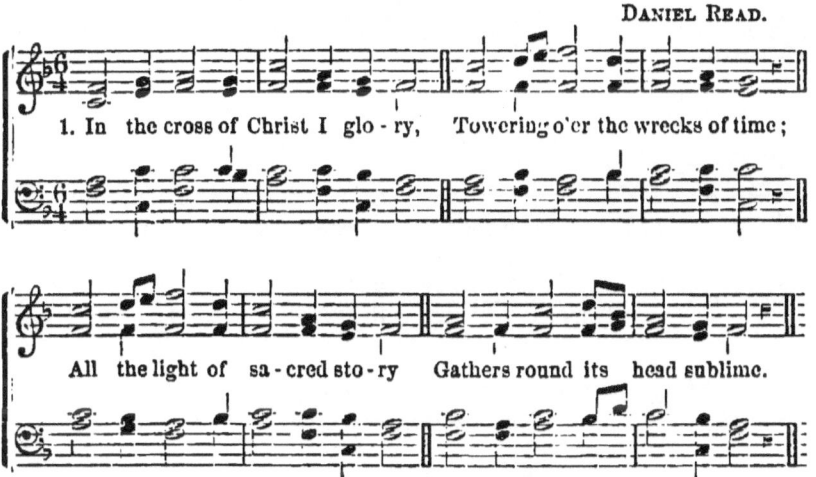

No. 11. "*God forbid that I should glory, save in the cross of our Lord.*"

2 When the woes of life o'ertake me,
    Hopes deceive, and fears annoy,
  Never shall the cross forsake me:
    Lo! it glows with peace and joy.

3 When the sun of bliss is beaming
    Light and love upon my way,
  From the cross the radiance streaming
    Adds new lustre to the day.

4 Bane and blessing, pain and pleasure,
    By the cross are sanctified;
  Peace is there, that knows no measure,
    Joys that through all time abide.

THE PILGRIM INVITED.

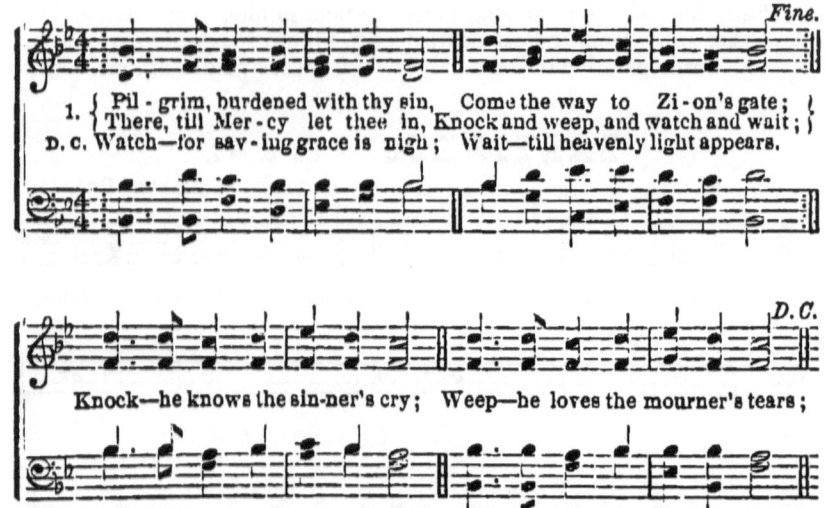

1. { Pil - grim, burdened with thy sin, Come the way to Zi - on's gate;
    There, till Mer - cy let thee in, Knock and weep, and watch and wait; }
D. C. Watch—for sav - ing grace is nigh; Wait—till heavenly light appears.

Knock—he knows the sinner's cry; Weep—he loves the mourner's tears;

No. 12. *" Turn, turn ye, for why will ye die ?"*

2 Hark! it is the Bridegroom's voice:
　Welcome, pilgrim, to thy rest;
　Now within the gate rejoice,
　　Safe and sealed, and bought and blest:
　Safe—from all the lures of vice;
　　Sealed—by signs the chosen know;
　Bought—by love and life the price;
　　Blest—the mighty debt to owe.

3 Holy pilgrim! what for thee
　In a world like this remain?
　From thy guarded breast shall flee
　　Fear and shame, and doubt and pain:
　Fear—the hope of heaven shall fly;
　　Shame—from glory's view retire;
　Doubt—in certain rapture die;
　　Pain—in endless bliss expire.

OH, HOW I LOVE JESUS.*

No. 13.
2 How can I forget thee,
 How can I forget thee
 How can I forget thee,
 Dear Lord, remember me.

* *May be sung after any hymn, where thought proper.*

WITH ME ABIDE.

Arr. by PHILLIPS.

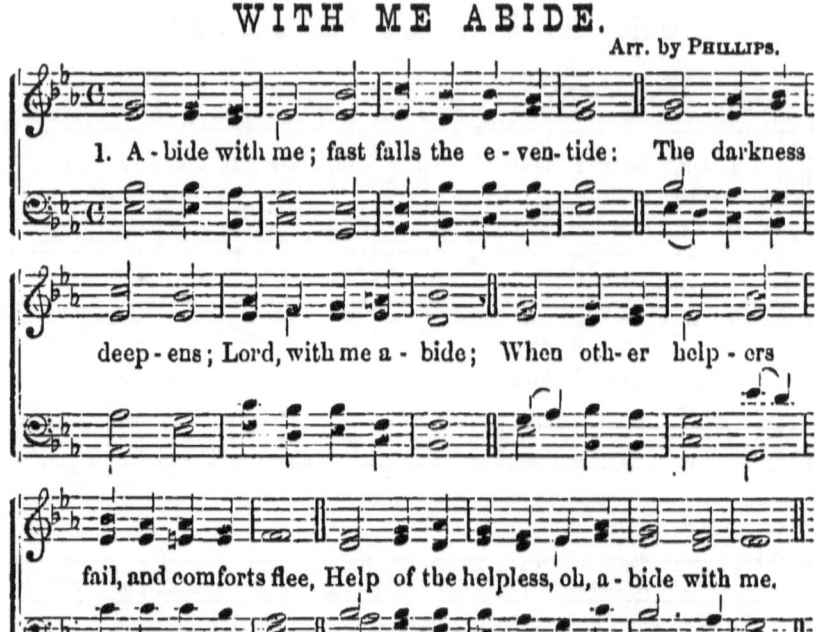

1. A-bide with me; fast falls the e-ven-tide: The darkness deep-ens; Lord, with me a-bide; When oth-er help-ers fail, and comforts flee, Help of the helpless, oh, a-bide with me.

No. 14. *"Abide with us; for it is towards evening, and the day is far spent."*

2 Swift to its close ebbs out life's little day;
Earth's joys grow dim, its glories pass away;
Change and decay in all around I see,
O thou who changest not—abide with me.

3 Thou on my head in early youth didst smile,
And, though rebellious and perverse meanwhile,
Thou hast not left me oft as I left thee;
On to the close, O Lord, abide with me.

4 I need thy presence every passing hour,
What but thy grace can foil the tempter's power;
Who like thyself my guide and stay can be,
Through clouds and sunshine—oh, abide with me.

5 Hold on thy cross before my closing eyes;
Shine through the gloom, and point me to the skies;
Heaven's morning breaks, and earth's vain shadows flee,
In life and death, O Lord, abide with me.

WAITING BY THE RIVER.

DR. THOS. HASTINGS.

1. I am wait-ing by the riv-er, And my heart has waited long;
Now I think I hear the cho-rus Of the an-gels' welcome song;
Oh, I see the dawn is breaking On the hill-tops of the blest,
"Where the wicked cease from troubling, And the weary be at rest."

No. 15. "*There shall be no more death.*"

2.
Far away beyond the shadows
Of this weary vale of tears,
There the tide of bliss is sweeping
Thro' the bright and changeless years;
Oh! I long to be with Jesus,
In the mansions of the blest,
"Where the wicked cease from troubling,
And the weary be at rest."

3.
They are launching on the river,
From the calm and quiet shore,
And they soon will bear my spirit
Where the weary sigh no more;
For the tide is swiftly flowing,
And I long to greet the blest,
"Where the wicked cease from troubling,
And the weary be at rest."

BLESS US TO-NIGHT.

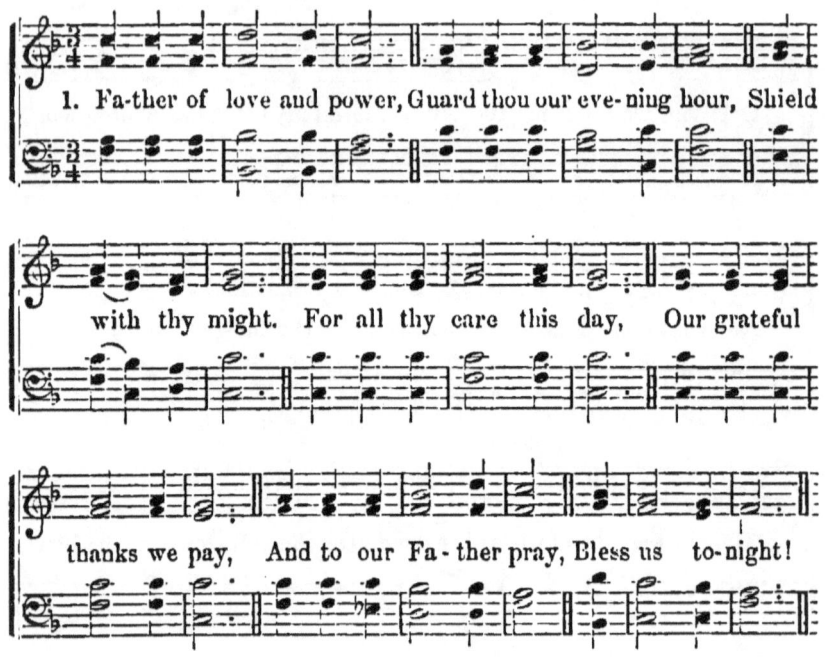

1. Fa-ther of love and power, Guard thou our eve-ning hour, Shield with thy might. For all thy care this day, Our grateful thanks we pay, And to our Fa-ther pray, Bless us to-night!

No. 16. *"He will bless them that fear the Lord."*

2 Jesus, Emmanuel,
  Come in thy love to dwell
    In hearts contrite;
  For many sins we grieve,
  But we thy grace receive,
  And in thy word believe,—
    Bless us to-night.

3 Spirit of truth and love,
  Life-giving, holy dove,
    Shed forth thy light;
  Heal every sinner's smart,
  Still every throbbing heart,
  And thine own peace impart,—
    Bless us to-night.

NEW HAVEN. 6s & 4s.

Dr. Thos. Hastings.

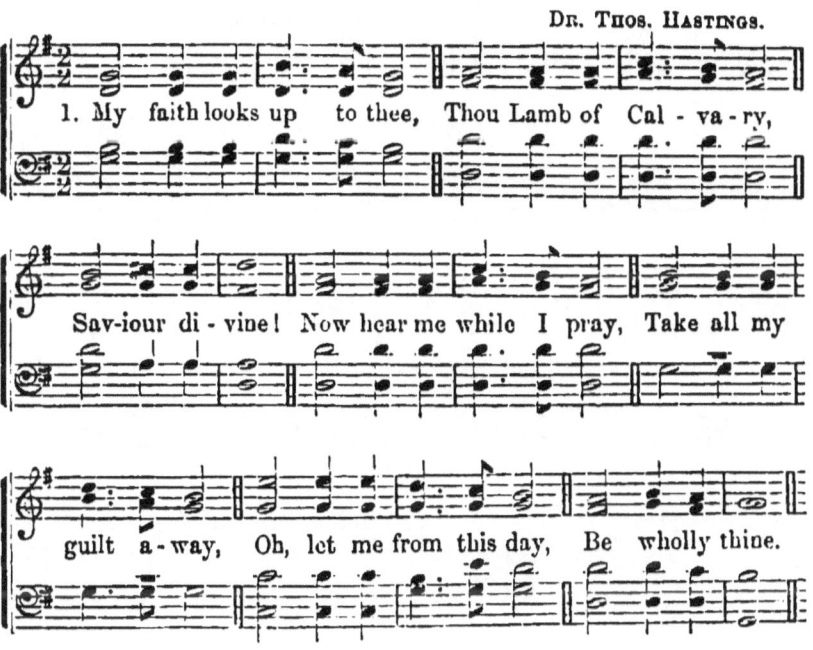

1. My faith looks up to thee, Thou Lamb of Cal-va-ry, Sav-iour di-vine! Now hear me while I pray, Take all my guilt a-way, Oh, let me from this day, Be wholly thine.

No. 17.   "*Have faith in God.*"

2 May thy rich grace impart
Strength to my fainting heart;
My zeal inspire :
As thou hast died for me
Oh, may my love to thee
Pure, warm, and changeless be—
A living fire.

3 While life's dark maze I tread,
And griefs around me spread,
Be thou my guide;
Bid darkness turn to day ;
Wipe sorrow's tears away,
Nor let me ever stray
From thee aside.

MACEDONIAN CRY.

Arr. by Philip Phillips.

1. Yes, my native land, I love thee; All thy scenes, I love them well;
Friends, connections, happy country! Can I bid you all farewell?
Can I leave you—Can I leave you, Far in heathen lands to dwell?

No. 18. *"Come over into Macedonia, and help us."*

2 Yes, I hasten from you gladly,
From the scenes I lov'd so well—
Far away, ye billows, bear me;
Lovely native land, farewell!
Pleased I leave thee,
Far in heathen lands to dwell.

3 In the desert let me labor;
On the mountains let me tell
How he died—the blessed Saviour—
To redeem a world from hell!
Let me hasten,
Far in heathen lands to dwell.

4 Bear me on, thou restless ocean;
Let the winds my canvass swell—
Heaves my heart with warm emotion,
While I go far hence to dwell.
Glad I bid thee,
Native land, Farewell! farewell!

SWEET HOUR OF PRAYER.

WM. B. BRADBURY *

1. Sweet hour of prayer! sweet hour of prayer! That calls me from a world of care. And bids me at my Father's throne Make all my wants and wish-es known: In sea-sons of dis-tress and grief, My soul has oft-en found re-lief;
D. C. And oft escaped the tempter's snare By thy re-turn, sweet hour of prayer; And oft es-caped the tempt-er's snare By thy re-turn, sweet hour of prayer.

No. 19. "*Evening, morning, and noon will I pray.*"

2. ‖: Sweet hour of prayer! :‖
Thy wings shall my petition bear
To him, whose truth and faithfulness
Engage the waiting soul to bless ;
And since he bids me seek his face,
Believe his word, and trust his grace,
‖: I'll cast on him my every care,
And wait for thee, sweet hour of prayer! :‖

3. ‖: Sweet hour of prayer! :‖
May I thy consolation share,
Till from Mount Pisgah's lofty height
I view my home, and take my flight:
This robe of flesh I'll drop, and rise
To seize the everlasting prize;
‖: And shout, while passing thro' the air,
Farewell, farewell, sweet hour of prayer! :‖

* From "*Fresh Laurels,*" by permission of BIGLOW & MAIN.

MERIBAH. C. P. M.

Dr. LOWELL MASON.

1. When thou, my righteous Judge, shalt come To take thy ransomed people home, Shall I a-mong them stand? Shall such a worthless worm as I, Who sometimes am a-fraid to die, Be found at thy right hand?

No. 20. *Pleading for acceptance.*

2 I love to meet thy people now,
Before thy feet with them to bow,
  Though vilest of them all:
But—can I bear the piercing tho't?—
What if my name should be left out,
  When thou for them shalt call?

3 O Lord, prevent it by thy grace;
Be thou my only hiding-place,
  In this, th' accepted day;
Thy pardoning voice, oh, let me hear,
To still my unbelieving fear,
  Nor let me fall, I pray.

4 Let me among the saints be found
Whene'er the archangel's trump shall sound,
  To see thy smiling face;
Then loudest of the crowd I'll sing,
While heaven's resounding mansions ring
  With shouts of sovereign grace.—*Ovington's Sel.*

Hallowed Songs, Revised. 27

NETTLETON. 8s & 7s. Double.
Dr. Nettleton.

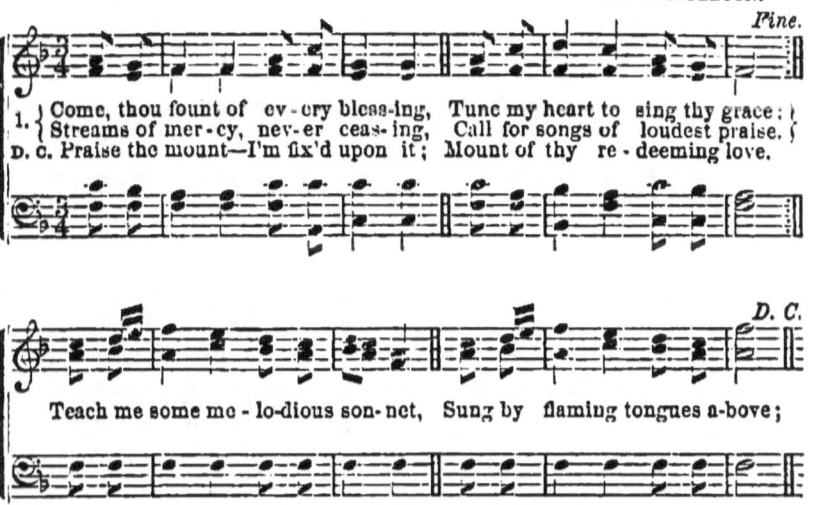

1. Come, thou fount of ev-ery bless-ing, Tune my heart to sing thy grace;
Streams of mer-cy, nev-er ceas-ing, Call for songs of loudest praise.
D. C. Praise the mount—I'm fix'd upon it; Mount of thy re-deeming love.

Teach me some me-lo-dious son-net, Sung by flaming tongues a-bove;

No. 21. *"God is a spirit; and they that worship him must worship him in spirit and in truth."*

2 Here I'll raise mine Ebenezer;
Hither by thy help I'm come;
And I hope, by thy good pleasure,
Safely to arrive at home.
Jesus sought me when a stranger,
Wand'ring from the fold of God.
He, to rescue me from danger,
Interposed his precious blood.

3 Oh! to grace how great a debtor
Daily I'm constrained to be!
Let thy goodness, like a fetter,
Bind my wand'ring heart to thee;
Prone to wander, Lord, I feel it,—
Prone to leave the God I love;
Here's my heart, oh, take and seal it;
Seal it for thy courts above.

GUIDE US, SHEPHERD. 8s, 7s & 4s.

Wm. B. Bradbury.

1. Sav-iour, like a shepherd lead us, Much we need thy tend'rest care;
In thy pleasant pastures feed us, For our use thy folds pre-pare.
Blessed Je-sus, Blessed Je-sus, Thou hast bought us, thine we are;
Blessed Je-sus, Blessed Je-sus, Thou hast bought us, thine we are.

No. 22.   *"Saviour, like a shepherd lead us."*

2 We are thine, do thou befriend us,
  Be the Guardian of our way;
Keep thy flock, from sin defend us,
  Seek us when we go astray.
    Blessed Jesus,
Hear, oh, hear us, when we pray.

3 Thou hast promised to receive us,
  Poor and sinful though we be;
Though hast mercy to relieve us,
  Grace to cleanse, and power to free.
    Blessed Jesus,
We will early turn to thee.

4 Early let us seek thy favor,
  Early let us do thy will;
Blessed Lord and only Saviour,
  With thy love our bosom fill.
    Blessed Jesus,
Thou hast loved us, love us still.

NEARER, MY GOD, TO THEE. (Bethany.) 6s & 4s.*
DR. LOWELL MASON.

No. 23.

2 Though like a wanderer,
    Daylight all gone,
  Darkness be over me
    My rest a stone,
  Yet in my dreams I'd be
    Nearer, my God, &c.

3 There let the way appear,
    Steps up to heaven;
  All that thou sendest me
    In mercy given,
  Angels to beckon me,
    Nearer, my God, &c.

4 Then with my waking thoughts,
    Bright with thy praise,
  Out of my stony griefs,
    Bethel I'll raise;
  So by my woes to be
    Nearer, my God, &c.

5 Or, if on joyful wing,
    Cleaving the sky,
  Sun, moon, and stars forgot,
    Upward I fly.
  Still, all my song shall be,
    Nearer, my God, &c.

* *From the* "ASAPH," *by permission of* MASON BROTHERS.

No. 24. "*O clap your hands together, all ye people, O sing unto God with the voice of melody.*"

    2 Jesus, our great High Priest,
       Hath full atonement made ;
      Ye weary spirits, rest;
       Ye mournful souls, be glad :
    The year of jubilee is come ;
    Return, ye ransomed sinners, home.

3 Extol the Lamb of God,—
 The all-atoning Lamb;
 Redemption in his blood
  Throughout the world proclaim;
The year of jubilee is come;
Return, ye ransomed sinners, home.

ARISE, MY SOUL.

No. 25. *"Abba, Father."* Tune—"Lenox."

1 Arise, my soul, arise;
 Shake off thy guilty fears;
 The bleeding sacrifice
  In my behalf appears;
Before the throne my Surety stands,
My name is written on his hands.

2 He ever lives above
 For me to intercede
 His all-redeeming love,
  His precious blood, to plead;
His blood atoned for all our race,
And sprinkles now the throne of grace.

3 Five bleeding wounds he bears,
 Received on Calvary;
 They pour effectual prayers,
  They strongly plead for me:—
Forgive him, oh, forgive, they cry,
Nor let that ransomed sinner die.

4 The Father hears him pray,
 His dear anointed One:
 He cannot turn away
  The presence of his Son:
His spirit answers to the blood,
And tells me I am born of God.

5 My God is reconciled;
 His pard'ning voice I hear;
 He owns me for his child;
  I can no longer fear:
With confidence I now draw nigh,
And Father, Abba, Father, cry.—*C. Wesley.*

WOODWORTH. L. M.

WM. B. BRADBURY.

1. Just as I am,... with-out.. one plea, But that thy blood was shed for me, And that thou bidst me come to thee, O Lamb of God, I come, I come!

No. 26.   *Going to Jesus.*

2 Just as I am—poor, wretched, blind;
Sight, riches, healing of the mind,
Yea, all I need in thee to find,
O Lamb of God, I come, I come!

3 Just as I am, thou wilt receive,
Wilt welcome, pardon, cleanse, relieve!
Because thy promise I believe,
O Lamb of God, I come, I come!

4 Just as I am—thy love unknown
Has broken every barrier down;
Now to be thine, yea, thine alone,
O Lamb of God, I come, I come!—*Charlotte Elliott.*

Hallowed Songs, Revised. 33

COME, YE DISCONSOLATE. 30th P. M.
S. WEBBE.

1. Come, ye dis-con-so-late, wher-e'er ye lan-guish,
Come to the mer-cy-seat, fer-vent-ly kneel;
Here bring your wounded hearts, here tell your an-guish;
Earth has no sor-row that heaven can-not heal.

No. 27. *"God is our refuge and strength: a very present help in trouble."*

2 Joy to the desolate, light of the straying,
Hope of the penitent, fadeless and pure;—
Here speaks the Comforter, tenderly saying—
Earth has no sorrow that heaven cannot cure.

3 Here see the bread of life; see waters flowing
Forth from the throne of God, pure from above;
Come to the feast of love; come, ever knowing—
Earth has no sorrow but heaven can remove.

INVITATION. 8s & 7s. Double.

1. Hear, O sinner, mer-cy hails you, Now with sweetest voice she calls:
Bids you haste to seek the Saviour Ere the hand of jus-tice falls.

Chorus.
Turn to the Lord, and seek sal-vation; Sound the praise of his dear name;
Glo-ry, hon-or, and sal-va-tion, Christ the Lord is come to reign.

No. 28.   "*The voice of mercy.*"

2 See! the storm of vengeance gath'ring
O'er the path you dare to tread;
Hark! the awful thunder rolling
Loud and louder o'er your head.
Turn to the Lord, &c.

3 Haste, O sinner! to the Saviour,
Seek his mercy while you may;
Soon the day of grace is over;
Soon your life will pass away.
Turn to the Lord, &c.—*Reed.*

COME, YE SINNERS.

No. 29. *The invitation.* TUNE—"INVITATION."

1 Come, ye sinners, poor and needy,
   Weak and wounded, sick and sore;
 Jesus ready stands to save you,
   Full of pity, love, and power:
     He is able,
   He is willing: doubt no more.

Chorus.—Turn to the Lord and seek salvation;
   Sound the praise of his dear name;
 Glory, honor, and salvation,
   Christ the Lord is come to reign.

2 Now, ye needy, come and welcome;
   God's free bounty glorify;
 True belief and true repentance,—
   Every grace that brings you nigh,—
     Without money,
   Come to Jesus Christ, and buy.

Chorus.—Turn to the Lord, &c.

3 Let not conscience make you linger;
   Nor of fitness fondly dream:
 All the fitness he requireth
   Is to feel your need of him:
     This he gives you,—
   'Tis the Spirit's glimm'ring beam.

Chorus.—Turn to the Lord, &c.

4 Come, ye weary, heavy laden,
   Bruised and mangled by the fall;
 If you tarry till you're better,
   You will never come at all;
     Not the righteous,—
   Sinners Jesus came to call.

Chorus.—Turn to the Lord, &o

PENITENCE. 7s, 6s & 8s.

W. H. OAKLEY.

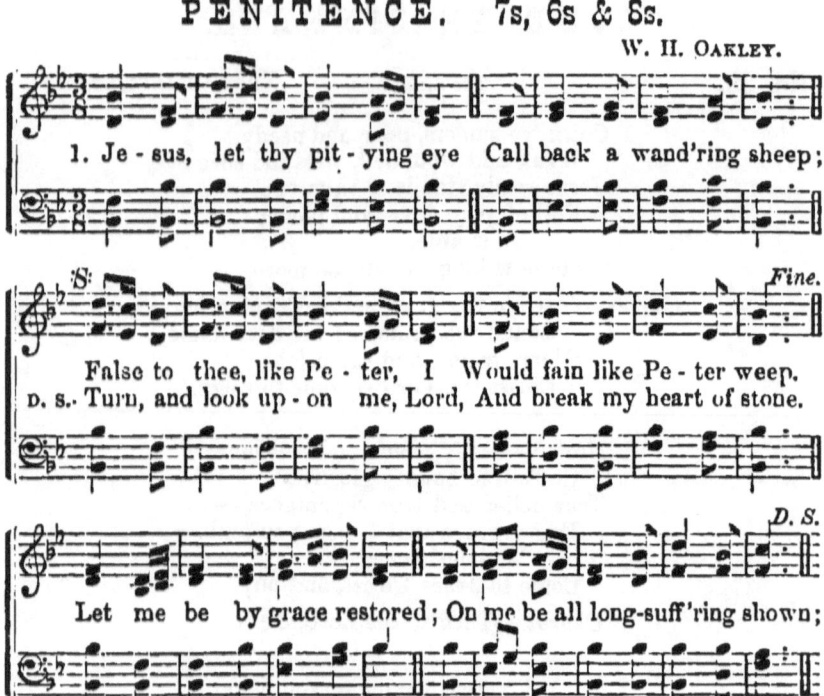

1. Jesus, let thy pitying eye Call back a wand'ring sheep;
False to thee, like Peter, I Would fain like Peter weep.
Let me be by grace restored; On me be all long-suff'ring shown;
D. S.— Turn, and look upon me, Lord, And break my heart of stone.

No. 30.   *Humility and contrition.*

2 Saviour, Prince, enthroned above,
  Repentance to impart,
Give me, through thy dying love,
  The humble, contrite heart:
Give what I have long implored,
  A portion of thy grief unknown:
Turn, and look upon me, &c.

3 For thine own compassion's sake,
  The gracious wonder show;
Cast my sins behind thy back,
  And wash me white as snow:
If thy bowels now are stirr'd,
  If now I do myself bemoan,
Turn, and look upon me, &c.—*C. Wesley.*

LEBANON. S. M.

J. ZUNDEL.

1. I was a wandering sheep, I did not love the fold;
I did not love my Shepherd's voice, I would not be con-troll'd:
I was a wayward child, I did not love my home,
I did not love my Father's voice, I loved a-far to roam.

No. 31.

2 The Shepherd sought his sheep,
   The Father sought his child;
They followed me o'er vale and hill,
   O'er deserts waste and wild:
They found me nigh to death,
   Famish'd, and faint, and lone;
They bound me with the bands of love,
   They saved the wandering one.

3 Jesus my Shepherd is,
   'Twas he that loved my soul,
'Twas he that washed me in his blood,
   'Twas he that made me whole:
'Twas he that sought the lost,
   That found the wandering sheep.
'Twas he that brought me to the fold,
   'Tis he that still doth keep.

Bonar.

ARIEL. C. P. M.

Dr. Lowell Mason.

1. Oh, could I speak the matchless worth, Oh, could I sound the glories forth, Which in my Saviour shine! { I'd soar, and touch the heavenly strings, And vie with Gabriel, while he sings, } In notes al-most di-vine, In notes al - most di - vine.

No. 32. *The unsearchable riches of Christ.*

2 I'd sing the precious blood he spilt.
My ransom from the dreadful guilt
   Of sin and wrath divine:
I'd sing his glorious righteousness,
In which all perfect, heavenly dress
   My soul shall ever shine.

3 I'd sing the characters he bears,
And all the forms of love he wears,
   Exalted on his throne:
In loftiest songs of sweetest praise,
I would to everlasting days
   Make all his glories known.

4 Well, the delightful day will come
  When my dear Lord will bring me home
    And I shall see his face ;
  Then with my Saviour, Brother, Friend,
  A blest eternity I'll spend,
    Triumphant in his grace.—*Medley.*

AUTUMN. 8s & 7s. Double.
Spanish.

1. Je-sus, I my cross have taken, All to leave, and follow thee;
Nak-ed, poor, despised, forsak-en, Thou, from hence, my all shalt be.
D. S. Wait-ing for the Spirit's seal-ing, Longing on-ly thine to be

Chorus, to each verse.

Here be-fore thine al-tar kneeling, Je-sus, Lord, I look to thee;

No. 33.   *Jesus, I my cross have taken.*

2.
Perish every fond ambition,
 All I've sought, or hoped, or known;
Yet how rich is my condition!
 God and heaven are still my own.

3.
Let the world despise and leave me,
 They have left my Saviour, too;
Human hearts and looks deceive me;
 Thou art not, like them, untrue:

4.
And while thou shalt smile upon me,
 God of wisdom, love, and might,
Foes may hate, and friends may scorn me;
 Show thy face, and all is bright.

5.
Man may trouble and distress me,
 'T will but drive me to thy breast;
Life with trials hard may press me,
 Heaven will bring me sweeter rest.

6.
Oh! 'tis not in grief to harm me,
 While thy love is left to me;
Oh! 'twere not in joy to charm me,
 Were that joy unmixed with thee.—*Miss Grant.*

SICILIAN HYMN. 8s & 7s.

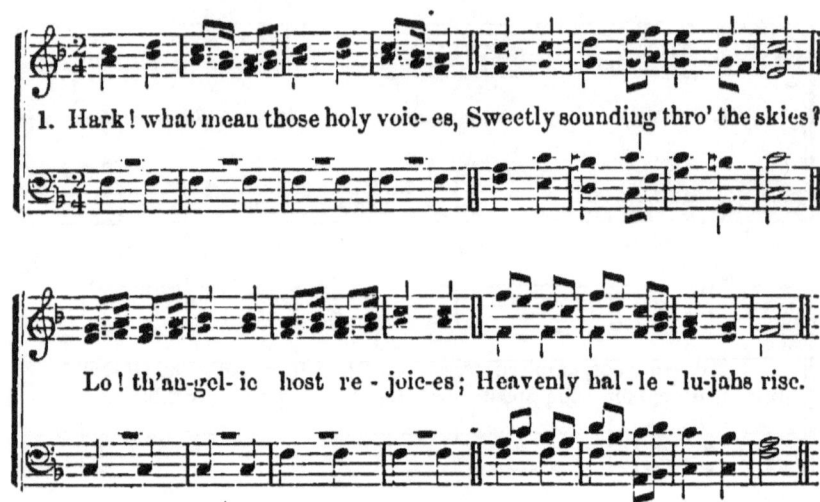

1. Hark! what mean those holy voic-es, Sweetly sounding thro' the skies?
Lo! th'an-gel-ic host re-joic-es; Heavenly hal-le-lu-jahs rise.

No. 34.   *Peace on earth—good-will to men.*

2 Listen to the wondrous story,
  Which they chant in hymns of joy:
 Glory in the highest, glory,
  Glory be to God most high!

3 Peace on earth, good-will from heaven
  Reaching far as man is found;
 Souls redeem'd, and sins forgiven!—
  Loud our golden harps shall sound.

4 Christ is born, the great Anointed;
  Heaven and earth his praises sing;
 Oh, receive whom God appointed,
  For your Prophet, Priest, and King.

5 Hasten, mortals, to adore him;
  Learn his name, and taste his joy;
 Till in heaven ye sing before him,—
  Glory be to God most high!—*Cawood.*

CHRISTIAN UNION.

Dr. Thos. Hastings.* *Nov.*, 1869.

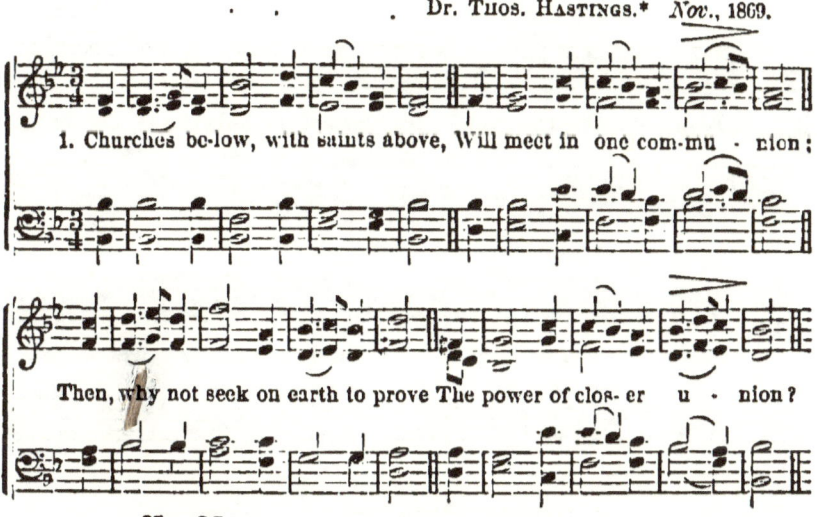

1. Churches be-low, with saints above, Will meet in one com-mu - nion;
Then, why not seek on earth to prove The power of clos- er u - nion?

No. 35.

2 Together bound for higher spheres,
    Far from this earth's commotion,—
  Fraternal love, 'mid smiles and tears,
    Should blend with our devotion.

3 Though diff'rent forms and diff'rent rites
    And methods are prevailing;
  The love of Christ each soul invites
    To energies unfailing.

4 Could all the friends of Christ be found,
    With hearts and hands combining;
  How would the grace of God abound,
    And heavenly light be shining.

5 Welcome the day when we shall see
    That union, firm and glorious!
  Then shall the Gospel message be
    Through all the world victorious.

* *The venerable author, now having lived to see the Church of his choice united into one glorious Body (Old and New School Presbyterian), adds another "Legacy of his Harmony," in the above beautiful hymn of Christian Union.*

BEAUTIFUL CROSS.

S. J. VAIL.

1. Beauti- ful cross by faith I see, Planted on Cal - va - ry for me;
Cross of the suffering Lamb of God, Under thy pressing weight he trod.
Beauti- ful cross, so dear to me, Beauti- ful cross of Cal - va - ry.

No. 36.

2 Beautiful faith that lifts me up,
Where I may taste the bitter cup;
Beautiful faith that bids me bear
Crosses and ills, his love to share;
Beautiful faith, when tempest toss'd;
Beautiful faith in Jesus' cross.

3 Beautiful cross of Calvary,
Oh! how my spirit clings to thee;
Beautiful faith that brings thee near;
Beautiful love that makes thee dear;
Beautiful cross, and faith, and love,
Sending me up to heaven above.

THERE IS AN HOUR.

From the German.

1. There is an hour of peace-ful rest, To mourning wand'rers given: There is a joy for souls distress'd, A balm for ev-ery wounded breast, 'Tis found a-lone in heaven.

No. 37.

2 There is a home for weary souls
   By sin and sorrow driven,
   When toss'd on life's tempestuous shoals,
   Where storms arise and ocean rolls,
   And all is drear but heaven.

3 There faith lifts up the tearless eye,
   To brighter prospects given;
   And views the tempest passing by,
   The evening shadows quickly fly,
   And all serene in heaven.

4 There fragrant flowers immortal bloom,
   And joys supreme are given:
   There rays divine disperse the gloom;
   Beyond the confines of the tomb
   Appears the dawn of heaven.

LOVED ONES GONE BEFORE.

S. C. FOSTER.

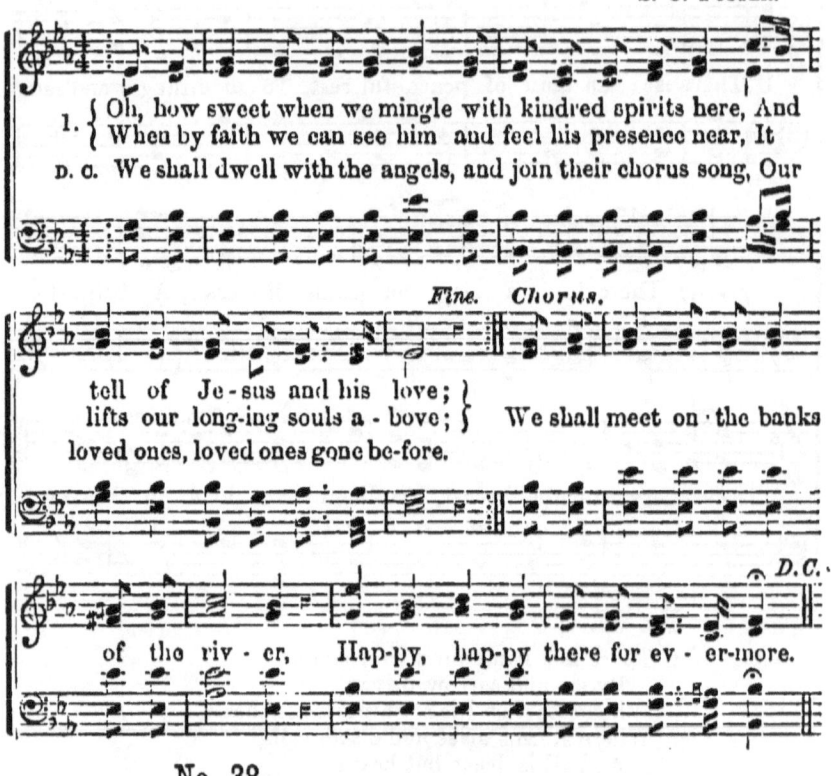

1. { Oh, how sweet when we mingle with kindred spirits here, And
   { When by faith we can see him and feel his presence near, It
D. C. We shall dwell with the angels, and join their chorus song, Our

tell of Je-sus and his love; }
lifts our long-ing souls a-bove; } We shall meet on the banks
loved ones, loved ones gone be-fore.

of the riv-er, Hap-py, hap-py there for ev-er-more.

No. 38.

2 We are pilgrims to Zion, though trials we must bear,
  We'll count them blessings in disguise;
  Though the cross may be heavy, the crown we soon shall wear
  In heaven, where pleasure never dies.
     Cho.—We shall meet on the banks, &c.

3 When we walk through the valley and shadow of the tomb,
  Dear Saviour, thou wilt be our guide;
  Thy smile like a sunbeam shall light beyond the gloom,
  And keep the ransomed at thy side.
     Cho.—We shall meet on the banks, &c.

JESUS IS MINE.

T. E. PERKINS.

1. Fade, fade each earth-ly joy, Jesus is mine!
Break ev-ery ten-der tie,.. Jesus is mine!
D. S. Jesus a-lone can bless, Jesus is mine!
Dark is the wil-der-ness, Earth has no rest-ing-place,

No. 39. *Jesus is mine.*

2 Tempt not my soul away,
Jesus is mine!
Here would I ever stay,
Jesus is mine!
Perishing things of clay,
Born but for one brief day,
Pass from my heart away,
Jesus is mine!

3 Farewell, ye dreams of night,
Jesus is mine!
Lost in this dawning light,
Jesus is mine!
All that my soul has tried,
Left but a dismal void,
Jesus has satisfied,
Jesus is mine!

4 Farewell, mortality,
Jesus is mine!
Welcome, eternity,
Jesus is mine!
Welcome, O loved and blest,
Welcome, sweet scenes of rest,
Welcome, my Saviour's breast,
Jesus is mine!—*Bonar.*

JESUS LOVES ME.

Wm. B. Bradbury.*

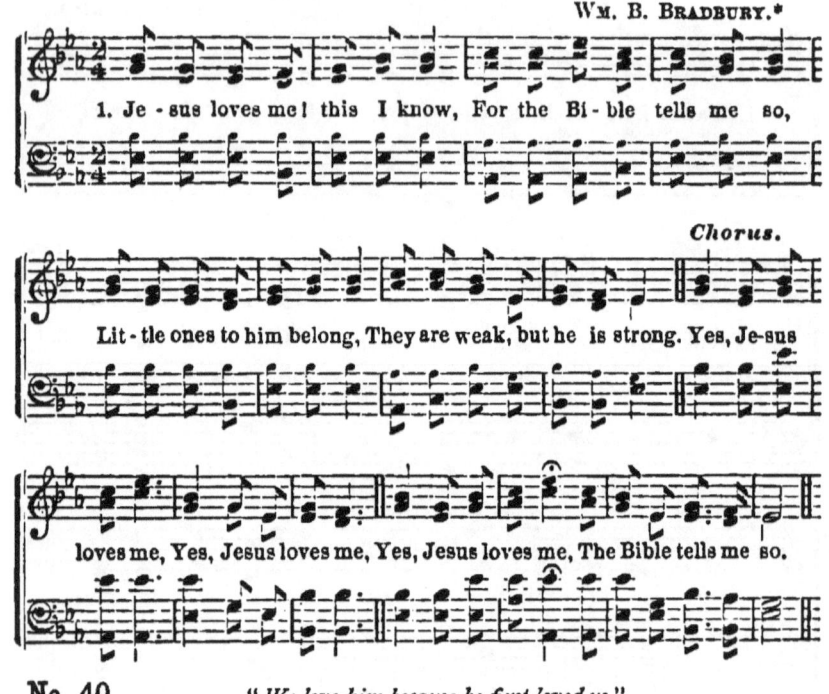

1. Jesus loves me! this I know, For the Bible tells me so, Little ones to him belong, They are weak, but he is strong. Yes, Jesus loves me, Yes, Jesus loves me, Yes, Jesus loves me, The Bible tells me so.

No. 40.   *" We love him because he first loved us."*

2 Jesus loves me! he who died,
   Heaven's gate to open wide;
   He will wash away my sin,
   Let his little child come in.—*Chorus.*

3 Jesus loves me! loves me still,
   Though I'm very weak and ill;
   From his shining throne on high,
   Comes to watch me where I lie.—*Chorus.*

4 Jesus loves me; he will stay
   Close beside me all the way;
   If I love him, when I die
   He will take me home on high —*Chorus.*

* *From " Praises of Jesus," by permission of* Biglow & Main.

ZION. 8s, 7s & 4s.

DR. THOS. HASTINGS.

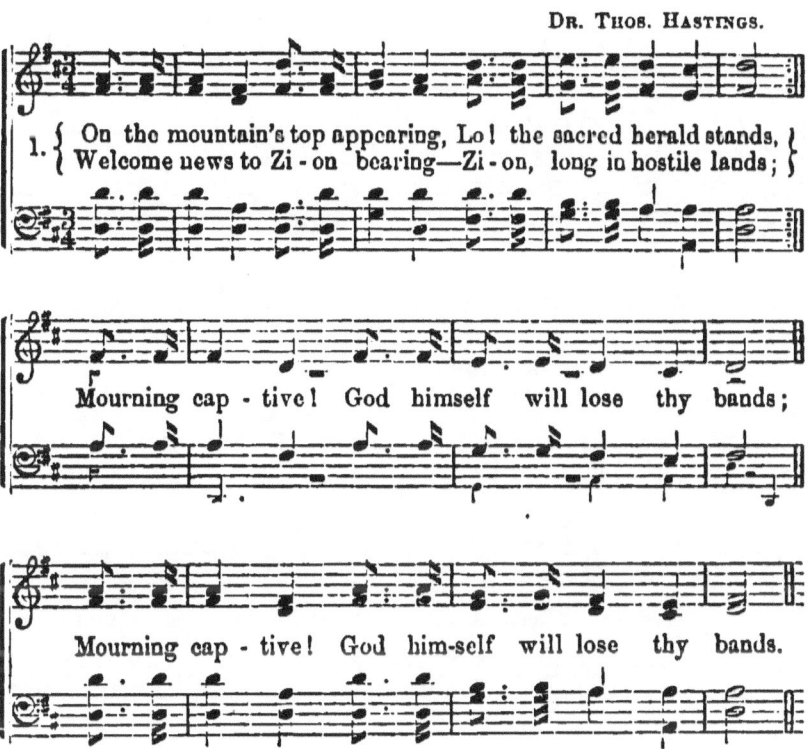

1. On the mountain's top appearing, Lo! the sacred herald stands,
Welcome news to Zi-on bearing—Zi-on, long in hostile lands;
Mourning cap-tive! God himself will lose thy bands;
Mourning cap-tive! God him-self will lose thy bands.

No. 41.   *Zion encouraged.*

2 Has thy night been long and mournful?
  Have thy friends unfaithful proved?
  Have thy foes been proud and scornful,
  By thy sighs and tears unmoved?
    Cease thy mourning;
  Zion still is well beloved.

3 God, thy God, will now restore thee;
  He himself appears thy Friend;
  All thy foes shall flee before thee;
  Here thy boasts and triumphs end:
    Great deliverance
  Zion's King shall surely send.

4 Enemies no more shall trouble,
  All thy wrongs shall be redress'd,
  For thy shame thou shalt have trouble,
  In thy Maker's favor bless'd;
    All thy conflicts
  End in everlasting rest.—*Kelly.*

HAPPY ZION. 8s, 7s & 4s.

I. B. WOODBURY.

1. Zi - on stands with hills sur - round-ed, Zi - on,
   All her foes shall be con - found-ed, Tho' the
   kept by power di - vine:
   world in arms com - bine: Hap - py Zi - on, Hap - py
   Zi - on— What a.... fav - ored lot is thine!

No. 42.   *Her enemies confounded.*

2 Every human tie may perish;
 Friend to friend unfaithful prove,
 Mothers cease their own to cherish;
 Heaven and earth at last removed;
  But no changes
  Can attend Jehovah's love.

3 In the furnace God may prove thee,
 Thence to bring thee forth more bright,
 But can never cease to love thee,—
 Thou art precious in his sight:
  God is with thee,—
  God, thine everlasting light.—*Kelly.*

GREENVILLE. 8s, 7s & 4s.

J. J. ROUSSEAU.

1. Lord, dismiss us with thy blessing, Fill our hearts with joy and peace;
Let us, each thy love pos-sessing, Triumph in re-deeming grace;
Oh, re-fresh us, Oh, re-fresh us, Traveling thro' this wilder-ness.

No. 43. *Dismission.*

2 Thanks we give and adoration,
  For thy gospel's joyful sound;
May the fruits of thy salvation
  In our hearts and lives abound:
    May thy presence
With us evermore be found.

3 So, whene'er the signal's given,
  Us from earth to call away,
Borne on angels' wings to heaven,
  Glad the summons to obey—
    May we, ready,
Rise and reign in endless day.—*Burder.*

4

THE HEAVENLY LAND.

Wm. B. Bradbury.

1. I love to think of the heavenly land, Where white-robed angels are;
   Where many a friend is gath-ered safe From fear and toil and care.

Refrain.
There'll be no part-ing, There'll be no part-ing,
There'll be no part-ing, There'll be no part-ing there.

No. 44. "*A better country, that is, an heavenly.*"

2 I love to think of the heavenly land,
   Where my Redeemer reigns,
Where rapturous songs of triumph rise,
   In endless, joyous strains.—*Refrain.*

3 I love to think of the heavenly land,
   The saints' eternal home,
Where palms, and robes, and crowns ne'er fade,
   And all our joys are one.—*Refrain.*

4 I love to think of the heavenly land,
   The greetings there we'll meet,
The harps—the songs forever ours—
   The walls—the golden streets.—*Refrain.*

5 I love to think of the heavenly land,
   That promised land so fair,
Oh, how my raptured spirit longs
   To be forever there.—*Refrain.*

Hallowed Songs, Revised. 51

MISSIONARY HYMN. 7s & 6s.
DR. LOWELL MASON.

1. From Greenland's i-cy mountains, From In-dia's co-ral strand;
Where A-fric's sun-ny fount-ains Roll down their golden sand;
From many an an-cient riv-er, From man-y a palmy plain,
They call us to de-liv-er Their land from er-ror's chain.

No. 45. *The cry of the heathen.*

2 What though the spicy breezes
   Blow soft o'er Ceylon's isle;
Though every prospect pleases
   And only man is vile:
In vain with lavish kindness
   The gifts of God are strown;
The heathen in his blindness
   Bows down to wood and stone.

3 Shall we, whose souls are lighted
   With wisdom from on high,
Shall we to men benighted
   The lamp of life deny?

Salvation!—O salvation!
   The joyful sound proclaim,
Till earth's remotest nation
   Has learn'd Messiah's name.

4 Waft, waft, ye winds, his story,
   And you, ye waters, roll,
Till, like a sea of glory,
   It spreads from pole to pole:
Till o'er our ransom'd nature
   The Lamb for sinners slain,
Redeemer, King, Creator,
   In bliss returns to reign.—*Heber.*

WEBB. 26th P. M.

G. J. WEBB.

1. The morning light is breaking; The darkness dis-ap-pears;
The sons of earth are wak-ing To pe-ni-ten-tial tears:
D. S. Of na-tions in com-mo-tion, Prepared for Zi-on's war.
Each breeze that sweeps the ocean Brings tidings from a-far

No. 46.   "*O be joyful in the Lord, all ye lands*"

2.
See heathen nations bending
 Before the God we love,
And thousand hearts ascending
 In gratitude above;
While sinners, now confessing,
 The gospel call obey,
And seek the Saviour's blessing—
 A nation in a day.

3.
Blest river of salvation,
 Pursue thy onward way;
Flow thou to every nation,
 Nor in thy richness stay:
Stay not till all the lowly
 Triumphant reach their home:
Stay not till all the holy
 Proclaim—"The Lord is come!"

WATCHMAN.

Wm. B. Bradbury.

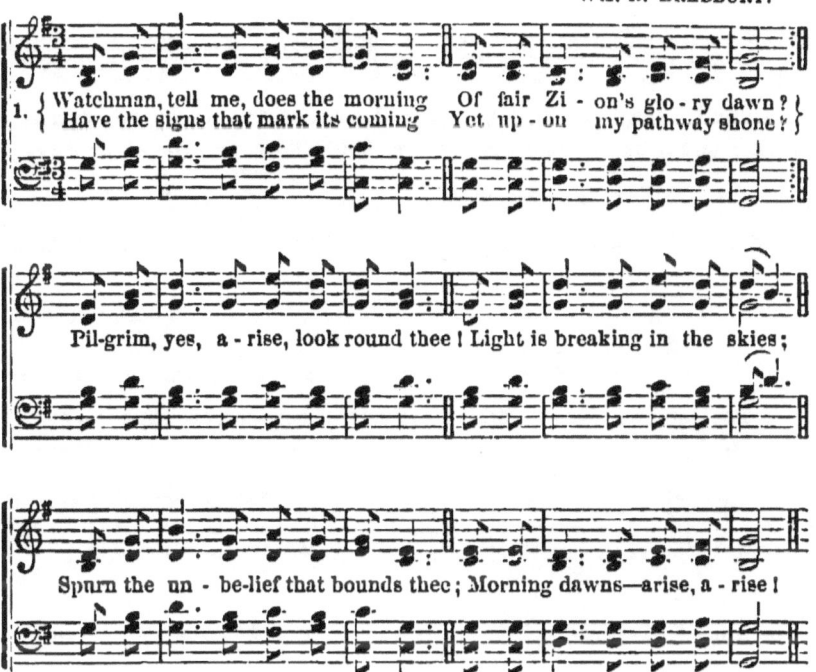

1. Watchman, tell me, does the morning Of fair Zi - on's glo - ry dawn?
   Have the signs that mark its coming Yet up - on my pathway shone?
   Pil-grim, yes, a - rise, look round thee! Light is breaking in the skies;
   Spurn the un - be-lief that bounds thee; Morning dawns—arise, a - rise!

No. 47.

2 Pilgrim in that golden city,
   Seated on his jasper throne,
   Zion's King, arrayed in beauty,
   Reigns in peace form zone to zone;
   There, on verdant hills and mountains,
   Where the golden sunbeams play,
   Purling streams and crystal fountains
   Sparkle in th' eternal day.

3 Pilgrim, see! the light is beaming
   Brighter still upon thy way;
   Signs thro' all the earth are gleaming,
   Omens of the coming day,
   When the last loud trumpet, sounding,
   Shall awake from earth and sea
   All the saints of God now sleeping,
   Clad in immortality.

4 Watchman, lo! the land we're nearing,
   With its vernal fruits and flowers,
   On just yonder; oh, how cheering
   Bloom forever Eden's bowers!
   Hark! the choral strains there ringing,
   Wafted on the balmy air;
   See the millions! hear them singing!
   Soon the pilgrims will be there.

NO SORROW THERE.

DUNBAR.

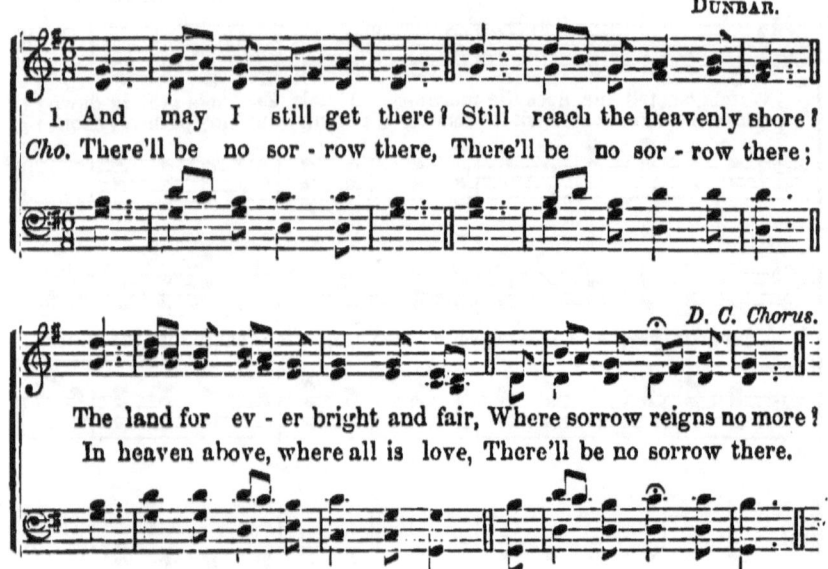

1. And may I still get there? Still reach the heavenly shore?
Cho. There'll be no sor - row there, There'll be no sor - row there;

The land for ev - er bright and fair, Where sorrow reigns no more?
In heaven above, where all is love, There'll be no sorrow there.

No. 48. *"Where the wicked cease from troubling, and the weary are at rest."*

2 Shall I, unworthy I,
    To fear and doubting given,
Mount up at last, and happy fly
    On angel's wings to heaven?
Cho.—There'll be no sorrow there, &c.

3 Hail, love divine and pure,
    Hail, mercy from the skies!
My hopes are bright, and now secure,
    Upborne by faith I rise.
Cho.—There'll be no sorrow there, &c.

4 I part with earth and sin,
    And shout the danger's past;
My Saviour takes me fully in,
    And I am his at last.
Cho.—There'll be no sorrow there, &c.

DUANE STREET. L. M.

Rev. G. COLES.

No. 49.   *The highway of holiness.*

3 This is the way I long have sought,
And mourn'd because I found it not;
My grief a burden long has been,
Because I was not saved from sin.

4 The more I strove against its power,
I felt its weight and guilt the more;
Till late I heard my Saviour say,—
Come hither, soul, I am the way.

5 Lo! glad I come; and thou, blest Lamb,
Shalt take me to thee, as I am;
Nothing but sin have I to give,—
Nothing but love shall I receive.

6 Then will I tell to sinners round
What a dear Saviour I have found;
I'll point to thy redeeming blood,
And say,—Behold the way to God.—*Cennick.*

CONSECRATION HYMN.

Mrs. Joseph F. Knapp.*

No. 50.

2 O Jesus, mighty Saviour,
  I trust in thy great name,
  I look for thy salvation,
  Thy promise now I claim.—*Cho.*

3 Oh, let the fire descending
  Just now upon my soul,
  Consume my humble offering,
  And cleanse and make me whole.
  Cho.

4 I am thine, O blessed Jesus,
  Wash'd by thy precious blood,
  Now seal me by thy Spirit
  A sacrifice to God.—*Cho.*—*Mary D. James.*

* *From "Notes of Joy."*

Hallowed Songs, Revised. 57

MARY MAGDALENE.
DUET FOR ALTO AND SOPRANO, WITHOUT ACCOMPANIMENT.*

1. To the hall of the feast came the sin-ful and fair, She heard in the cit-y that Je-sus was there; Un-heed-ing the splen-dor that zed on the board, She si-lent-ly knelt at the feet of the Lord.

. 51.

The frown and the murmur went round through them all,
That one so unhallowed should tread in that hall;
And some said the poor would be objects more meet,
As the wealth of her perfume she showered on his feet.

She heard but the Saviour—she spoke but with tears;
She dared not look up to the Heaven of his eyes,
And the hot tears gushed forth at each heave of her breast,
As her lips to his sandals were throbbingly pressed.

n the sky after tempest, as shineth the bows,
In the glare of the sunbeams as melteth the snows,
He looked on the lost one. "her sins were forgiven."
And Mary went forth in the beauty of heaven.

* *From the "Song Crown."*

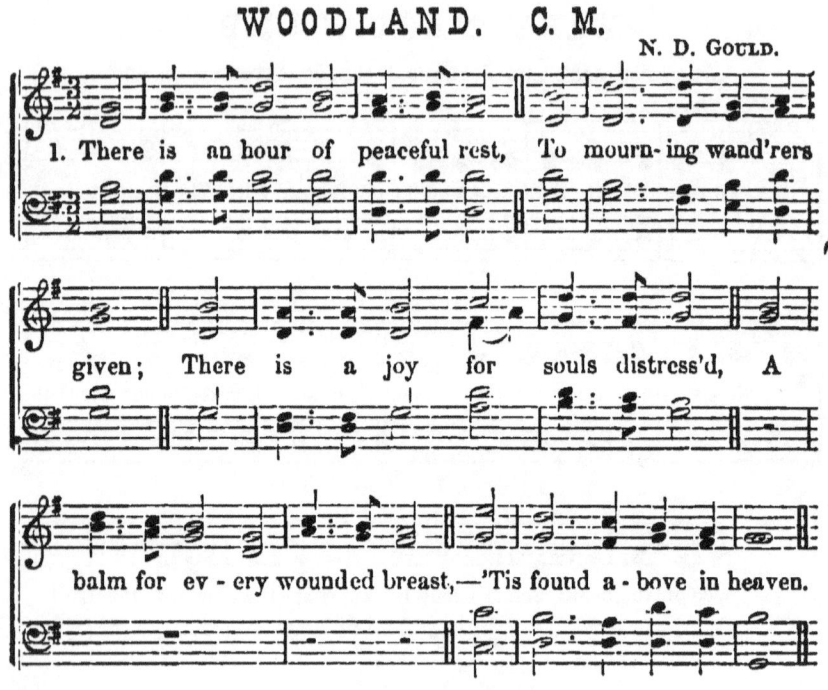

No. 52.   *The land of rest.*

2 There is a home for weary souls
   By sin and sorrow driven,
  When tossed on life's tempestuous shoals,
  Where storms arise and ocean rolls,
   And all is drear but heaven.

3 There faith lifts up the tearless eye,
   To brighter prospects given;
  And views the tempest passing by,
  The evening shadows quickly fly,
   And all serene in heaven.

4 There fragrant flowers immortal bloom,
   And joys supreme are given;
  There rays divine disperse the gloom;
  Beyond the confines of the tomb
   Appears the dawn of heaven.—*Tappan.*

ENON'S ISLE. 8s. Double.
I. B. WOODBURY.

1. Oh, when shall we sweetly remove, Oh, when shall we enter our rest,—
D. C. Where saints our Immanu-el sing, And cherub and seraph a-dore?
Re-turn to the Zi-on a-bove, The moth-er of spirits distress'd;—
That cit-y of God the great King, Where sorrow and death are no more,

No. 53. *"And to be with Christ, which is far better."*

2 But angels themselves cannot tell
The joys of that holiest place,
Where Jesus is pleased to reveal
The light of his heavenly face:
When, caught in the rapturous flame,
The sight beatific they prove;
And walk in the light of the Lamb,
Enjoying the beams of his love.

3 Thou know'st in the spirit of prayer
We long thy appearing to see,
Resign'd to the burden we bear,
But longing to triumph with thee:
'Tis good at thy word to be here;
'Tis better in thee to be gone,
And see thee in glory appear,
And rise to a share in thy throne.—*C. Wesley.*

DE FLEURY. 8s. Double.

1. How tedious and tasteless the hours When Jesus no longer I see!
D. C. But when I am happy in him, December's as pleasant as May.

Sweet prospects, sweet birds, and sweet flowers, Have all lost their sweetness to [me;—

The midsummer sun shines but dim, The fields strive in vain to look gay;

No. 54.   *All-sufficiency of Jesus.*

2 His Name yields the richest perfume,
  And sweeter than music his voice;
His presence disperses my gloom,
  And makes all within me rejoice;
I should, were he always thus nigh,
  Have nothing to wish or to fear;
No mortal so happy as I,—
  My summer would last all the year.

3 Content with beholding his face,
  My all to his pleasure resign'd,
No changes of season or place
  Would make any change in my mind:

While blest with a sense of his love,
  A palace a toy would appear;
And prisons would palaces prove,
  If Jesus would dwell with me there.

4 Dear Lord, if indeed I am thine,
  If thou art my sun and my song,
Say, why do I languish and pine?
  And why are my winters so long?
O drive these dark clouds from my sky;
  Thy soul-cheering presence restore;
Or take me to thee up on high,
  Where winter and clouds are no
    more.—*Newton.*

Hallowed Songs, Revised.

OAK. 6s & 4s.

Dr. L. MASON.

1. I'm but a stran-ger here, Heaven is my home; Earth is a des-ert drear, Heaven is my home; Dan-ger and sor-row stand, Round me on ev-ery hand; Heav'n is my fath-er-land, Heav'n is my home.

No. 55. *Heaven is my home.*

2.
What though the tempest rage,
 Heaven is my home;
Short is my pilgrimage,
 Heaven is my home.
Time's cold and wintry blast
 Soon will be overpast;
I shall reach home at last,
 Heaven is my home.

3.
There, at my Saviour's side,
 Heaven is my home;
I shall be glorified,
 Heaven is my home.
There are the good and blest,
Those I loved most and best,
There too, I soon shall rest,
 Heaven is my home.

CHRIST AT THE WHEEL.

DEDICATED TO PHILIP PHILLIPS.

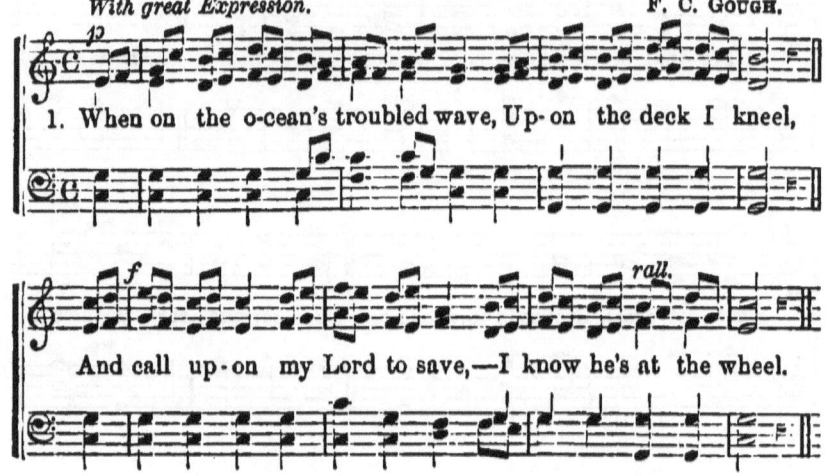

With great Expression.   F. C. GOUGH.

1. When on the o-cean's troubled wave, Up-on the deck I kneel,
And call up-on my Lord to save,—I know he's at the wheel.

No. 56.

2 That through the tempest he will guide
   My soul as deems him best;
Bear up my life on raging tide,
   And land me with the blest.

3 With loving care will lead me o'er
   The dangers of the way,
And to me open wide the door
   Which leads to endless day.

4 Though on the waters or the land,
   I may be tempest toss'd,
He holds the rudder in his hand,
   That I may not be lost.

5 The helmsman of redeeming grace,
   Who with his life did seal
Salvation to a dying race,
   Is ever at the wheel.—*W. H. Phillips.*

LYONS. 6s & 5s.

HAYDN.

1. Tho' troubles as-sail, and dangers affright, Tho' friends should all fail, and foes all u-nite, Yet one thing se-cures us, what-ev-er be-tide, The promise assures us,—The Lord will provide.

No. 57.   *The Lord will provide.*

2 The birds, without barn or storehouse, are fed;
From them let us learn to trust for our bread:
His saints what is fitting shall ne'er be denied,
So long as 'tis written,—The Lord will provide.

3 When Satan appears to stop up our path,
And fills us with fears, we triumph by faith;
He cannot take from us (though oft he has tried)
The heart-cheering promise,—The Lord will provide.

4 He tells us we're weak,—our hope is in vain;
The good that we seek we ne'er shall obtain:
But when such suggestions our graces have tried,
This answers all questions,—The Lord will provide.—*Newton.*

I'M A PILGRIM.

1. I'm a pilgrim, and I'm a stranger, I can tarry, I can tarry but a night; Do not detain me, for I am going To where the fountains are ever flowing.

D. C. I'm a pilgrim, &c.

No. 58.   *A pilgrim and stranger.*

2 There the glory is ever shining;
　I am longing, I am longing for the sight;
Here in this country so dark and dreary,
I have been wand'ring forlorn and weary.
I'm a pilgrim, and I'm a stranger;
　I can tarry, I can tarry but a night.

3 There's the city to which I journey;
　My Redeemer, my Redeemer is its light;
There is no sorrow, nor any sighing,
There is no sin there, nor any dying.
I'm a pilgrim, and I'm a stranger;
　I can tarry, I can tarry but a night

THERE IS JOY FOR YOU.

S. J. VAIL.*

No. 59.

2 Let me drink sweet draughts of mercy
  From the fountain flowing free,
  Let me drink and live forever
  Where my Saviour I may see.—*Cho.*

3 Tell me not, ye weary-laden,
  There is nought but sorrow here,
  For the Lord hath sent his angels,
  And his chosen need not fear.—*Cho.*

4 Keep your lamps well trimmed and burning
  And the wedding garments on,
  For there's none that know the moment
  Of the coming of the Son.—*Cho.*—*Mrs. M. A. Kidder.*

* *From " Chapel Melodies."*

UNITY. 6s & 5s.

Dr. Lowell Mason.

1. When shall we meet a-gain?—Meet ne'er to sev-er?
When will peace wreathe her chain Round us for ev-er?
Our hearts will ne'er re-pose Safe from each blast that blows
In this dark vale of woes— Nev-er— no, nev-er!

No. 60.   *Reunion in heaven.*

2 When shall love freely flow
   Pure as life's river?
When shall sweet friendship glow
   Changeless forever?
Where joys celestial thrill,
Where bliss each heart shall fill,
And fears of parting chill,
   Never—no, never!

3 Up to that world of light
   Take us, dear Saviour;
May we all there unite,
   Happy forever:
Where kindred spirits dwell,
There may our music swell,
And time our joys dispel,
   Never—no, never!

MOUNT VERNON.* 8s & 7s.

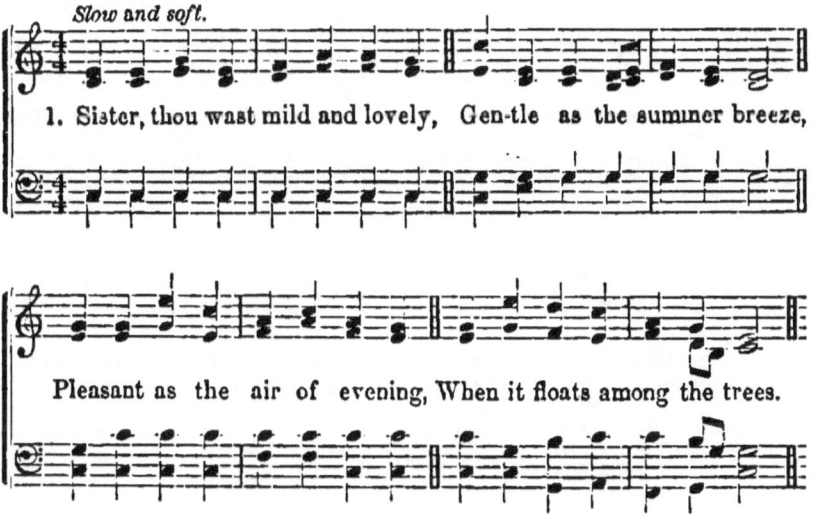

1. Sister, thou wast mild and lovely, Gen-tle as the summer breeze,
Pleasant as the air of evening, When it floats among the trees.

No. 61.

2 Peaceful be thy silent slumber,
    Peaceful in the grave so low;
  Thou no more wilt join our number,
    Thou no more our songs shalt know.

3 Dearest sister, thou hast left us,
    Here thy loss we deeply feel,
  But 'tis God that hath bereft us,
    He can all our sorrow heal.

4 Yet again we hope to meet thee,
    When the day of life is fled,
  Then, in heaven, with joy to greet thee,
    Where no farewell tear is shed

* *This tune may be sung as a Duet by Treble voices.*

IVES. 7s. Double.

Arranged by E. IVES.

1. Who are these in bright ar-ray, This ex-ult-ing, hap-py throng,
Round the al-tar night and day, Hymning one tri-umphant song?
D. S. Wis-dom, rich-es to ob-tain, New do-min-ion ev-ery hour.
Worth-y is the Lamb, once slain, Bless-ing, hon-or, glo-ry, power,

No. 62. *Perfect love dispels all fears.*

2.
These through fiery trials trod;
  These from great afflictions came;
Now, before the throne of God,
  Sealed with his almighty name:
Clad in raiment pure and white,
  Victor palms in every hand:
Thro' their great Redeemer's might,
  More than conquerors they stand.

3.
Hunger, thirst, disease unknown,
  On immortal fruits they feed:
Then the Lamb, amidst the throne,
  Shall to living fountains lead:
Joy and gladness banish sighs:
  Perfect love dispels all fears;
And forever from their eyes,
  God shall wipe away their tears.
        Montgomery.

HOMEWARD BOUND.

J. W. DADMUN.

No. 63. *Homeward bound.*

2 Wildly the storm sweeps us on as it roars; We're homeward bound;
Look! yonder lie the bright heavenly shores; We're homeward bound;
Steady! O pilot! stand firm at the wheel,
Steady! we soon shall outweather the gale,
Oh! how we fly 'neath the loud creaking sail, We're homeward bound.

3 We'll tell the world as we journey along, We're homeward bound;
Try to persuade them to enter our throng, We're homeward bound,
Come, trembling sinner, forlorn and oppressed,
Join in our number, oh, come and be blest;
Journey with us to the mansions of rest, We're homeward bound.

4 Into the harbor of heaven now we glide, We're home at last
Softly we drift on its bright silver tide, We're home at last;
Glory to God! all our dangers are o'er;
We stand secure on the glorified shore,
Glory to God! we will shout evermore, We're at home at last.

Rev. W. F. Warren.

MERDIN. 7s, 6s & 7s.

Dr. L. Mason.

1. Burst, ye emerald gates, and bring To my rap-tured vis-ion,
All the ecstatic joys that spring Round the bright e-lys-ian;
Lo! we lift our long-ing eyes, Break, ye in-ter-ven-ing skies!
Sons of righteousness, a-rise, Ope the gates of Par-a-dise.

No. 64. *The great salvation.*

2 Floods of everlasting light!
   Freely flash before him;
Myriads, with supreme delight,
   Instantly adore him;
Angels trumps resound his fame;
Lutes of lucid gold proclaim
All the music of his name;
Heaven echoing the theme.

3 Four-and-twenty elders rise
   From their princely station;
Shout his glorious victories,
   Sing the great salvation;

Cast their crowns before his throne,
Cry, in reverential tone,
Glory be to God alone,
Holy! Holy! Holy One.

4 Hark! the thrilling symphonies
   Seem, methinks, to seize us;
Join we, too, the holy lays—
   Jesus, Jesus, Jesus!
Sweetest sound in seraph's song,
Sweetest note on mortal tongue,
Sweetest carol ever sung—
Jesus, Jesus, flow along.

FREDERICK. 11s.

GEO. KINGSLEY.

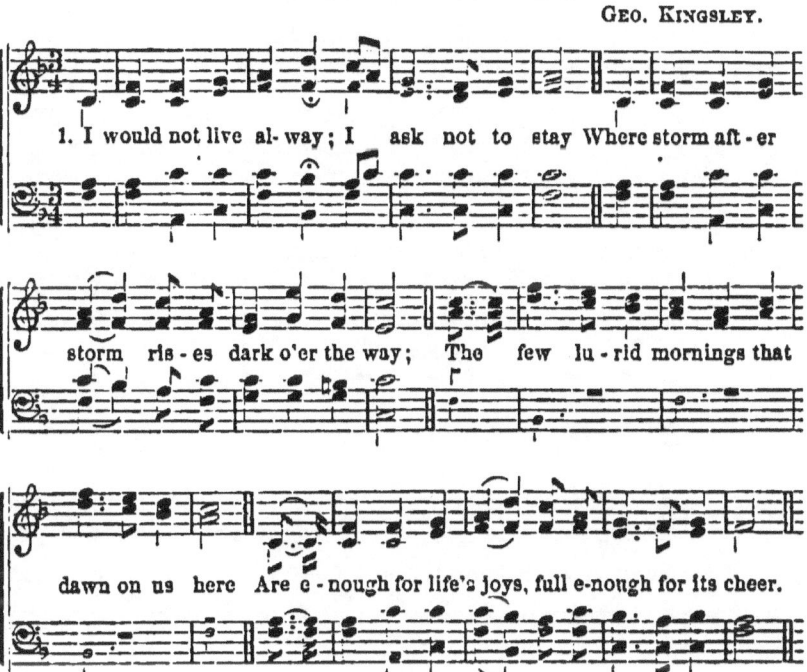

1. I would not live al-way; I ask not to stay Where storm aft-er storm ris-es dark o'er the way; The few lu-rid mornings that dawn on us here Are e-nough for life's joys, full e-nough for its cheer.

No. 65. *I would not live alway.*

2 I would not live alway; no—welcome the tomb!
Since Jesus hath lain there, I dread not its gloom:
There sweet be my rest till he bid me arise,
To hail him in triumph descending the skies.

3 Who, who would live alway, away from his God—
Away from yon heaven, that blissful abode,
Where rivers of pleasure flow bright o'er the plains,
And the noontide of glory eternally reigns?

4 There saints of all ages in harmony meet,
Their Saviour and brethren transported to greet;
While anthems of rapture unceasingly roll,
And the smile of the Lord is the feast of the soul.—*Muhlenburg.*

SHINING SHORE.

Geo. F. Root.

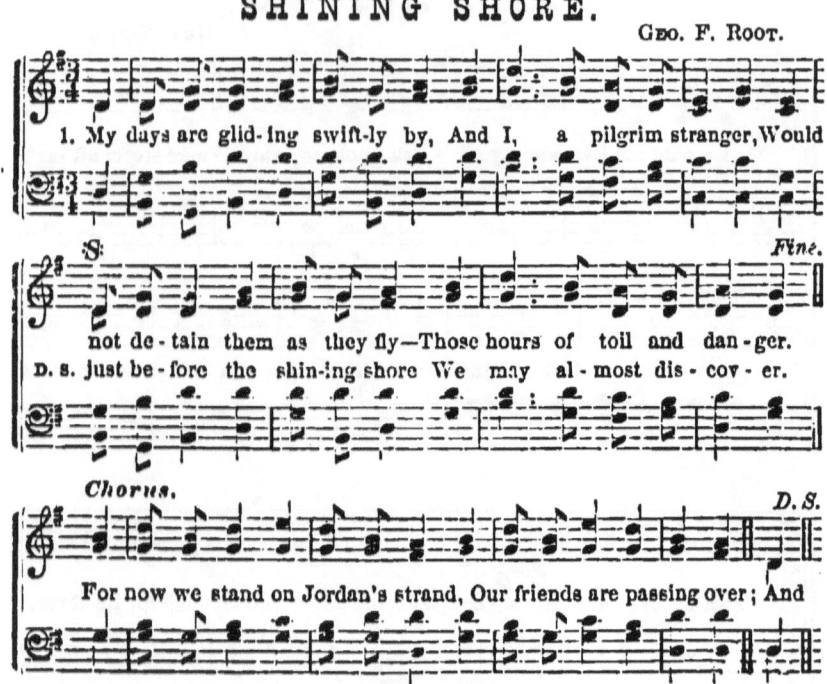

No. 66.

The shining shore.

2 We'll gird our loins, my brethren dear,
    Our heavenly home discerning:
    Our absent Lord has left us word,
    Let every lamp be burning.
      For now we stand, &c.

3 Should coming days be cold and dark,
    We need not cease our singing;
    That perfect rest naught can molest
    Where golden harps are ringing.
      For now we stand, &c.

4 Let sorrow's rudest tempest blow,
    Each chord on earth to sever,
    Our King says come, and there's our home,
    Forever! oh, forever!
      For now we stand, &c.

LOOKING HOME.

Wm. B. Bradbury.

No. 67. *Looking home.*

2 Soon the glorious day will dawn,
　Heavenly pleasures bringing;
　Night will be exchanged for morn,
　Sighs give place to singing.

3 Oh! to be at home again,
　All for which we're sighing,
　From all earthly want and pain
　To be swiftly flying.

4 Blessed home! oh, blessed home!
　All for which we're sighing,
　Soon our Lord will bid us come
　To our Father's kingdom.

HAMDEN. 8s, 7s & 4.
Dr. L. Mason.

1. Guide me, O thou great Je-ho-vah, Pilgrim thro' this barren land: I am weak, but thou art mighty; Hold me with thy powerful hand; Bread of heav-en, Feed me till I want no more.

No.

The pilgrim's guide and guardian.

2 Open now the crystal fountain,
 Whence the healing waters flow;
 Let the fiery, cloudy pillar
 Lead me all my journey through:
  Strong Deliverer,
 Be thou still my strength and shield.

3 When I tread the verge of Jordan,
 Bid my anxious fears subside;
 Bear me through the swelling current,
 Land me safe on Canaan's side;
  Songs of praises
 I will ever give to thee

Hallowed Songs, Revised. 75

LOVING-KINDNESS. L. M.

1. Awake, my soul, in joy-ful lays, And sing thy great Redeemer's praise; He just-ly claims a song from me: His lov-ing-kindness, oh, how free! His loving-kindness, loving-kindness, His lov-ing-kindness, oh, how free!

No. 69.   *Christ's loving-kindness.*

2 He saw me ruined by the fall,
Yet loved me, notwithstanding all;
He saved me from my lost estate;
His loving-kindness, oh, how great!

3 Tho' numerous hosts of mighty foes,
Though earth and hell my way oppose,
He safely leads my soul along:
His loving-kindness, oh, how strong!

4 I often feel my sinful heart
Prone from my Saviour to depart;
But though I oft have him forgot,
His loving-kindness changes not.

5 Soon shall I pass the gloomy vale,
Soon all my mortal powers must fail;
Oh, may my last, expiring breath
His loving-kindness sing in death.
Medley.

SWEET REST.

Wm. B. Bradbury.

1. Come, brethren, don't grow wea-ry, But let us jour-ney on:
   The pass-ing scenes all tell us That death will sure-ly come;
   The moments will not tar-ry; This life will soon be gone:
   These bod-ies soon will mould-er In th' dark and wea-ry tomb:

Chorus.
There is sweet rest in heav'n, There is sweet rest in heav'n, There is sweet rest in heav'n,........ sweet rest, There is sweet rest, There is sweet rest in heav'n.

No. 70. *Sweet rest in heaven.*

2 Loved ones have gone before us,
　They beckon us away,
O'er aerial plains they're soaring,
　Blest in eternal day;
But we are in the army,
　And dare not leave our post;
We'll fight until we conquer
　The foes' most mighty host.

3 Our Captain's gone before us,
　He kindly calls us home
To yonder world of glory,
　And sweetly bids us come.
The world, the flesh, and Satan,
　Will strive to hedge our way,
But we'll o'ercome these powers,
　If we hourly watch and pray.
　　　　　　　Unknown.

BEAUTIFUL ZION.

1. Beauti-ful Zi - on, built a - bove, Beauti-ful cit - y that I love,
Beauti-ful gates of pear-ly white, Beauti-ful tem-ple—God its light;
Beauti-ful gates of pear-ly white, Beauti-ful tem-ple—God its light.

No. 71.

2 Beautiful heaven, where all its light,
Beautiful angels, clothed in white,
Beautiful strains, that never tire,
Beautiful harps through all the choir.

3 Beautiful crowns on every brow,
Beautiful palms the conquerors show,
Beautiful robes the ransomed wear,
Beautiful all who enter there.

4 Beautiful throne of Christ our King,
Beautiful songs the angels sing,
Beautiful rest, all wanderings cease,
Beautiful home of perfect peace.

* *From the "Oriola," by permission of* BIGLOW & MAIN.

SHALL WE MEET.

Philip Phillips.

1. Shall we meet be-yond the riv-er, Where the sur-ges cease to roll?
   Where, in all the bright for-ev-er, Sor-row ne'er shall (*Omit*.......)

press the soul? Shall we meet? shall we meet? Shall we meet be-

yond the riv-er, Where the sur-ges cease.... to roll?

No. 72.   *Shall we meet beyond the river.*

2 Shall we meet in that blest harbor,
   When our stormy voyage is o'er?
Shall we meet and cast the anchor
   By the fair celestial shore?

3 Shall we meet in yonder city,
   Where the towers of crystal shine,
Where the walls are all of jasper,
   Built by workmanship divine?

4 Where the music of the ransomed
   Rolls its harmony around,

And creation swells the chorus,
   With its sweet melodious sound?

5 Shall we meet with many a loved one,
   That was torn from our embrace?
Shall we listen to their voices,
   And behold them face to face?

6 Shall we meet with Christ our Saviour,
   When he comes to claim his own?
Shall we know his blessed favor,
   And sit down upon the throne?

HAPPY DAY. L. M.

1. O happy day, that fix'd my choice On thee, my Saviour and my God!
Well may this glowing heart rejoice, And tell its raptures all abroad.

Happy day, happy day, When Jesus washed my sins away;
D. S. Happy day, happy day, When Jesus washed my sins away.

He taught me how to watch and pray, And live rejoicing every day:

No. 73.   *Vows remembered and renewed.*

2 O happy bond, that seals my vows
   To him who merits all my love;
Let cheerful anthems fill his house,
   While to that sacred shrine I move.

3 'Tis done, the great transaction's done,
   I am my Lord's, and he is mine;
He drew me, and I follow'd on,
   Charm'd to confess the voice divine.

4 Now rest, my long-divided heart;
   Fix'd on this blissful centre, rest;
Nor ever from thy Lord depart:
   With him of every good possess'd.

5 High Heaven, that heard the solemn vow,
   That vow renew'd shall daily hear,
Till in life's latest hour I bow,
   And bless in death a bond so dear.—*Doddridge.*

SAFE WITHIN THE VAIL.

Arr. by J. C. MIDDLETON.

1. "Land a - head!" Its fruits are waving O'er the hills of fadeless green;
And the liv - ing wa-ters lav - ing Shores where heav'nly forms are seen.

Chorus.
Rocks and storms I'll fear no more, When on that e - ter - nal shore.
Drop the an - chor! furl the sail! I am safe within the vail.

No. 74.

2 Onward, bark! the cape I'm rounding,
See, the blessed wave their hands;
Hear the harps of God resounding
From the bright immortal bands.

3 There, let go the anchor, riding
On this calm and silv'ry bay;

Sea-ward fast the tide is gliding,
Shores in sunlight stretch away.

4 Now we're safe from all temptation,
All the storms of life are past;
Praise the Rock of our salvation,
We are safe at home at last!

HARWELL. 8s & 7s.

Dr. Lowell Mason.

1. Hail, my ev-er blessed Je-sus! On-ly thee I wish to sing;
   To my soul thy name is precious, Thou my Prophet, Priest, and King.
D. C. Love I much, I've much forgiv-en— I'm a mir-a-cle of grace!

Oh, what mercy flows from heaven! Oh, what joy and happiness!
Oh, what mer-cy flows from heaven! Oh, what joy and happi-ness!

No. 75.   *Blessed Jesus.*

2 Once with Adam's race in ruin,
   Unconcerned in sin I lay;
Swift destruction still pursuing,
   Till my Saviour passed that way.
Witness, all ye host of heaven,
   My Redeemer's tenderness;
Love I much, I've much forgiven—
   I'm a miracle of grace!

3 Shout, ye bright, angelic choir,
   Praise the Lamb enthroned above,
Whilst, astonished, I admire
   God's free grace and boundless love.
That blest moment I received him,
   Filled my soul with joy and peace;
Love I much, I've much forgiven—
   I'm a miracle of grace!

ELTHAM. 7s. Double.

DR. LOWELL MASON.

1. Hasten, Lord, the glorious time,
   When, beneath Messiah's sway,
   Every nation, every clime,
   Shall the gospel call obey.
   Mightiest kings his power shall own;
   Heathen tribes his name adore;
   Satan and his host, o'erthrown,
   Bound in chains, shall hurt no more.

No. 76.   *Christ's universal reign.*

2 Then shall wars and tumults cease;
   Then be banished grief and pain;
   Righteousness, and joy, and peace,
   Undisturbed, shall ever reign.
   Bless we, then, our gracious Lord;
   Ever praise his glorious name;
   All his mighty acts record,—
   All his wondrous love proclaim.

THE FARTHER SHORE.

S. J. Vail.

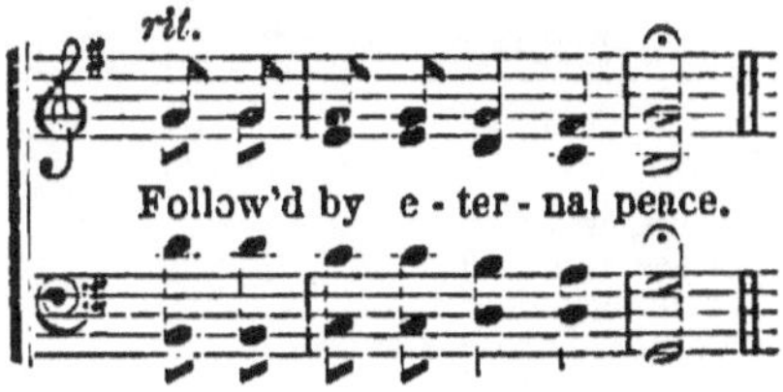

1. When we pass thro' yon-der riv-er, When we reach the farth-er shore, There's an end of war for-ev-er; We shall see our foes no more: All our con-flicts then shall cease, All our con-flicts then shall cease, Follow'd by e-ter-nal peace.

No. 77.

2.
After warfare, rest is pleasant;
Oh, how sweet the prospect is!
Though we toil and strive at present,
Let us not repine at this;
‖: Toil, and pain, and conflict past, :‖
All endear repose at last.

3.
When we gain the heavenly regions,
When we touch the heavenly shore—
Blessed thought—no hostile legions
Can alarm or trouble more:
‖: Far beyond the reach of foes, :‖
We shall dwell in sweet repose.

4.
O that hope; how bright, how glorious
'Tis his people's blest reward;
In the Saviour's strength victorious,
They at length behold their Lord:
‖: In his kingdom they shall rest, :‖
In his love be fully blest.

No. 78.

2 Stand up for Jesus, Christian, stand!
Sound forth his name o'er sea and land!
Spread ye his glorious Word abroad,
Till all the world shall own him Lord!—*Chorus.*

3 Stand up for Jesus, Christian, stand!
Lift high the cross with steadfast hand!
Till heathen lands with wondering eye
Its rising glory shall descry.—*Chorus.*

4 Stand up for Jesus, Christian, stand!
Soon with the blest immortal band
We'll dwell for aye, life's journey o'er,
In realms of light on heaven's bright shore.—*Chorus.*

* From "S. S. Casket," by permission.

TALMAR. 8s & 7s.

I. B. Woodbury.

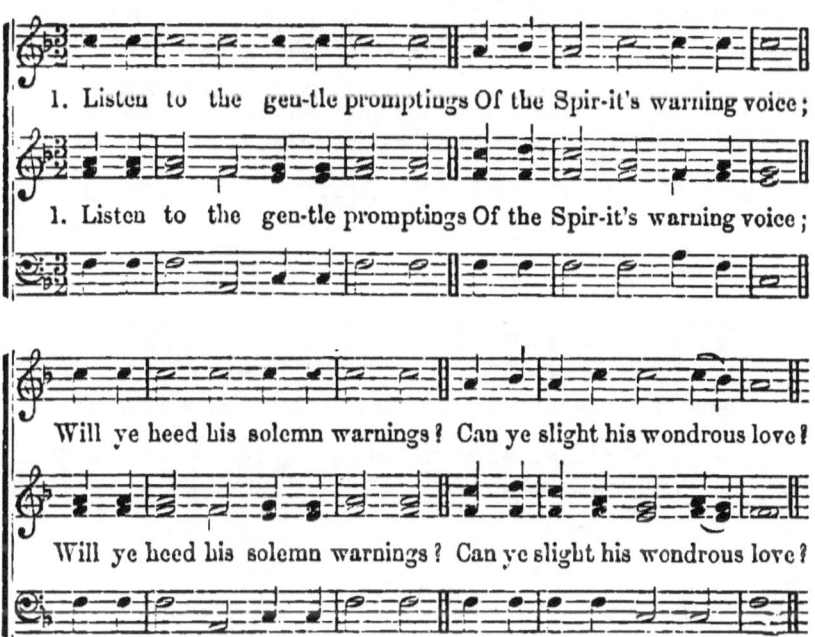

1. Listen to the gentle promptings Of the Spirit's warning voice;
Will ye heed his solemn warnings? Can ye slight his wondrous love?

No. 79.

2 Sweetly calling on the erring,
   Pardons offered without price;
Come, and round the altar kneeling,
   Oh, receive the offered grace.

3 Joy and hope the troubled conscience
   Will allay with soothing peace;
Press ye, then, to realms of glory;
   Run with joy the offered race.

4 Hesitate no longer, sinner,
   Lest the Spirit, sad and grieved,
Should forsake thee now and ever,
   Never more to be deceived.

WILL YOU GO?

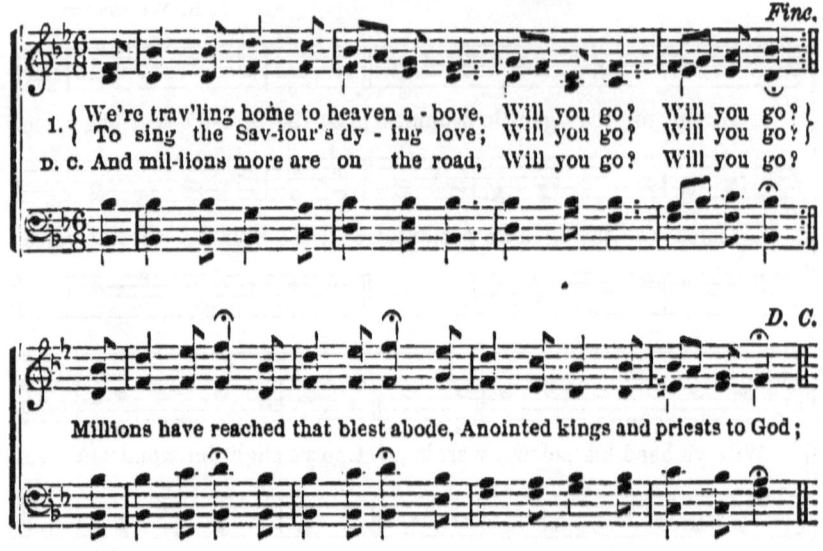

1. We're trav'ling home to heaven a-bove, Will you go? Will you go?
   To sing the Sav-iour's dy-ing love; Will you go? Will you go?
D.C. And mil-lions more are on the road, Will you go? Will you go?

Millions have reached that blest abode, Anointed kings and priests to God;

No. 80.   *Will you go?*

2 We're going to walk the plains of light; Will you go?
Far, far from the curse of death and night; Will you go?
The crown of life we then shall wear,
The conqueror's palm we then shall bear,
And all the joys of heaven we'll share; Will you go?

3 The way to heaven is straight and plain; Will you go?
Repent, believe, be born again; Will you go?
The Saviour cries aloud to thee,
"Take up your cross and follow me,
And thou shalt my salvation see." Will you go?

4 Oh, could I hear some sinner say, "I will go;"
Oh, could I hear him humbly pray "Make me go;"
And all his old companions tell,
"I will not go with you to hell,
I long with Jesus Christ to dwell; Let me go.

SWEET LAND OF REST.

1. Sweet land of rest, for thee I sigh! When will the moment come,
And dwell with Christ at home,........ And dwell with Christ at home;
When I shall lay my armor by, And dwell with Christ at home;
When I shall lay my armor by, And dwell with Christ at home.

No. 81. *Sweet land of rest.*

2 No tranquil joys on earth I know,
No peaceful, sheltering dome;
This world's a wilderness of woe,
:||: This world is not my home; :||:
This world's a wilderness of woe,
This world is not my home.

3 To Jesus Christ I sought for rest,
He bade me cease to roam;
But fly for succor to his breast,
:||: And he'd conduct me home; :||:
But fly for succor to his breast,
And he'd conduct me home.

4 Weary of wand'ring round and round
This vale of sin and gloom,
I long to leave th' unhallowed ground,
:||: And dwell with Christ at home; :||:
I long to leave th' unhallowed ground,
And dwell with Christ at home.

LOVE DIVINE.

J. H. WILCOX.

1. Love di-vine, all love ex-cell-ing, Joy of heaven, to earth come down!
Fix in us thy humble dwell-ing; All thy faith-ful mercies crown;
Je-sus, thou art all compas-sion, Pure, unbound-ed love thou art;
Vis-it us with thy sal va-tion, En-ter ev-ery trembling heart.

No. 82.

2 Breathe, oh, breathe thy loving Spirit
   Into every troubled breast;
Let us all thy grace inherit,
   Let us find thy promised rest;
Take away the love of sinning,
   Take our load of guilt away;
End the work of thy beginning,
   Bring us to eternal day.

THE SHINING WAY.

S. MAIN.

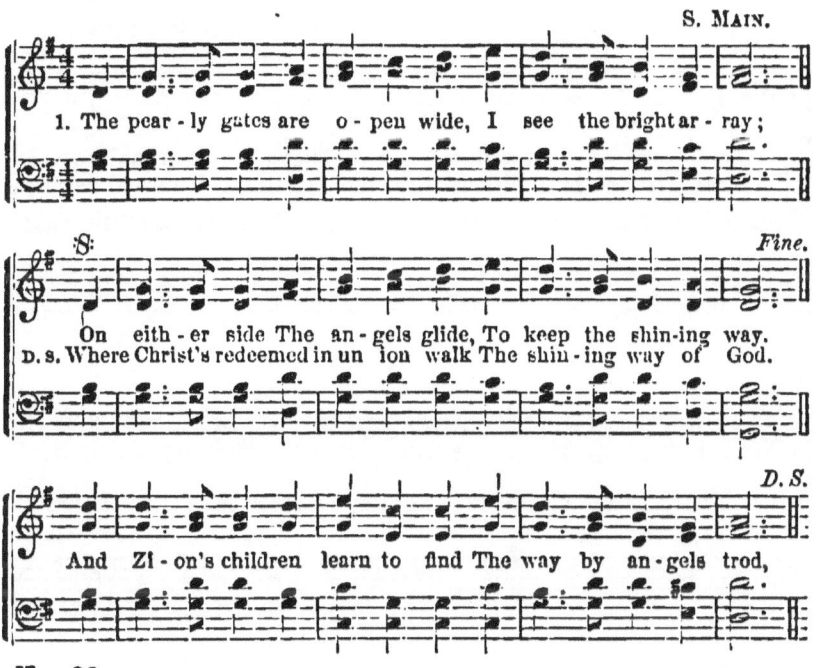

No. 83. *The shining way.*

2 When storms arise, and darkness clouds
    The faithful pilgrim's way,
The angels glide On either side,
    To drive the clouds away.
And brighter gleams the morning light
    Behind the gentle rod;
For Christ's redeemed more clearly see
    The shining way of God.

3 And soon they walk the golden streets,—
    Not slighted and alone,
On either side The angels glide,
    To lead them to the throne:
And there they wear a starry crown,
    While mortals tire and plod;
For Christ's redeemed are kings who praise
    The shining way of God.—*John P. Ellis.*

WILLOW-DALE. C. M. Double.

W<small>M</small>. B. B<small>RADBURY</small>.

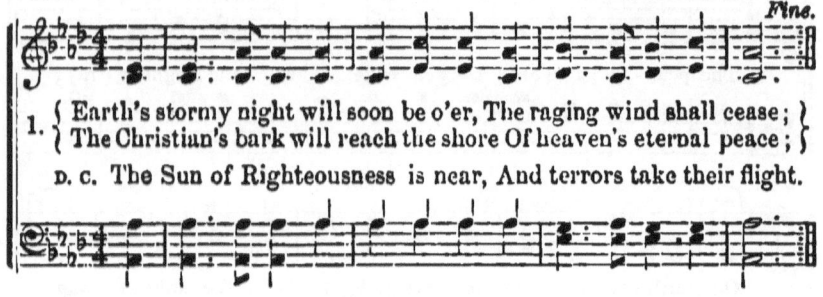

1. Earth's stormy night will soon be o'er, The raging wind shall cease;
The Christian's bark will reach the shore Of heaven's eternal peace;
D. C. The Sun of Righteousness is near, And terrors take their flight.

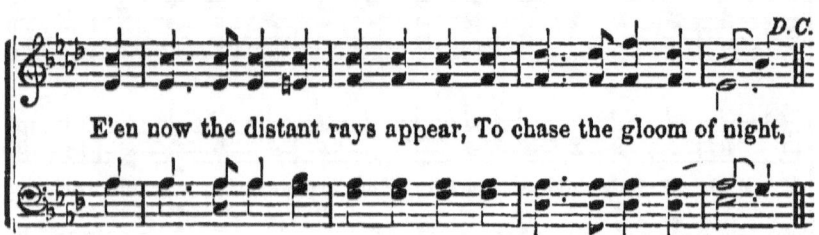

E'en now the distant rays appear, To chase the gloom of night,

No. 84.   *Earth's shadowy years.*

2 The precious jewels Jesus sent
  To be our solace here,
Were only for a season lent,
  They're shining brighter there.
And we shall soon their lovely forms
  In glorious robes behold;
Shall sing with them in angels' songs,
  With harps of shining gold.

3 Earth's shadowy years will soon
    be o'er—
  Heaven's blissful morn arise,
And sorrow's night will then no
    more
  O'ercloud our weeping eyes.

Then will the Lord of life and love
  Unveil his beaming face;
And never from our sight remove
  The bright celestial rays.

4 In that blest place no loved ones
    part;
  No mourning there, no sighs;
For God himself will gently wipe
  All sorrow from their eyes.
There everlasting peace and joy,
  And transport shall be thine;
Praise shall our utmost powers em-
    ploy
  In melody divine.

Hallowed Songs, Revised. 91

ALETTA. 7s. 6 lines.
Wm. B. Bradbury.

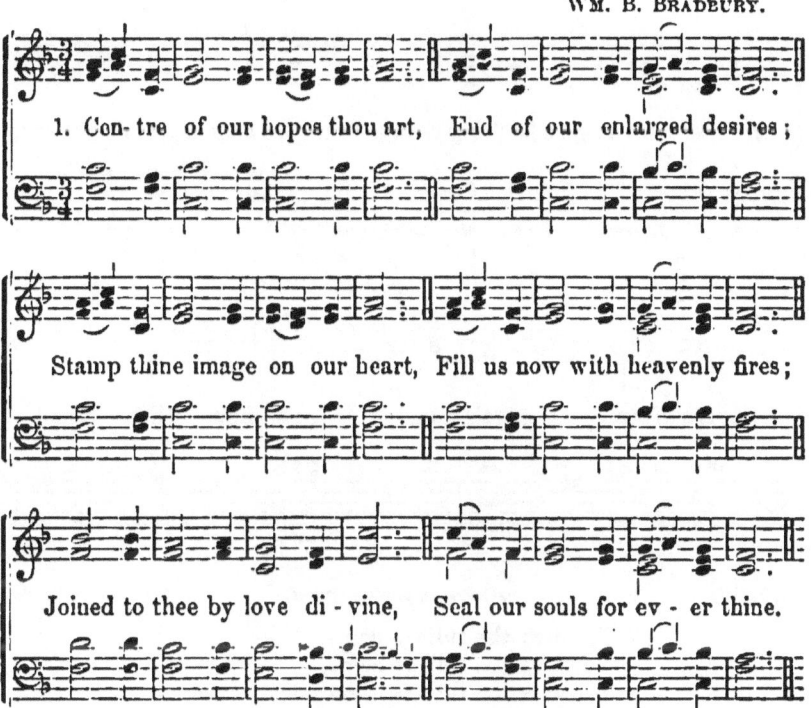

1. Cen- tre of our hopes thou art, End of our enlarged desires;
Stamp thine image on our heart, Fill us now with heavenly fires;
Joined to thee by love di-vine, Seal our souls for ev - er thine.

No. 85.   *Hand in hand to heaven.*

2 All our works in thee be wrought—
Leveled at one common aim;
Every word and every thought
Purge in the refining flame;
Lead us through the paths of peace,
On to perfect holiness.

3 Let us altogether rise,
To thy glorious life restored:
Here regain our paradise,
Here prepare to meet our Lord;
Here enjoy the earnest given;
Travel hand in hand to heaven.

ANGELS HOVERING ROUND.

No. 86. *Angels hovering round.*

2 To carry the tidings home,
To carry the tidings home,
To carry the tidings, the tidings home.

3 To the new Jerusalem,
To the new Jerusalem,
To the new, the new Jerusalem.

4 Poor sinners are coming home,
Poor sinners are coming home,
Poor sinners, sinners are coming home.

5 And Jesus bids them come,
And Jesus bids them come,
And Jesus, Jesus bids them come.

6 There's glory all around,
There's glory all around,
There's glory, glory all around.

GOING HOME. L. M.

1. { My heavenly home is bright and fair; Nor pain, nor
   { Its glittering towers the sun out-shine; That heavenly
   death can enter there; } I'm going home, I'm going
   mansion shall be mine; } To die no more, to die no
   home, I'm going home, to die no more;
   more, I'm going home, to die no more.

No. 87.   *The heavenly home.*

2 My Father's house is built on high,
  Far, far above the starry sky:
  When from this earthy prison free,
  That heavenly mansion mine shall be
      I'm going home, &c.

3 Let others seek a home below,
  Which flames devour, or waves o'erflow
  Be mine a happier lot to own
  A heavenly mansion near the throne.
      I'm going home, &c.

GOD IS LOVE.

Moderato Legato.  W. H. ROBERTS.

1. Depth of mer-cy! can there be Mer-cy still re-served for me?
Can my God his wrath forbear? Me, the chief of sinners, spare?

Chorus. Faster—Staccato.

God is love! I know, I feel; Jesus weeps, and loves me still;

Smoothly. *Repeat pp*

Je - sus weeps, He weeps, and loves me still.

No. 88. *Mercy for the chief of sinners.*

2 I have long withstood his grace
Long provoked him to his face:
Would not hearken to his calls;
Grieved him by a thousand falls.
God is love, &c.

3 Now incline me to repent;
Let me now my sins lament;
Now my foul revolt deplore,
Weep, believe, and sin no more.
God is love, &c.

4 There for me the Saviour stands;
Shows his wounds, and spreads his hands;
God is love! I know, I feel;
Jesus weeps, and loves me still.
God is love, &c.—*C. Wesley.*

LORD, REVIVE US.

1. Sav-iour, vis-it thy plan-ta-tion, Grant us,
   All will come to des-o-la-tion, Un-less

Chorus.

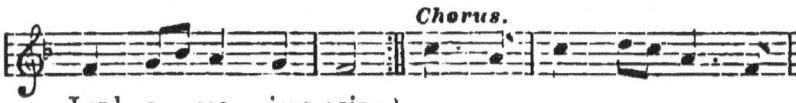

Lord, a gra-cious rain;
thou re-turn a-gain. Lord, re-vive us, oh, re-

vive us; Lord, re-vive thy work in me; Good Lord, re-

vive us, oh, re-vive us; All our help must come from thee.

No. 89.   *Prayer for revival.*

2 Keep no longer at a distance,
   Shine upon us from on high,
  Lest for want of thine assistance,
   Every plant should droop and die,
     Lord, revive us, &c.

3 Let our mutual love be fervent,
   Make us prevalent in prayers;
  Let each one esteemed thy servant,
   Shun the world's bewitching snares.
     Lord, revive us, &c.

4 Break the tempter's fatal power,
   Turn the stony heart to flesh;
  And begin, from this good hour
   To revive the work afresh.
     Lord, revive us, &c.—*Newton.*

WHO'S LIKE JESUS.

No. 90.

MORE LIKE JESUS.

F. C. GOUGH.

1. More like Je-sus, more like Je-sus would I be: More like Je-sus in sub-mis-sion, Like him trustful, un-re-pin - - ing, Pa-tient like him, like him in hu-mil-i-ty, like him in hu-mil-i-ty.

No. 91.

2 More like Jesus, more like Jesus would I be;
  More like Jesus in his meekness,
  Like him gentle and forgiving;
Harmless like him, like him in his charity.

3 More like Jesus, more like Jesus would I be;
  More like Jesus, watchful, prayerful,
  Like him striving, ever doing;
Earnest like him, like him in fidelity.

4 Blessed Jesus, come, and make me all like thee;
  Make me like thee in my spirit,
  In my walk and conversation,
Make me like thee, like thee in all purity.

5 Then in heaven let me ever dwell with thee;
  To behold thee in thy glory,
  And to praise thee, O my Saviour,
Where thy smile shall wrap my soul in ecstacy.

Rev. F. Merrick, D.D.

CONGREGATIONAL CHORUS.

"Let the people praise thee, O God, let all the people praise thee."

PHILIP PHILLIPS.

1. Yes, let our con-gre-ga-tions sing, And let our earth-ly tem-ples ring With hymns of joy from ev-ery soul, In ev-ery church from pole to pole, Let all u-nit-ed join, and raise This old fa-mil-iar song of praise:

CORONATION. *Chorus to 1st Verse.*
Firm.

1. Oh, for a thousand tongues to sing My great Redeemer's praise: The glo-ries of my God and King, The triumphs of his grace;

Hallowed Songs, Revised. 99

The glo-ries of my God and King, The triumphs of.... his grace.

OLD HUNDRED. *Chorus to 2d Voice.*

Praise God, from whom all blessings flow; Praise him, all creatures here be-low; Praise him a-bove, ye heaven-ly host; Praise Fa-ther, Son, and Ho-ly Ghost.

No. 92.
2 O rapturous music, how sublime!
 I wept and thought the olden time
 Of Watts' and Wesley's earnest throng
 Had with its flame inspired the song;
 Oh, let us sing with one accord,
 Join heart and voice to praise the Lord.
  CHORUS.—Praise God, &c.

FOREVER WITH THE LORD.

I. B. Woodbury.

Near - er home, near - er home, A day's march nearer home.

No. 93.

2 My Father's house on high,
   Home of my soul, how near,
At times, to faith's aspiring eye
   Thy golden gates appear!
Ah, then my spirit faints
   To reach the land I love;
The bright inheritance of saints—
   Jerusalem above;
Home above, home above,
   Jerusalem above.

3 Yet doubts still intervene,
   And all my comfort flies:
Like Noah's dove, I flit between
   Rough seas and stormy skies:
Anon the clouds depart,
   The wind and waters cease,
While sweetly o'er my gladden'd heart
   Expands the bow of peace;
Bow of peace, bow of peace,
   Expands the bow of peace.

4 So, when my latest breath
   Shall rend the vail in twain,
By death I shall escape from death,
   And life eternal gain;
Knowing "as I am known,"
   How shall I love that word,
And oft repeat before the throne,
   "Forever with the Lord;"
With the Lord, with the Lord,
   "Forever with the Lord."

COME, CROWN AND THRONE.

"Having promise of the life that now is, and of that which is to come."

G. B. LOOMIS.*

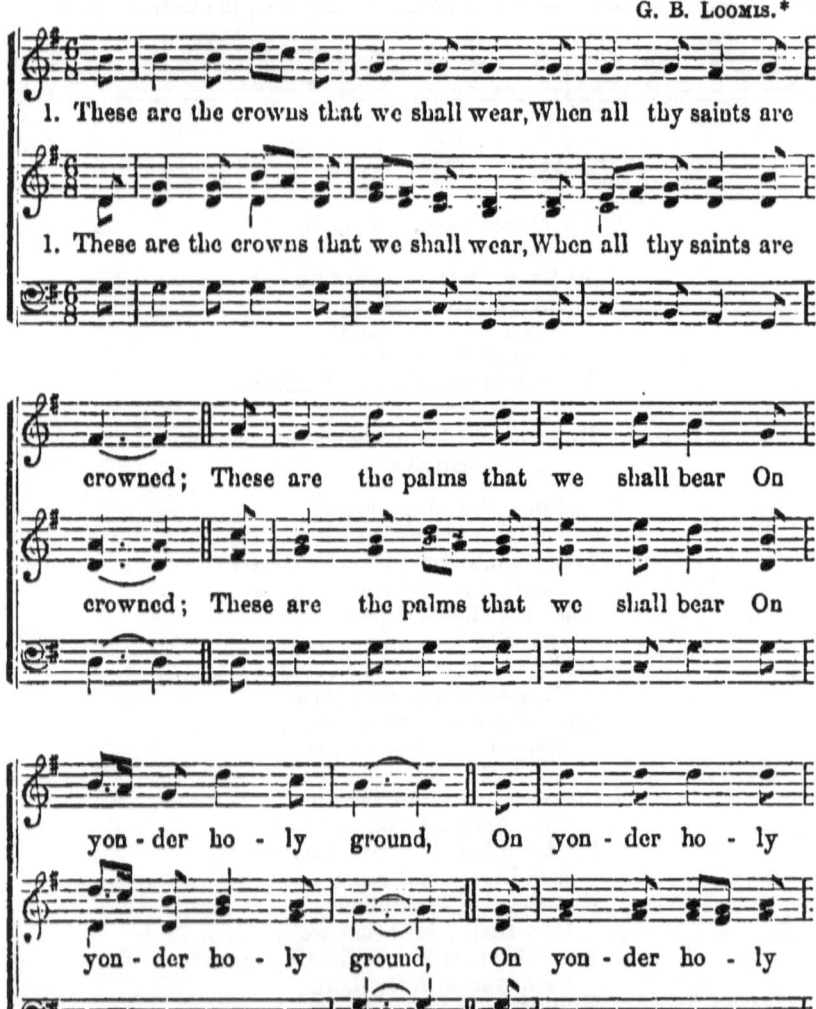

1. These are the crowns that we shall wear, When all thy saints are crowned; These are the palms that we shall bear On yon-der ho-ly ground, On yon-der ho-ly ground, On yon-der ho-ly

* *From "Singing Pilgrim."*

No. 94.

2 These are the robes, unsoiled and white,
   Which we shall then put on,
   When foremost 'mong the sons of light,
   We sit on yonder throne.

3 That is the city of the saints,
   Where we so soon shall stand,
   When we shall strike these desert-tents,
   And quit this desert-land.

4 Then welcome toil, and care, and pain!
   And welcome sorrow, too!
   All toil is rest, all grief is gain,
   With such a prize in view.

5 Come, crown and throne; come, robe and palm;
   Burst forth, glad stream of peace!
   Come, holy city of the Lamb!
   Rise, Sun of Righteousness!—*Bonar.*

THE LIVING WELL.

"Whosoever drinketh of the water that I shall give him, shall never thirst."

PHILIP PHILLIPS.*

1. On the cross where Christ hung bleeding, Streams of love for-ev-er flow; Thro' the Saviour's in-ter-ced-ing, We that bless-ed stream may know. Oh, my heart, be filled completely, And in grateful love re-joice! Je-sus speaks so gently, sweetly, Lis-ten to his

* From "Singing Pilgrim."

No. 95.

2 Though our way is often dreary,
    And in gloom the sky is clad:
Though the steps grow faint and weary,
    And the heart is sick and sad;
There's a well of living pleasure,
    Every night and morning too,
Flowing in exhaustless measure,
    Ever blessing, ever new. Drink, &c.

3 We may ever have that fountain,
    Welling with exhaustless flow,
In the valley, on the mountain,
    Wheresoe'er our steps may go
As we drink, a holy beauty
    Fills our souls, so washed and blest,
And our hands grow strong for duty,
    And our weary hearts find rest. Drink, &c.

THE FUTURE REST.

"Fear not, little flock, for it is your Father's good pleasure to give you the kingdom."

S. J. VAIL.

1. We shall meet no more to sev-er, By - and-by, by - and-by;
And the darkness will be o - ver, By - and-by, by - and-by;
With the toilsome journey done, And the glorious bat - tle won,
We shall shine forth as the sun, By - and-by, by - and-by.

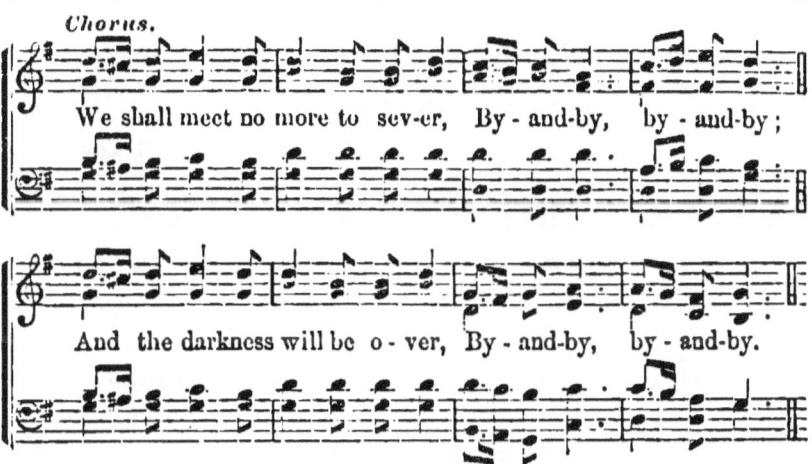

No. 96.

2 Done with all the earth's delusion,
   By-and-by, by-and-by:
War and strife and sin's confusion,
   By-and-by, by-and-by;
We shall rest our pilgrim feet
On the shores where loved ones meet,
There to dwell in bliss complete,
   By-and-by, by-and-by.—*Chorus.*

3 We shall see and be like Jesus
   By-and-by, by-and-by;
He a crown of life will give us,
   By-and-by, by-and-by;
And the angels who fulfill
All the mandates of his will,
Shall attend and love us still,
   By-and-by, by-and-by.—*Chorus.*

4 Then with robes of snowy whiteness,
   By-and-by, by-and-by;
And with crowns of dazzling brightness,
   By-and-by, by-and-by;
There our storms and perils passed,
And with glory ours at last,
We'll possess the kingdom vast,
   By-and-by, by-and-by.—*Chorus.*

SHALL WE GATHER AT THE RIVER.

"I will gather you from all nations."

Rev. R. Lowry.*

* From "Happy Voices."

No. 97.

2 On the margin of the river,
  Washing up its silver spray,
We will walk and worship ever,
  All the happy, golden day.—*Chorus.*

3 Ere we reach the shining river,
  Lay we every burden down;
Grace our spirits will deliver,
  And provide a robe and crown.—*Chorus.*

4 At the smiling of the river,
  Mirror of the Saviour's face,
Saints whom death will never sever
  Lift their songs of saving grace.—*Chorus.*

5 Soon we'll reach the silver river,
  Soon our pilgrimage will cease;
Soon our happy hearts will quiver
  With the melody of peace.—*Chorus.*

I WILL SING FOR JESUS.

"Singing and making melody in your heart to the Lord."

PHILIP PHILLIPS.*

* From "*The Singing Pilgrim.*"

Hallowed Songs, Revised.

No. 98.

2 Can there overtake me
   Any dark disaster,
While I sing for Jesus,
   My blessed, blessed Master?
    Cho.—Oh, help me sing, &c.

3 I will sing for Jesus!
   His name alone prevailing,
Shall be my sweetest music,
   When heart and flesh are failing.
    Cho.—Oh, help me sing, &c.

4 Still I'll sing for Jesus!
   Oh, how will I adore him,
Among the cloud of witnesses,
   Who cast their crowns before him.
    Cho.—Oh, help me sing, &c

Mrs. Ellen H. Gates.

112 Hallowed Songs, Revised.

LET ME GO.

Rev. L. HARTSOUGH*.

1. Let me go where saints are going, To the mansions of the blest; Let me go where my Re-deem-er Has pre-pared his peo-ple's rest; I would gain the realms of brightness, Where they dwell for ev-er-more; I would gain the realms of day! Bear me

CHORUS. Let me go! 'tis Je-sus calls me; Let me gain the realms of day! Bear me

* By permission of Rev. H. MATTISON.

Hallowed Songs, Revised. 113

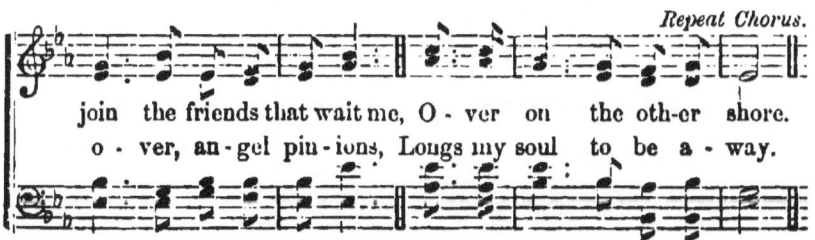

join the friends that wait me, O-ver on the oth-er shore.
o-ver, an-gel pin-ions, Longs my soul to be a-way.

No. 99.
2 Let me go where none are weary,
   Where is raised no wail or woe;
Let me go, and bathe my spirit
   In the raptures angels know:
Let me go! for bliss eternal
   Lures my soul away, away;
And the victors' song triumphant
   Thrills my heart—I cannot stay.—*Cho.*

3 Let me go! why should I tarry?
   What has earth to keep me here?
What, but cares and toils and sorrows?
   What, but death and pain and fear?
Let me go! for hopes most cherished
   Blasted round me often lie;
Oh! I've gathered brightest flowers,
   But to see them fade and die.—*Cho.*

4 Let me go where tears and sighing
   Are for evermore unknown;
Where the joyous songs of glory
   Call me to a happier home:
Let me go!—I'd cease this dying;
   I would gain life's fairer plains;
Let me join the myriad harpers!
   Let me chant their rapt'rous strains!—*Cho.*

5 Let me go! there is a glory
   That my soul hath longed to know:
I am thirsting for the waters
   That from crystal fountains flow:
There is where the angels tarry;
   There the saved forever throng;
There the brightness wearies never;
   There I'll sing Redemption's song.—*Cho.*

8

HOME OF THE SOUL.

"*And there shall in nowise enter into it any thing that defileth.*"

Moderato e Affettuoso.   PHILIP PHILLIPS.*

1. I will sing you a song of that beau-ti-ful land, The far-a-way home of the soul, Where no storms ev-er beat on the glit-ter-ing strand, While the years of e-ter-ni-ty roll, While the years of e-ter-ni-ty roll; Where no storms ev-er beat on the

* *From "Singing Pilgrim."*

Hallowed Songs, Revised. 115

glit - ter - ing strand, While the years of e - ter - ni - ty roll.

No. 100.

2 Oh, that home of the soul, in my visions and dreams,
    Its bright jasper walls I can see,
Till I fancy but thinly the vale intervenes
    Between the fair city and me.

3 There the great tree of life in its beauty doth grow,
    And the river of life floweth by,
For no death ever enters that city you know,
    And nothing that maketh a lie.

4 That unchangeable home is for you and for me,
    Where Jesus of Nazareth stands;
The King of all kingdoms forever is he,
    And he holdeth our crowns in his hands.

5 Oh, how sweet it will be in that beautiful land,
    So free from all sorrow and pain!
With songs on our lips, and with harps in our hands,
    To meet one another again.—*Mrs. Ellen H. Gates.*

"Now I saw in my Dream that these two men went in at the Gate; and lo, as they entered, they were transfigured, and they had Raiment put upon them that shone like Gold. There was also that met them with Harps and Crowns, and gave to them, the Harps to praise withal, and the Crowns in token of honor Then I heard in my Dream that all the Bells in the City rang again for joy, and that it was said unto them, *Enter ye into the joy of your Lord.* Now just as the Gates were opened to let in the men, I looked in after them, and behold, the City shone like the Sun; the Streets also were paved with Gold, and in them walked many men, with Crowns on their heads, Palms in their hands, and Harps to sing praises withal. After that they shut up the gates, which when I had seen I wished myself among them."

THE WORLD IS MY PARISH.

"Lo! I am with you alway, even unto the end of the world."

PHILLIPS AND O'KANE.*

* *From "Singing Pilgrim."*

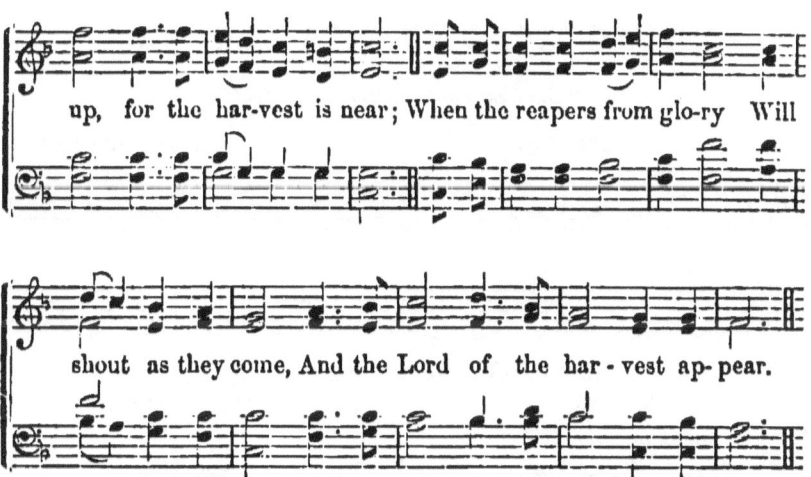

up, for the har-vest is near; When the reapers from glo-ry Will shout as they come, And the Lord of the har-vest ap-pear.

No. 101.

2 Our field is the world, and our work is before us,
  To each is appointed a message to bear;
At home or abroad, in the cottage or palace,
  Wherever directed, our mission is there.
    Our field is the world, &c.

3 Perhaps we are called from the highways and hedges,
  To gather the lowly, despised, and oppressed;
If this be our duty, then why should we falter,
  We'll do it, and trust to our Saviour the rest.
    Our field is the world, &c.

4 O'er islands that sleep in the wave-crested ocean,
  We'll scatter the truth, and its fruit it shall bear;
O'er ice-covered regions, and rock-girded mountains,
  The Lord will protect, as his children are there
    Our field is the world, &c.

5 Instead of the thorn shall the myrtle be planted;
  The desert shall blossom and bloom as the rose;
The palm tree rejoicing shall spread forth her branches:
  The lamb and the lion together repose
    Our field is the world, &c.—*Fanny Crosby.*

CLING TO THE MIGHTY ONE.

"But cleave unto the Lord your God."

Earnest and Pleading.   Philip Phillips.*

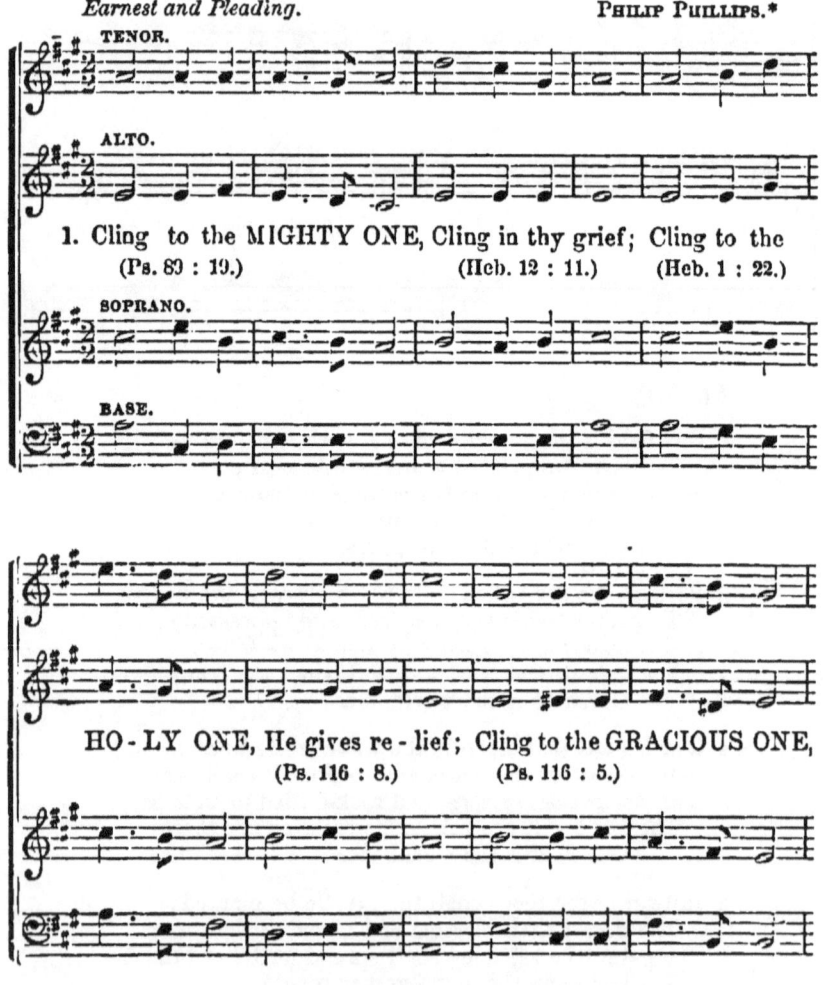

1. Cling to the MIGHTY ONE, Cling in thy grief; Cling to the
(Ps. 89 : 19.)   (Heb. 12 : 11.)   (Heb. 1 : 22.)

HO - LY ONE, He gives re - lief; Cling to the GRACIOUS ONE,
(Ps. 116 : 8.)   (Ps. 116 : 5.)

* *From " Singing Pilgrim."*

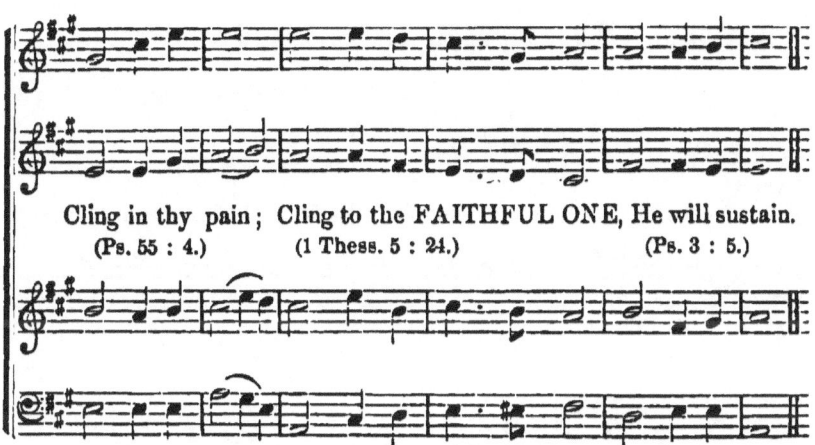

Cling in thy pain; Cling to the FAITHFUL ONE, He will sustain.
(Ps. 55 : 4.)   (1 Thess. 5 : 24.)   (Ps. 3 : 5.)

No. 102.

2 Cling to the LOVING ONE, Cling in thy woe;
(Heb. 7 : 25.)   (Ps. 86 : 7.)
Cling to the LIVING ONE, Through all below;
(1 John 4 : 16.)   (Rom. 8 : 38, 39.)
Cling to the PARDONING ONE, He speaketh peace;
(Is. 4 : 7.)   (John 14 : 27.)
Cling to the HEALING ONE, Anguish shall cease.
(Exod. 15 : 26.)   (Ps. 118 : 3.)

3 Cling to the BLEEDING ONE, Cling to his side;
(1 John 1 : 7.)   (John 20 : 27.)
Cling to the RISEN ONE, In him abide;
(Rom. 6 : 9.)   (John 15 : 4.)
Cling to the COMING ONE, Hope shall arise;
(Rev. 22 : 20.)   (Titus 2 : 13.)
Cling to the REIGNING ONE, Joy lights thine eyes.
(Ps. 97 : 1.)   (Ps. 16 : 2.)

No. 103.

2 Work, for the night is coming;
Work through the sunny noon;
Fill brightest hours with labor;
Rest comes sure and soon.
Give every flying minute
Something to keep in store;
Work, for the night is coming,
When man works no more.

3 Work, for the night is coming,
Under the sunset skies;
While their bright tints are glowing,
Work, for daylight flies.
Work, till the last beam fadeth,
Fadeth to shine no more:
Work, while the night is darkening,
When man's work is o'er.

OH, SAY, SHALL WE MEET YOU ALL THERE?

S. J. VAIL, *by permission.*

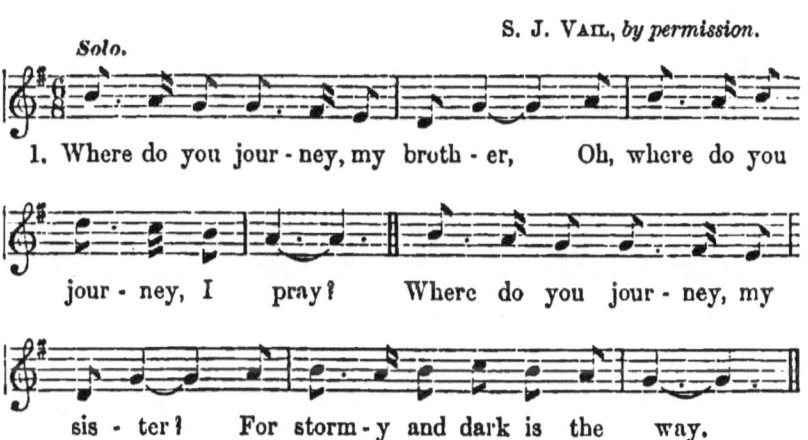

No. 104.

2.

Solo. What is your mission, my brother,
    What is your mission below?
What is your mission, my sister,
    As journeying onward you go?
Duet. Our mission is practising mercy,
    Sweet charity, patience, and love,
And following the footsteps of Jesus,
    That lead to the mansions above.
Cho. Oh, say, shall we meet, &c.

3.

Solo. Oh, yes! you will meet us, my brother,
    God helping our weakness and sin;
Bearing the cross, we, my sister,
    The crown will endeavor to win.
Duet. We'll walk through the vale and the shadow,
    Through suff'rings, and trials, and care,
And when you get safely to glory,
    You'll meet, yes, you'll meet us all there!
Cho. Oh, say, shall we meet, &c.—*Minnie Waters.*

CLIMBING UP ZION'S HILL.

"*They shall mount up with wings as eagles, and they shall walk and faint not.*"

PHILIP PHILLIPS.*

1. I'm try-ing to climb up Zi-on's hill, For the Saviour whispers, "Love me;" Tho' all beneath is dark as death, Yet the stars are bright a-bove me. Then up-ward still, to Zi-on's hill, To the land of joy and beau-ty, My

* *From "Singing Pilgrim."*

Hallowed Songs, Revised.

path before shines more and more, As it nears the gold-en cit - y.

Solo, or Semi-chorus.   *Duet, or 2d Semi-chorus.*

I'm climbing up Zi - on's hill,   I'm climbing up Zi - on's

Full Chorus.   *Repeat Chorus.*

hill,   Climbing, climb-ing, climbing up Zi - on's hill.

No. 105.

2 I know I'm but a little child,
   My strength will not protect me;
   But then I am the Saviour's Lamb,
   And he will not neglect me.
Then all the time I'll try to climb
   This holy hill of Zion,
For I am sure the way is pure,
   And on it comes "no lion."—*Cho.*

3 Then come with me, we'll upward go,
   And climb this hill together;
   And as we walk we'll sweetly talk,
   And sing as we go thither.
Then mount up still God's holy hill,
   Till we reach the pearly portals,
Where raptured tongues proclaim the songs
   Of the shining-robed immortals.—*Cho.*

Rev. John G. Chaffee.

WE SHALL SLEEP, BUT NOT FOREVER.

S. J. Vail. *By permission.**

1. We shall sleep, but not for-ev-er, There will be a glorious dawn;

We shall meet to part, no, nev-er! On the re-sur-rec-tion morn!

From the deep-est caves of o-cean, From the des-ert and the plain,

From the val-ley and the mountain, Countless throngs shall rise again.

* *From "Musical Leaves."*

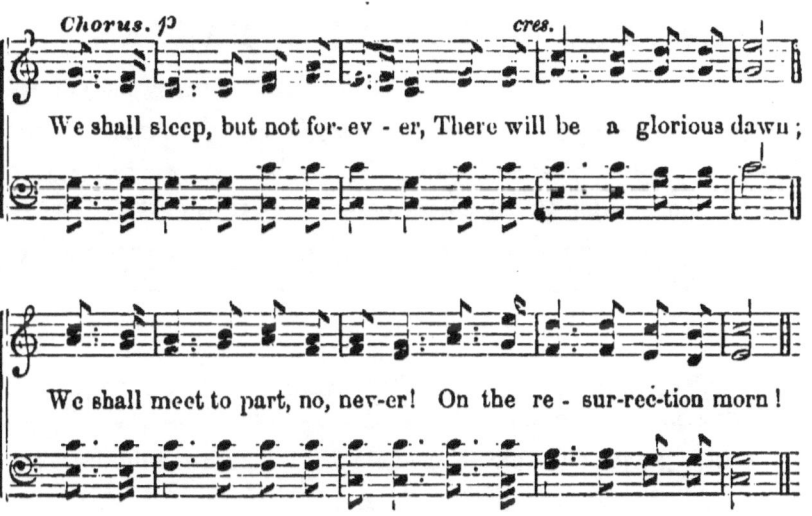

No. 106.

2 When we see a precious blossom,
   That we tended with such care,
Rudely taken from our bosom,
   How our aching hearts despair!
Round its little grave we linger,
   Till the setting sun is low,
Feeling all our hopes have perished
   With the flower we cherished so.
   Cho.—We shall sleep, etc.

3 We shall sleep, but not forever,
   In the lone and silent grave;
Blessed be the Lord that taketh,
   Blessed be the Lord that gave.
In the bright, eternal city
   Death can never, never come!
In his own good time he'll call us
   From our rest to Home, sweet Home.
   Cho.—We shall sleep, etc.

Mrs. M. A. Kidder.

WORKING FOR THE MASTER.

Philip Phillips.*

1. I'm working for the Master— O glorious work divine!
Thro' grace I'll labor in the field While breath and life are mine;
I'm working for the Master, And this my boast shall be:
The consecrated cross of him, Who bled and died for me.

* Written for Mr. Phillips for an opening piece at his "Evenings of Sacred Song."

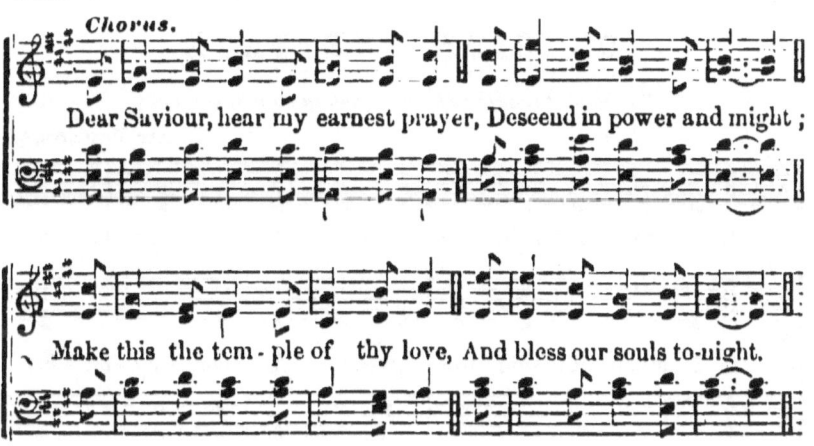

Dear Saviour, hear my earnest prayer, Descend in power and might;
Make this the tem-ple of thy love, And bless our souls to-night.

No. 107.

2 If strains, like mine so simple,
  Can reach thy gracious ear,
Oh, grant the christian hope they breathe,
  Some careless soul may hear;
If I am counted worthy,
  To sing these songs for thee,
The least among thy children, Lord,
  I am content to be.
Cho.—Dear Saviour, hear my earnest prayer,
  Descend in power and might,
Oh, turn some wanderer to thy fold,
  Convert one soul to-night.

3 Thy name, O precious Jesus,
  My constant theme below;
Thy love that crowns the angels' song
  I'll sing where'er I go;
While on my journey homeward,
  My greatest joy shall be
To labor in the vineyard here,
  And gather souls for thee.
Cho.—Dear Saviour, hear my earnest prayer,
  Descend in power and might,
Convert some thoughtless sinner now,
  Seal thine one soul to-night.—*Fanny Crosby.*

OUTSIDE THE GATE.

"Him that cometh unto me, I will in no wise cast out.

PHILIP PHILLIPS.*

* From "Musical Leaves."

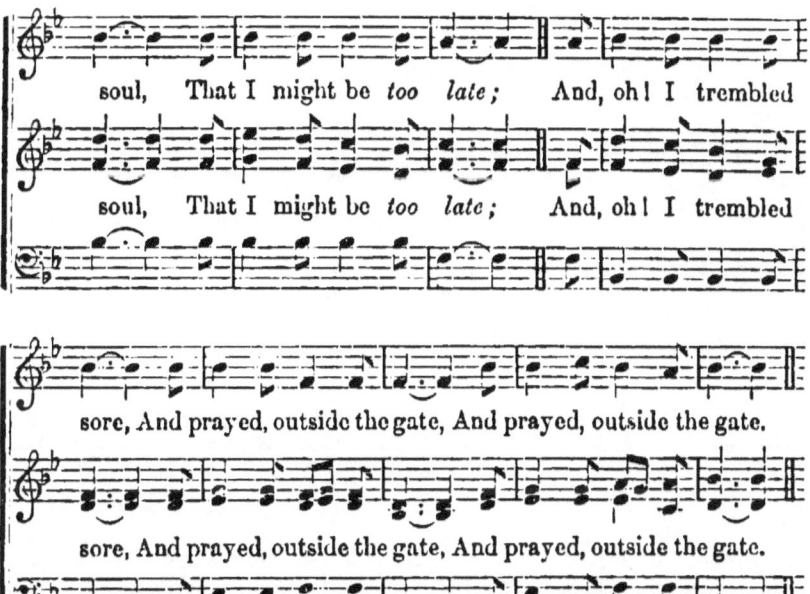

No. 108.

2 "Mercy!" I loudly cried;
   "Oh, give me rest from sin!"
   "I will," a voice replied;
   And Mercy let me in.
   She bound my bleeding wounds,
   And carried all my sin;
   She eased my burdened soul,
   And then she took me in.

3 In Mercy's guise, I knew
   The Saviour long abused;
   Who often sought my heart,
   And wept when I refused.
   Oh! what a blest return
   For ignorance and sin!
   I stood outside the gate,
   And Jesus let me in!—*Josephine Pollard.*

THE VALLEY OF BLESSING.

WM. G. FISCHER.

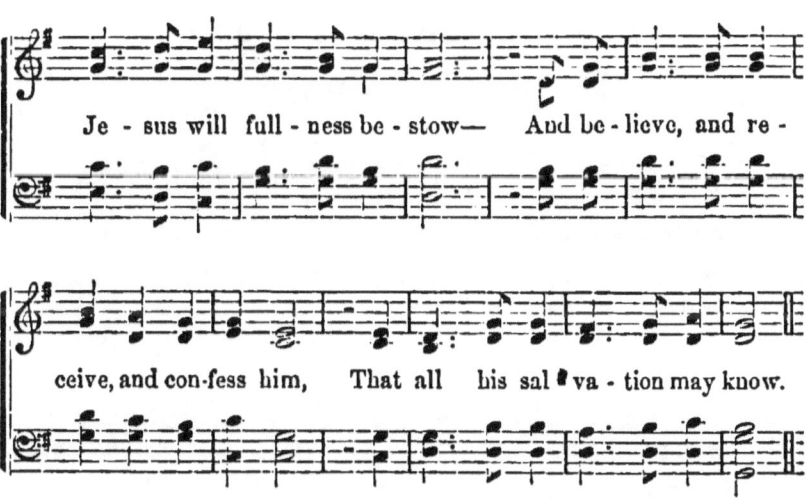

No. 109.

2 There is peace in the valley of blessing so sweet,
 And plenty the land doth impart;
 And there's rest for the weary-worn traveler's feet,
 And joy for the sorrowing heart.
  CHORUS.—Oh, come to this valley, &c.

3 There is love in the valley of blessing so sweet,
 Such as none but the blood-washed may feel;
 When heaven comes down redeemed spirits to greet,
 And Christ sets his covenant seal.
  CHORUS.—Oh, come to the valley, &c.

4 There's a song in the valley of blessing so sweet,
 That angels would fain join the strain—
 As, with rapturous praises, we bow at his feet,
 Crying, "Worthy the Lamb that was slain!"
  CHORUS.—Oh, come to this valley of blessing so sweet,
   Where Jesus will fullness bestow—
   And believe, and receive, and confess him,
   That all his salvation may know.
     Annie Wittenmyer.

'TIS BLESSED TO GIVE.

" God loveth the cheerful giver."

PHILIP PHILLIPS.*

1. As God has kind-ly blessed us, To oth-ers let us give;
Not with a grudg-ing spir-it, Or that our deeds may live;
Not with a vain am-bi-tion, To win the praise of men,
No mer-it in a kind-ness That claims reward a-gain.

* From the "New Standard Singer."

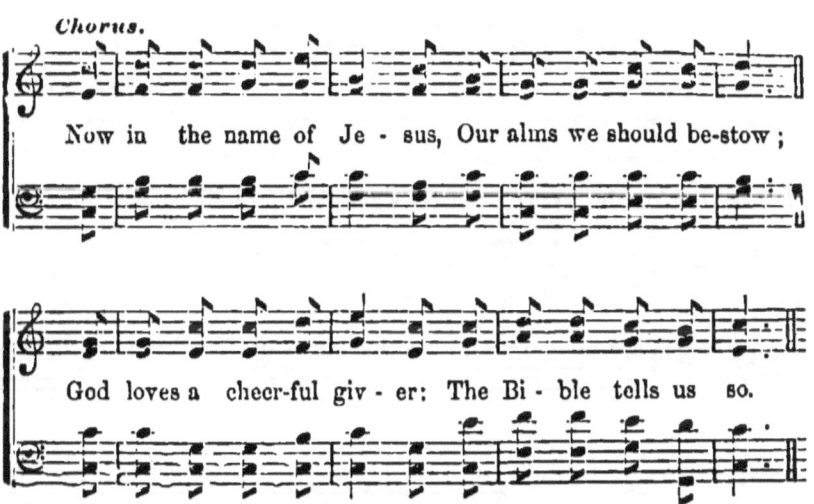

No. 119.

2 Now in the world before us
  A glorious field we see;
And in our Master's vineyard
  How active we should be,
The Sabbath schools around us,
  For help they loudly call;
Home missions, too, remember,
  And freely give to all.—*Chorus.*

3 The cause of foreign missions
  Our zealous care demands;
We'll send the blessed Bible
  To distant heathen lands,
That they may hear of Jesus,
  Whom we so dearly love;
May leave their senseless idols,
  And worship God above.—*Chorus.*

I'M KNEELING AT THE DOOR.

T. E. PERKINS.*

1. I'm kneeling, Lord, at mercy's gate, With trembling hope and fear,

I've waited long, and still I wait, Thy gracious voice to hear.

Thy precious word has bid me seek The joys thou hast in store;

* From the "Sabbath Carols," by permission.

No. 111.

2 None ever empty turned away,
  Who truly sought thy face:
And I, my Saviour, come to-day,
  To seek thy pardoning grace.
Thy precious blood is all my plea:
  This can my soul restore:
Wilt thou in mercy speak to me,
  I'm kneeling at the door.—*Chorus.*

3 And when the ransomed millions stand
  On Zion's flowery hill,
With palms of victory in their hand,
  Waiting their Master's will;
Oh, may I bear the living green,
  And that dear name adore,
Whose love the sinner did redeem,
  While kneeling at the door.—*Chorus.*

THE WATER OF LIFE.

"I will give unto him that is athirst of the fountain of the water of life freely."

WM. B. BRADBURY.*

1. Jesus the water of life will give Freely, freely, freely;
Come to that fountain, oh, drink and live, Freely, freely, freely;

Jesus the water of life will give Freely to those who love him;
Come to that fountain, oh, drink and live, Flowing for those that [OMIT.]

love him. The Spirit and the Bride say, Come; Freely, freely, freely;

And he that is thirsty, let him come, And drink of the water of life...

* *From "Fresh Laurels," by permission of* BIGLOW & MAIN.

Hallowed Songs, Revised. 139

Full Chorus.

The fountain of life is flow-ing, Flowing, free-ly flow-ing; The fountain of life is flow-ing, Is flowing for you and for me...

No. 112.

2 Jesus has promised a home in heaven,
 Freely, freely, freely;
Jesus has promised a home in heaven
 Freely to those that love him;
Treasures unfading will there be given,
 Freely, freely, freely;
Treasures unfading will there be given
 Freely to those that love him.
  The Spirit and the Bride, &c.

3 Jesus has promised a robe of white,
 Freely, freely, freely;
Jesus has promised a robe of white
 Freely to those that love him;
Kingdoms of glory and crowns of light,
 Freely, freely, freely;
Kingdoms of glory and crowns of light
 Freely to those that love him,
  The Spirit and the Bride, &c.

4 Jesus has promised eternal day,
 Freely, freely, freely;
Jesus has promised eternal day
 Freely to those that love him;
Pleasure that never shall pass away,
 Freely, freely, freely;
Pleasure that never shall pass away,
 Freely to those that love him.
  The Spirit and the Bride, &c.

KEEP ON PRAYING.

"Pray without ceasing."

T. E. PERKINS.*

1. Long my spir-it pined in sor-row, Watching, waiting all in vain;
Waiting for a gold-en morrow, Free from earthly care and pain.
When I heard a sweet voice saying, In the ac-cents of a friend,
Cheer up, brother, "keep on praying," Keep on praying to the end.

* *From the " Sabbath Carol."*

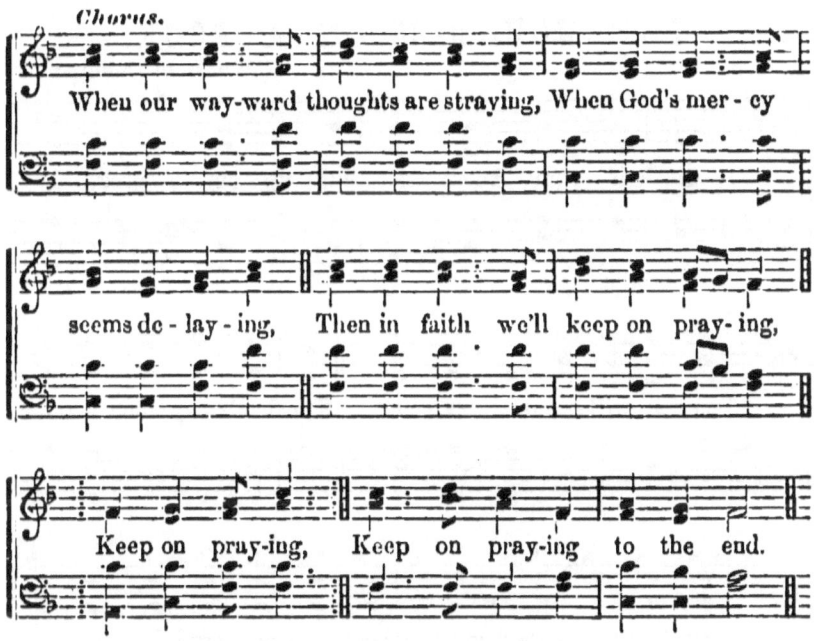

No. 113.

2 Ye, who sigh for holy pleasures,
  Ye, who mourn your load of sin,
"Keep on praying," heavenly treasures
  In the end you're sure to win.
Wrestle with the Lord of glory,
  Lay your troubles at his feet,
Plead with faith in Calvary's story
  Till your joys are all complete.—*Cho.*

3 How the angel-band rejoices,
  When a kneeling mortal prays;
Hear them cry in heavenly voices,
  "Keep on praying," all your days:
Pray until you reach fair Canaan,
  Reach the pearly gates of day,
Then your bliss shall end in glory,
  And shall never pass away.—*Cho.*

Mrs. M. A. Kidder.

THE HOUSE UPON A ROCK.

WM. B. BRADBURY.*

1. Oh, if my house is built up-on a rock, I know it will stand for-ev-er; The floods may come, and the roll-ing thunder's shock May beat up-on my house that is found-ed on a rock, But it nev-er will fall, nev-er will fall, nev-er, nev-er, nev-er! My rock is

Full Chorus.

* *From " Golden Censer."*

No. 114.

2 Oh, if my house is built upon the sand,
   'Twill fall when the floods are swelling;
The winds will blow, and the tempest will descend,
   And beat upon my house that is built upon the sand,
And it surely will fall, never to rise, never, never, never!
    Chorus.—My rock is firm, &c.

3 Then let my house be built upon a rock,
   For there it will stand for ever;
The floods may come, and the rolling thunder's shock
   May beat upon my house that is founded on a rock.
But it never will fall, never will fall, never, never, never!
    Chorus.—My rock is firm, &c.

Chorus.

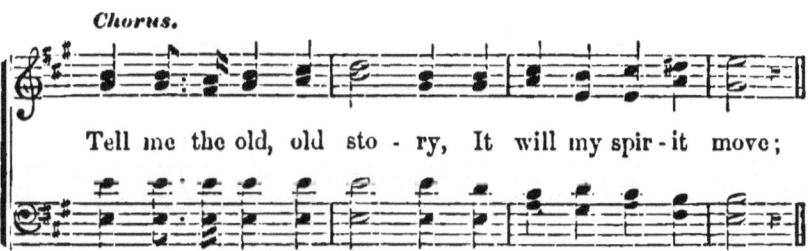

Tell me the old, old sto - ry, It will my spir-it move;

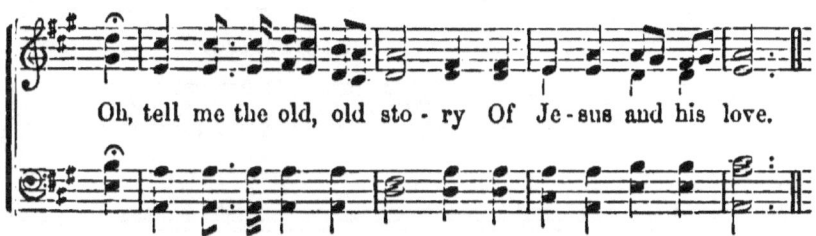

Oh, tell me the old, old sto - ry Of Je-sus and his love.

No. 115.

2 Tell me the story slowly,
    That I may take it in,
That wonderful redemption,
    God's remedy for sin.
Tell me the story often,
    For I forget so soon!
The "early dew" of morning
    Has passed away at noon.
    Cho.—Tell me the old, old story, &c.

3 Tell me the same old story,
    When you have cause to fear
That this world's empty glory
    Is costing me too dear.
Oh, yes, when that world's glory
    Is dawning on my soul,
Tell me the old, old story,
    "Christ Jesus makes thee whole!"
    Cho.—Tell me the old, old story, &c.

WEEP FOR THE FALLEN.

"Meekness, temperance—against such there is no law."

English.*

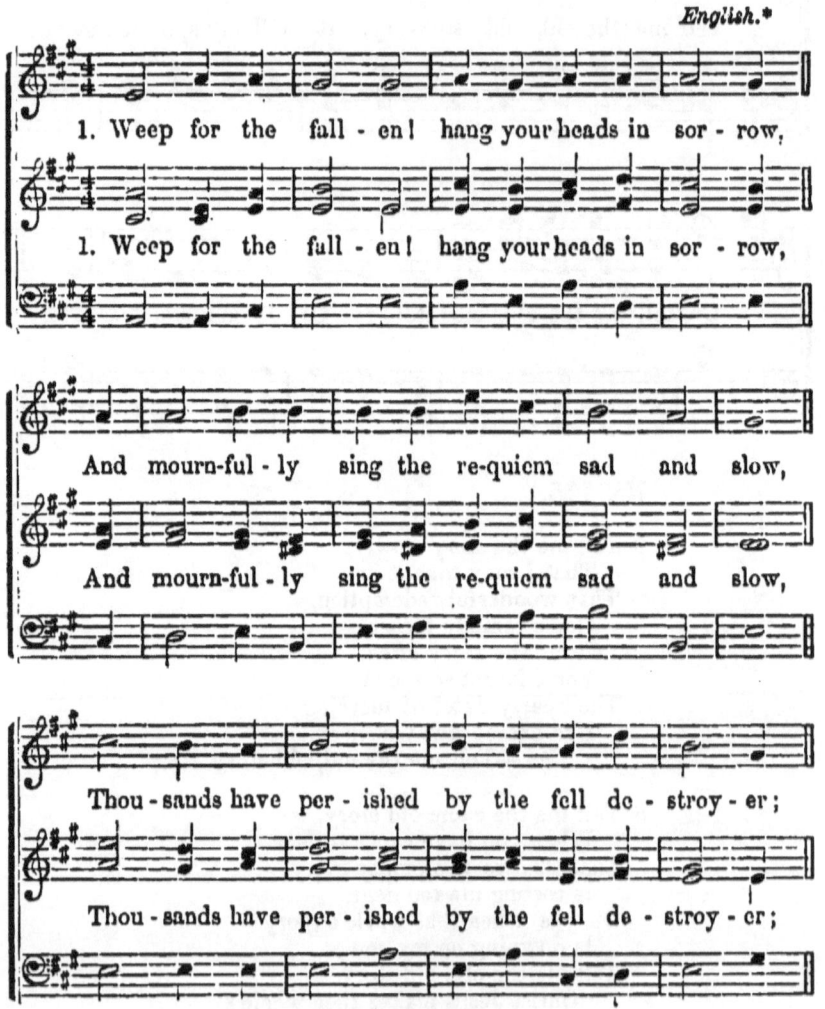

* From "Temperance Chimes."

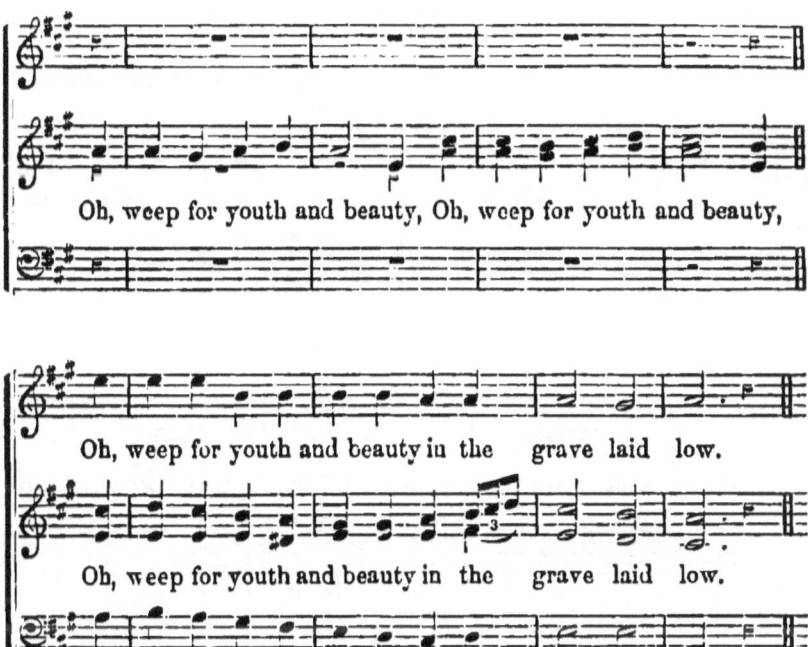

Oh, weep for youth and beauty, Oh, weep for youth and beauty, Oh, weep for youth and beauty in the grave laid low.

No. 116.

2 Voices of wailing tell our hopeless anguish,
    While sorrowing mothers bid us onward go:
Hark! to their accents, theirs the broken-hearted
    Who weep for youth and beauty in the grave laid low!

3 Hear how they bid us sound the timely warning,
    While yet there is hope to shun the cup of woe;
For is it nothing, ye who see no danger,
    To weep for youth and beauty in the grave laid low?

4 Weep for the fallen; but amid your sorrow
    Still point to the pledge that freedom can bestow,
Rescue the nation from the fell destroyer,
    For why should youth and beauty in the grave lie low!

EVENING SHADOWS.

S. J. Vail. *By permission.*

1. On-ly waiting till the shadows Are a lit-tle long-er grown;
On-ly waiting till the glimmer Of the day's last beam is flown;
Till the night of death is fad-ed From the heart once full of day;
Till the stars of heav'n are breaking Thro' the twilight soft and gray.

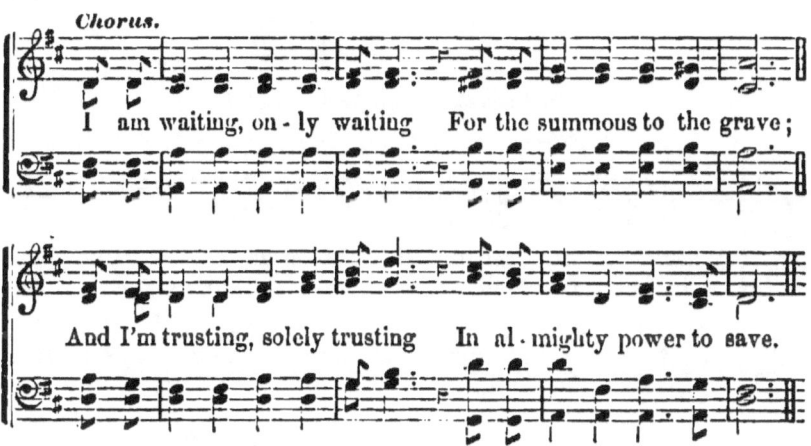

No. 148.

2 Only waiting till the reapers
   Have their last sheaf gather'd home;
For the summer time is ended,
   And the autumn winds have come;
Quickly, reapers, gather quickly
   The last ripe hours of my heart,
For the bloom of life is wither'd.
   And I hasten to depart.

3 Only waiting till the angels
   Open wide the mystic gate,
At whose feet I long have linger'd,
   Weary, poor, and desolate;
Even now I hear their footsteps,
   And their voices far away,
If they call me I am waiting,
   Only waiting to obey.

4 Only waiting till the shadows
   Are a little longer grown;
Only waiting till the glimmer
   Of the day's last beam is flown;
Then from out the gathering darkness,
   Holy, deathless stars will rise,
By whose light my soul will gladly
   Wing its passage to the skies.

Hallowed Songs, Revised. 151

No. 118.

2 Let cares like a wild deluge come,
   Let storms of sorrow fall—
   So I but safely reach my home,
   My God, my heaven, my all.
   Cho.—We will stand, &c.

3 There I shall bathe my weary soul
   In seas of heavenly rest,
   And not a wave of trouble roll
   Across my peaceful breast.
   Cho.—We will stand, &c.

CALLING US AWAY.

"Here we have no continuing city."

WALTER KITTRIDGE.*

1. Give me the wings of faith to rise With-in the veil, and see The saints a-bove, how great their joys, How bright their glo-ries be. Ma-ny are the friends, Who are wait-ing to-day, Hap-py on the gold-en strand;

Ma-ny are the voic-es Call-ing us a-way To
Ma-ny are the voic-es Call-ing us a-way To

* *From the "New Standard Singer."*

Hallowed Songs, Revised.

No. 119.

2 Once they were mourners here below,
And pour'd out cries and tears;
They wrestled hard, as we do now,
With sins, and doubts, and fears.
    Many are the friends, &c.

3 I ask them whence their vict'ry came:
They, with united breath,
Ascribe their conquest to the Lamb,—
Their triumph to his death.
    Many are the friends, &c.

BRIGHT HOME.*

"In my Father's house are many mansions."

* Air—"Home, sweet home."

Hallowed Songs, Revised. 155

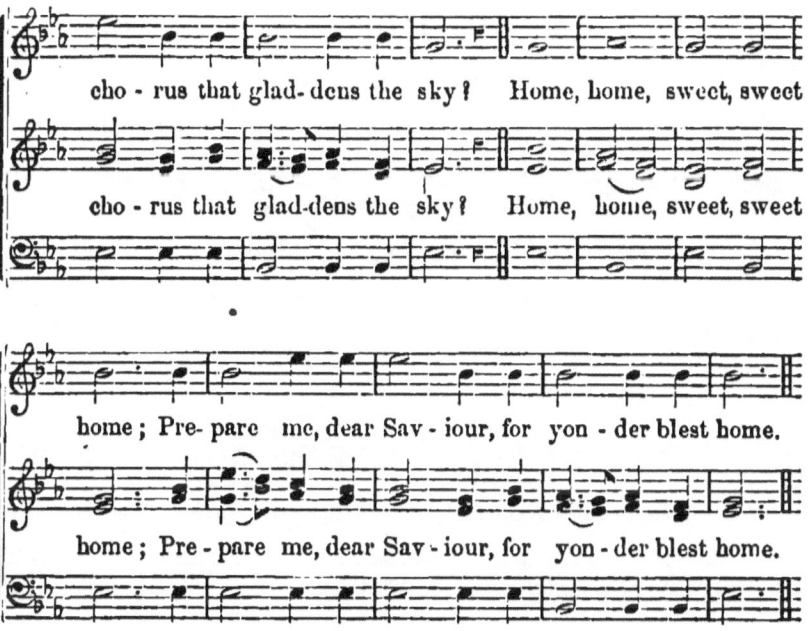

No. 120.

2 The home of the ransom'd, the land of the blest,
Where pilgrims shall enter a glorious rest;
Shall wander in gladness the pastures of green,
And drink the still waters of pleasures serene.
   Home, home, &c.

3 The home that our Saviour has gone to prepare—
No heart can conceive of the blessedness there,
Of raptures unending awaiting the just,
When pure in his likeness they rise from the dust.
   Home, home, &c.

4 We bless thee, dear Saviour, who call'st us to share
The beautiful home thou hast gone to prepare;
We trust in thy mercy, that, wash'd from our sin,
Through yonder bright gates we may all enter in.
   Home, home, &c.

No. 121.

2 Through his all-atoning merit,
    We no more are slaves to sin;
By his grace we yet may conquer
    Foes without and foes within.
Courage! let our hearts be valiant,
    And our armor brightly shine;
Take the helmet of salvation,
    Wield the sword of truth divine.—*Cho.*

3 See our glorious banner waving
    O'er the Christian's battle-ground;
Faithful at the posts of duty,
    Let us each and all be found.
See our glorious banner waving,
    To its colors boldly stand;
Lo! our "beacon" in the distance,
    Pointing to the promised land.—*Cho.*

4 We are on the banks of Jordan,
    Darkly though its waters flow,
Upward to the Mount of Zion,
    Shout triumphant as we go.
One more struggle, one more conquest,
    And our mortal strife shall cease;
Hallelujah! hallelujah!
    We shall gain the port of peace.—*Cho.*
                            Fanny Crosby.

No. 122.

2 Yes, I'll to my bosom press thee;
   Precious word, I'll hide thee here,
Sure my very heart will bless thee,
   For thou ever say'st, "good cheer!"
Speak, poor heart, and tell thy pond'rings,
   Tell how far thy rovings led,
When this book brought back thy wand'rings,
   Speaking life as from the dead.
      Blessed Bible! Blessed Bible!
      How thou dost my spirit cheer.

3 Yes, sweet Bible! I will hide thee
   Deep—yes, deeper in this heart;
Thou through all my life wilt guide me,
   And in death we will not part.
Part in death? no, never! never!
   Through death's vale I'll lean on thee;
Then in worlds above, forever,
   Sweeter still thy truths shall be.
      Blessed Bible! Blessed Bible!
      How thou dost my spirit cheer.—*Mrs. Phebe Palmer.*

BATTLING FOR THE LORD.

"I must work the works of him that sent me while it is day; the night cometh when no man can work."

T. E. PERKINS.

We'll work till Je-sus comes, And then we'll rest at home.

No. 123.

2 Under our captain Jesus Christ,
  Battling for the Lord!
We've listed for this mortal life,
  Battling for the Lord!—We'll work, &c.

3 We'll fight against the powers of sin,
  Battling for the Lord!
In favor of our heavenly King,
  Battling for the Lord!—We'll work, &c.

4 And when our warfare here is o'er,
  Battling for the Lord!
This strife we'll leave, and war no more,
  Battling for the Lord!—We'll work, &c.

5 Our friends and kindred there we'll meet,
  On the heavenly shore!
And ground our arms at Jesus' feet,
  On the heavenly shore!—We'll work, &c.

Philip Phillips.

Coda, for the last verse.

Home, home, sweet, sweet home! Prepare me, dear Saviour, for glory, my home.

GUIDE US, SAVIOUR.

"He will guide you into all truth."

T. C. O'KANE.*

* From "Singing Pilgrim."

Hallowed Songs, Revised.

No. 124.

2 Be our strength, for we are weakness;
   Be our wisdom and our guide;
  May we walk in love and meekness,
   Nearer to our Saviour's side.
  Naught can harm us, naught can harm us,
   While we thus in thee abide.

3 May thy watchful angels hover
   Round us, when there's evil near;
  May we hide beneath the cover
   Of thy wings, in time of fear;
  And in sorrow, and in sorrow,
   Comfort our sad hearts, and cheer.

4 And when death at last o'ertakes us,
   And we sink beneath his might,
  May the blessed morn awake us,
   Safe in yonder realms of light;
  There forever, there forever,
   Chant thy praise with angels bright.

                    Mrs. Bishop Thompson.

THAT WILL BE JOYFUL.

Fellowship of love.

No. 125.

2 Yes, happy thought! when we are free
From earthly grief and pain,
In heaven we shall each other see
And never part again.
  Chorus.—Oh, that will be joyful, &c.

3 Then let us each, in strength divine,
Still walk in wisdom's ways,
That we with those we love may join
In never-ending praise.
  Chorus.—Oh, that will be joyful, &c.—*Unknown.*

REST FOR THE WEARY.

Arr. by Rev. J. W. DADMUN.

No. 126.

2 He is fitting up my mansion,
　Which eternally shall stand,
　For my stay shall not be transient
　In that holy, happy land.—*Cho.*

3 Pain nor sickness ne'er shall enter,
　Grief nor woe my lot shall share;
　But in that celestial centre,
　I a crown of life shall wear.—*Cho.*

4 Death itself shall then be vanquished,
　And his sting shall be withdrawn;
　Shout for gladness, O ye ransomed.
　Hail with joy the rising morn.—*Cho.*

5 Sing, oh, sing, ye heirs of glory;
　Shout your triumph as you go;
　Zion's gate will open for you,
　You shall find an entrance through.—*Cho.*

WHAT ARE YOU GOING TO DO?

"*Wherewithal shall a young man cleanse his ways*," by heeding, etc., etc.

PHILIP PHILLIPS.*

1. Oh, what are you go-ing to do, brother? Say, what are you go-ing to do? You have thought of some useful la-bor, But what is the end in view? You are fresh from the home of your boy-hood, And just in the bloom of youth! Have you

* *One of the soul-stirring songs from the "Musical Leaves," and dedicated by the author to the Young Men's Christian Associations of the United States.*

Hallowed Songs, Revised.

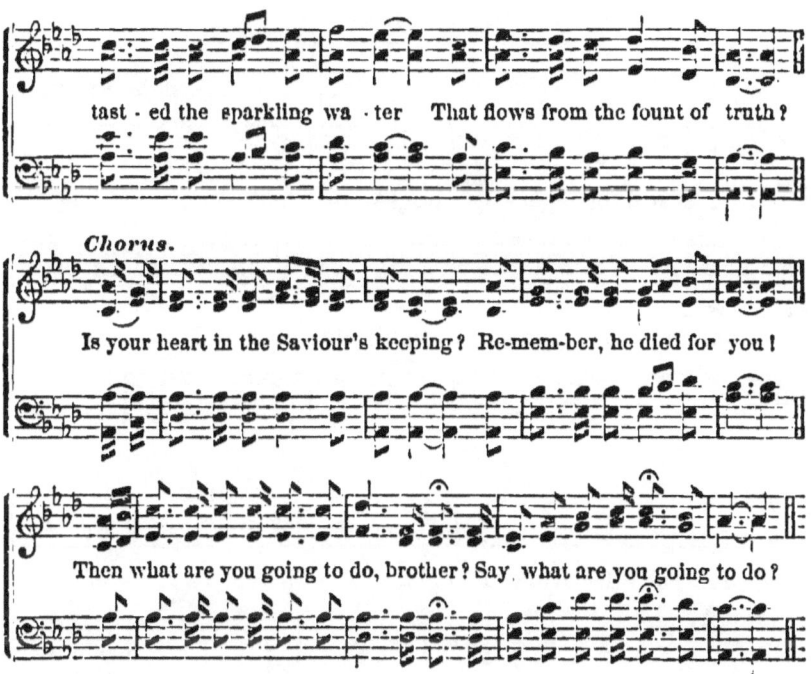

tast-ed the sparkling wa-ter That flows from the fount of truth?

Chorus.

Is your heart in the Saviour's keeping? Re-mem-ber, he died for you!

Then what are you going to do, brother? Say, what are you going to do?

No. 127.

2.
Oh, what are you going to do, brother?
 The morning of youth is past;
The vigor and strength of manhood,
 My brother, are yours at last.
You are rising in worldly prospects,
 And prospered in worldly things;—
A duty to those less favored.
 The smile of your fortune brings.
CHORUS.
Go, prove that your heart is grateful—
 The Lord has a work for you!
Then what are you going to do, brother?
 Say, what are you going to do?

3.
Oh, what are you going to do, brother?
 Your sun at its noon is high;
It shines in meridian splendor,
 And rides through a cloudless sky.
You are holding a high position,
 Of honor, of trust, and fame;—

Are you not willing to give the glory
 And praise to your Saviour's name?
CHORUS.
The regions that sit in darkness
 Are stretching their hands to you;
Then what are you going to do, brother?
 Say, what are you going to do?

4.
Oh, what are you going to do, brother?
 The twilight approaches now;—
Already your locks are silvered,
 And winter is on your brow.
Your talents, your time, your riches,
 To Jesus, your Master, give;
Then ask if the world around you
 Is better because you live.
CHORUS.
You are nearing the brink of Jordan,
 But still there is work for you;
Then what are you going to do, brother?
 Say, what are you going to do?

NEARER MY HOME.

John M. Evans.

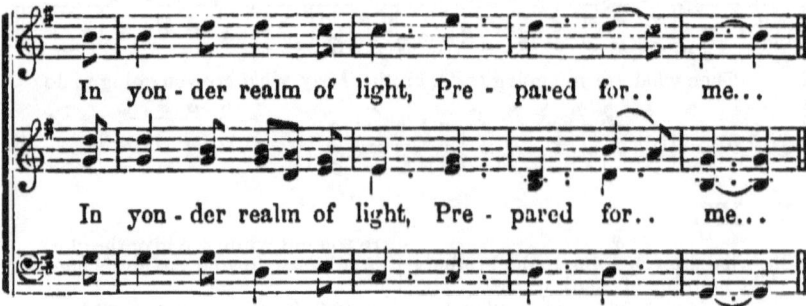

Hallowed Songs, Revised.

No. 128.

2 Oh, may I faithful prove,
   And keep the crown in view,
  And through the storms of life
   My way pursue.

3 Jesus, be thou my guide,
   My steps attend;
  Oh, keep me near thy side,
   Be thou my friend.

4 Be thou my shield and sun,
   My Saviour and my guide;
  And when my work is done,
   My great reward.—*Unknown.*

JOYFULLY.

"Joyfully onward."

1. Joy-ful-ly, joy-ful-ly on-ward I move, Bound to the land of bright spir-its a-bove; An-gel-ic chor-is-ters sing as I come, Joy-ful-ly, joy-ful-ly haste to thy home! Soon with my pil-grimage end-ed be-low, Home to the

No. 129.

2 Friends, fondly cherished, have passed on before;
Waiting, they watch me approaching the shore;
Singing to cheer me through death's chilling gloom,
Joyfully, joyfully haste to thy home.
Sounds of sweet melody fall on my ear;
Harps of the blessed, your voices I hear
Rings with the harmony heaven's high dome,—
Joyfully, joyfully haste to thy home.

3 Death, with thy weapons of war lay me low
Strike, king of terrors, I fear not the blow;
Jesus hath broken the bars of the tomb!
Joyfully, joyfully will I go home.
Bright will the morn of eternity dawn,
Death shall be banished, his sceptre be gone:
Joyfully, then, shall I witness his doom,
Joyfully, joyfully, safely at home.—*Rev. Wm. Hunter.*

THE LAND OF BEULAH.

"My immortal home."

Wm. B. Bradbury.*

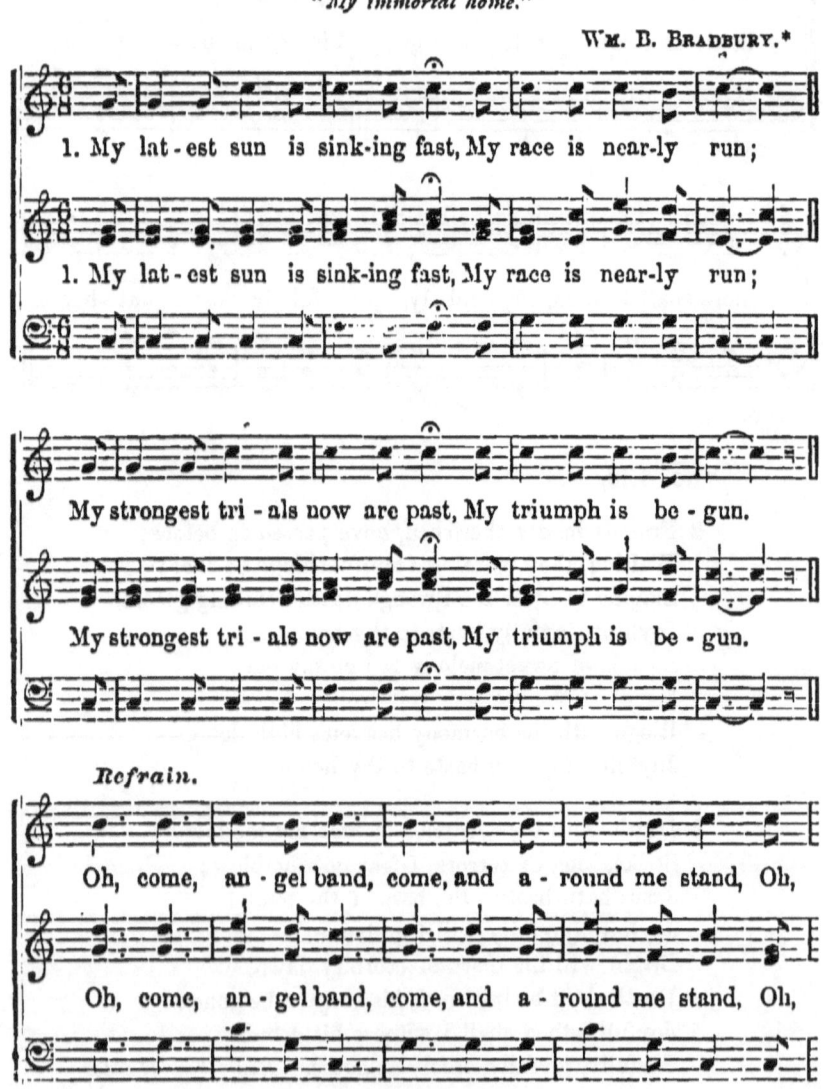

* *From " Golden Chain."*

No. 130.

2 I know I'm nearing the holy ranks
   Of friends and kindred dear;
   For I brush the dews on Jordan's banks,
   The crossing must be near.—*Refrain.*

3 I've almost gained my heavenly home,
   My spirit loudly sings;
   The holy ones, behold, they come!
   I hear the noise of wings.—*Refrain.*

4 Oh, bear my longing heart to Him,
   Who bled and died for me;
   Whose blood now cleanses from all sin,
   And gives me victory.—*Refrain.*—*Rev. J. Haskell*

A LIGHT IN THE WINDOW.

WM. B. BRADBURY.*

1. There's a light in the win-dow for thee, broth-er,
There's a light in the win-dow for thee;
A dear one has moved to the mansions a-bove,
There's a light in the win-dow for thee.

* From "*Golden Chain,*"

No. 131.

2 There's a crown, and a robe, and a palm, brother,
   When from toil and from care you are free;
   The Saviour has gone to prepare you a home,
   With a light in the window for thee.—*Cho.*

3 Oh, watch, and be faithful, and pray, brother,
   All your journey o'er life's troubled sea,
   Though afflictions assail you, and storms beat severe,
   There's a light in the window for thee.—*Cho.*

4 Then on, perseveringly on, brother,
   Till from conflict and suffering free;
   Bright angels now beckon you over the stream,
   There's a light in the window for thee.—*Cho.*

HE LEADETH ME.

WM. B. BRADBURY.

1. He lead-eth me! oh! blessed thought, Oh! words with heavenly comfort fraught, What-e'er I do, wher-e'er I be, Still 'tis God's hand that lead-eth me! He lead-eth me! he

Refrain.

No. 132.

2 Sometimes 'mid scenes of deepest gloom,
Sometimes where Eden's bowers bloom,
By waters still, o'er troubled sea—
Still 'tis his hand that leadeth me.
   He leadeth me, &c.

3 Lord, I would clasp thy hand in mine,
Nor ever murmur nor repine—
Content, whatever lot I see,
Since 'tis my God that leadeth me.
   He leadeth me, &c.

4 And when my task on earth is done,
When, by thy grace, the victory's won,
E'en death's cold wave I will not flee,
Since God through Jordan leadeth me.
   He leadeth me, &c.

SOLDIERS OF THE CROSS.*

1. Ye sol-diers of the Cross, rise and put your ar-mor on; March to the cit-y of the New Je-ru-sa-lem; Je-sus gives the or-der, and leads his peo-ple on Till vic-to-ry is

* From "Pilgrim's Songs."

No. 133.

2 The watchmen they are crying, attend the trumpet's sound,
Take the gospel banner, and the powers of hell surround,
Hearts and arms make ready, the battle is at hand;
Go forth at Christ's command.—*Chorus.*

3 Lay hold upon the Saviour by faith's victorious shield,
March on in order, till you win the glorious field,
Faint not by the way, till you've gained that peaceful shore,
Where war shall be no more.—*Chorus.*

4 Ne'er think the victory won, nor lay your armor down,
March on in duty till you gain the starry crown;
When the war is o'er, and the battle you have won,
Jesus will say, "Well done."—*Chorus.*

WATCH AND PRAY.

T. E. PERKINS.*

1. Soft-ly on the breath of eve-ning Comes the ten-der sigh of day; Lone-ly heart, by sor-row lad-en, 'Tis the time to pray. Wea-ry pil-grim,

* *From "Golden Promise."*

No. 134.

2 Pearly dews like tears are falling
   Gently on the sleeping flowers;
   Stars like angel eyes are beaming
   From celestial bowers.
      Weary pilgrim, &c.

3 'Tis the hour where hallowed feelings
   Chase our doubts and fears away;
   'Tis the hour of calm devotion:
   Pilgrim, watch and pray.
      Weary pilgrim, &c.

4 Though temptations dark oppress thee,
   Jesus guides thee on thy way;
   He will hear thy lightest whisper:
   Pilgrim, watch and pray.
      Weary pilgrim, &c.—*Fanny Crosby.*

I LOVE TO TELL THE STORY.

Written for Chaplain C. C. McCABE.   WM. G. FISCHER.

1. I love to tell the story Of unseen things above, Of Jesus and his glory, Of Jesus and his love. I love to tell the story, Because I know it's true, It satisfies my longings, As nothing else would do.

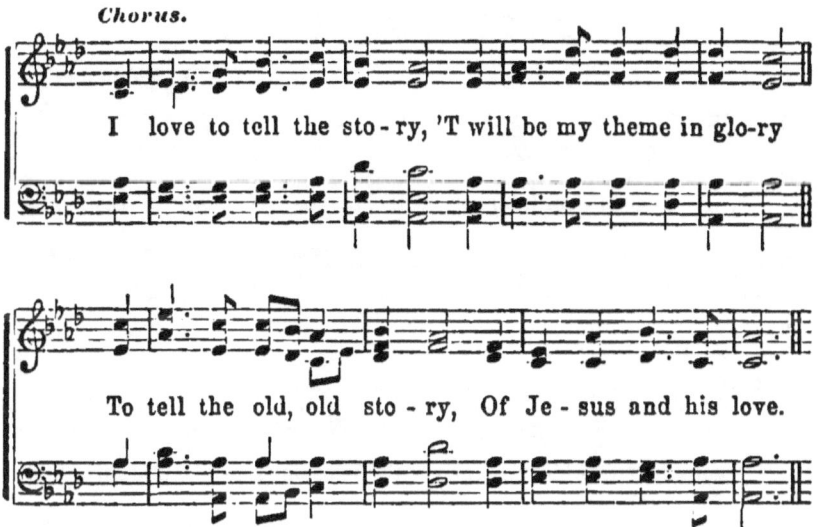

No. 135.

2 I love to tell the story:
   More wonderful it seems
   Than all the golden fancies
   Of all our golden dreams.
I love to tell the story:
   It did so much for me!
   And that is just the reason
   I tell it now to thee.—*Cho.*

3 I love to tell the story:
   'T is pleasant to repeat
   What seems, each time I tell it
   More wonderfully sweet.
I love to tell the story:
   For some have never heard
   The message of salvation
   From God's own holy word.—*Cho.*

4 I love to tell the story:
   For those who know it best
   Seem hungering and thirsting
   To hear it like the rest.
And when, in scenes of glory,
   I sing the NEW, NEW SONG,
   'T will be—the OLD, OLD STORY
   That I have loved so long.—*Cho.*

BEAUTIFUL LAND.

Wm. B. Bradbury.

1. A beau-ti-ful land by faith I see, A land of rest, from sor-row free, The home of the ransomed, bright and fair, And

beau-ti-ful an-gels, too, are there.

Chorus.

Will you go? Will you go?

Go to that beau-ti-ful land with me? Will you go?

Hallowed Songs, Revised.   187

No. 136.

2 That beautiful land, the city of light,
  It ne'er has known the shades of night;
  The glory of God, the light of day,
  Hath driven the darkness far away.—*Cho.*

3 In vision I see its streets of gold,
  Its beautiful gates I, too, behold,
  The river of life, the crystal sea,
  The ambrosial fruit of life's fair tree.—*Cho.*

4 The heavenly throng arrayed in white
  In rapture range the plains of light;
  And in one harmonious choir they praise
  Their glorious Saviour's matchless grace.—*Cho.*

TO-DAY THE SAVIOUR CALLS. 6s & 4s.

Dr. LOWELL MASON.

No. 137.

2 To-day the Saviour calls:
  Oh, listen now;
  Within these sacred walls
  To Jesus bow.

3 To-day the Saviour calls:
  For refuge fly;

The storm of justice falls,
  And death is nigh.

4 The Spirit calls to-day:
  Yield to his power:
  Oh, grieve him not away;
  'Tis mercy's hour.

CHRIST ON THE MOUNT.

Philip Phillips.*

* *From "Musical Leaves."*

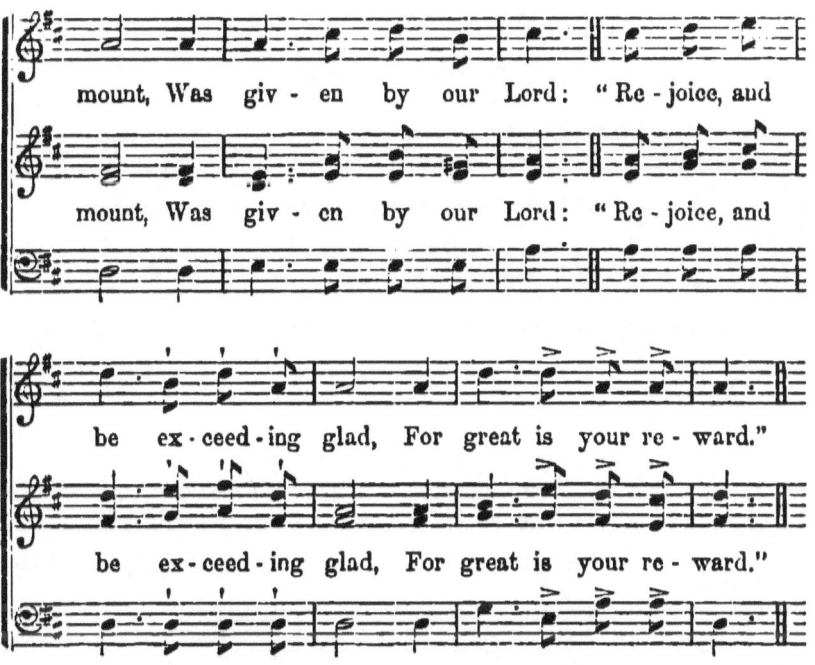

No. 138.

2 Ye poor in spirit, unto you
　How great the blessings given;
His choicest promises are yours,
　"Yours is the kingdom—Heav'n."—*Cho.*

3 The meek, and they for Jesus' sake,
　Who persecutions bear;
He promises a heavenly home,
　A crown of glory there.—*Cho.*

4 Be merciful, for unto such
　He spares his chast'ning rod;
Be pure in heart, our Saviour says,
　The pure shall dwell with God.—*Cho.*

Dr. E. G Sumner.

PORTLAND. 8s. Double.

The heavenly Jerusalem.

W. H. OAKLEY.

Hallowed Songs, Revised. 191

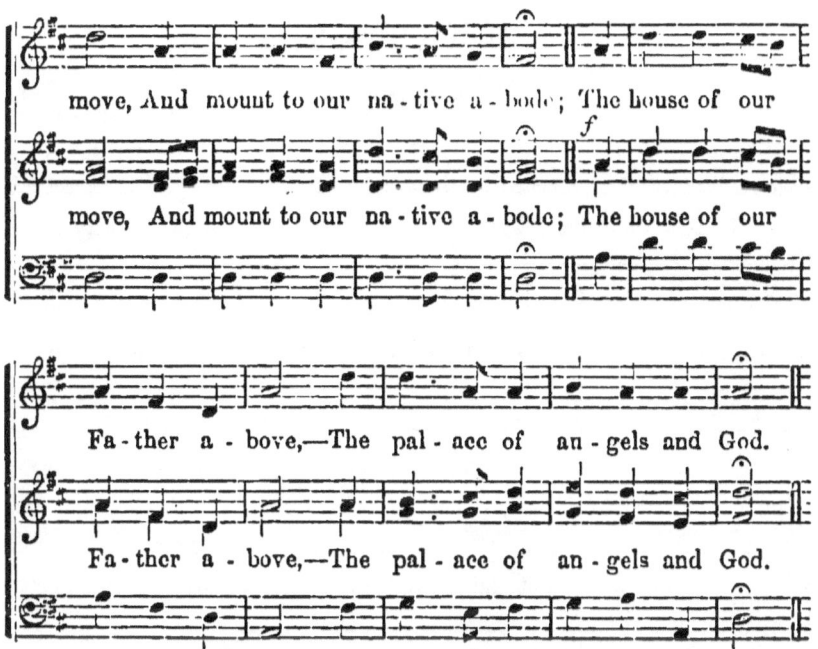

No. 139.
2 Our mourning is all at an end,
  When, raised by the life-giving Word,
We see the new city descend,
  Adorn'd as a bride for her Lord:
The city so holy and clean,
  No sorrow can breathe in the air:
No gloom of affliction or sin;
  No shadow of evil is there.

3 By faith we already behold
  That lovely Jerusalem here:
Her walls are of jasper and gold;
  As crystal her buildings are clear;
Immovably founded in grace,
  She stands as she ever hath stood,
And brightly her Builder displays,
  And flames with the glory of God.—*C. Wesley.*

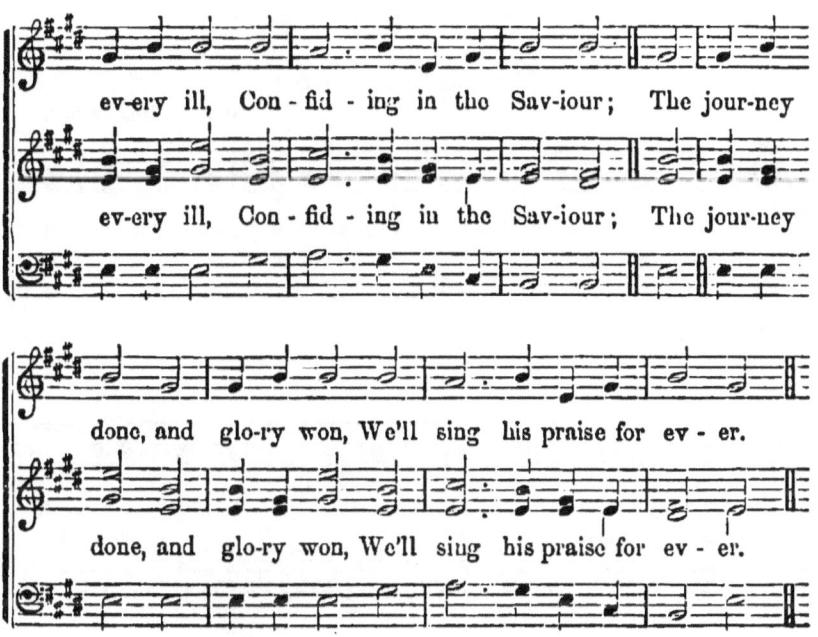

No. 140.

2 Though sore beset, not overcome,
   Cast down, but not despairing,
We're traveling toward a heavenly home,
   Our Master's standard bearing.
     Toil onward still, &c.

3 We'll one another's burdens bear,
   The toilsome journey cheering;
Our joys and all our sorrows share,
   Each day our home we're nearing.
     Toil onward still, &c.

4 Our Lord is God; his promise sure,
   His help shall fail us never;
And they that to the end endure
   Shall reign with him forever!
     Toil onward still, &c.

THE GOLDEN SHORE.

"A home beyond the tide."

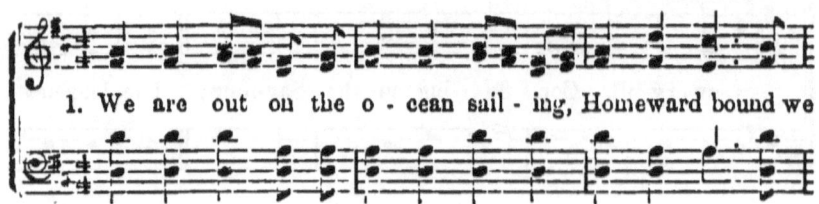

1. We are out on the o-cean sail-ing, Homeward bound we

sweetly glide; We are out on the o-cean sail-ing

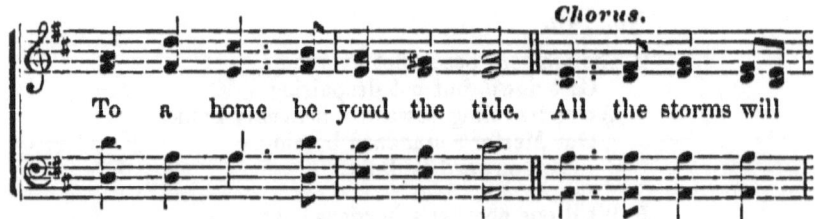

To a home be-yond the tide. *Chorus.* All the storms will

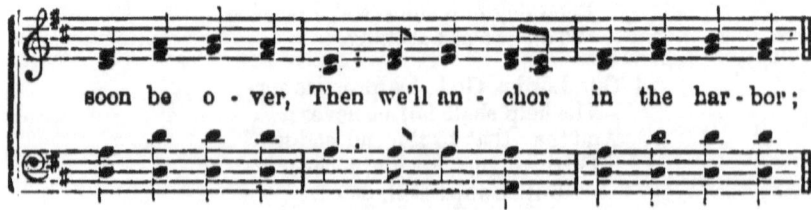

soon be o-ver, Then we'll an-chor in the har-bor;

No. 141.

2 Millions now are safely landed,
　Over on the golden shore;
Millions more are on the journey,
　Yet there's room for millions more.
　　All the storms, &c.

3 Spread your sails while heavenly breezes
　Gently waft our vessel on;
All on board are sweetly singing—
　Free salvation is the song.
　　All the storms, &c.

4 When we all are safely anchored,
　We will shout—our trials o'er;
We will walk about the city,
　And we'll sing for evermore.
　　All the storm, &c.

GO, AND TELL JESUS.

"And they went and told Jesus."

T. F. SEWARD.

1. Go, and tell Je - sus, wea - ry, sin - sick soul, He'll ease thee of thy bur-den, make thee whole; Look up to him, he on - ly can for-give, Believe on him and thou shalt surely live.

Chorus.

Go, and tell Je - sus, He on - ly can for - give;

No. 142.

2 Go, and tell Jesus, when your sins arise,
Like mountains of deep guilt before your eyes:
His blood was spilt, his precious life he gave,
That mercy, peace, and pardon you might have.

3 Go, and tell Jesus, he'll dispel thy fears,
Will calm thy doubts, and wipe away thy tears;
He'll take thee in his arm, and on his breast,
Thou may'st be happy, and forever rest.

NEVER SIN AGAIN.

"*No sin there.*"

T. E. PERKINS.

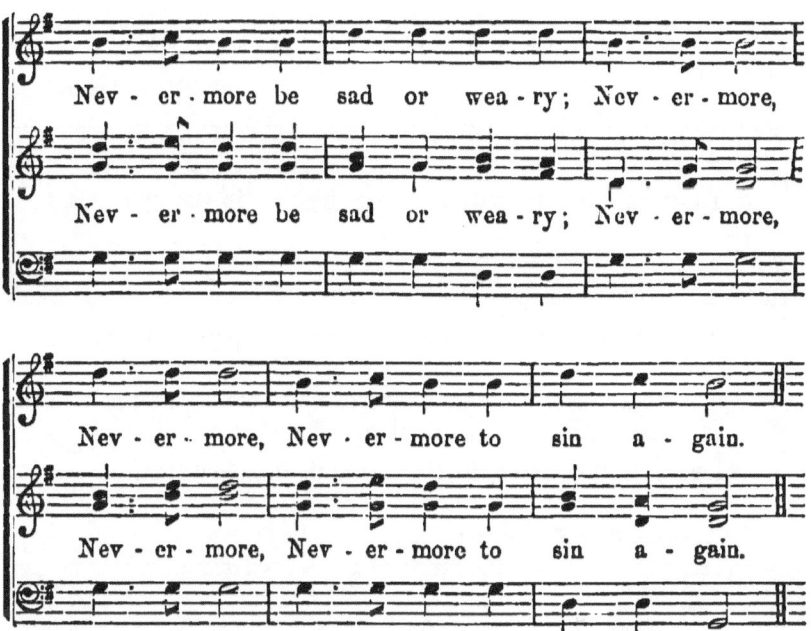

No. 143.

2 In it all is light and glory,
 O'er it shines a nightless day;
 Every trace of sin's sad story—
 All the curse has passed away.
  Nevermore, &c.

3 There the Lamb, our Shepherd, leads us
 By the streams of life along,
 On the freshest pastures feed us,
 Turns our sighing into song.
  Nevermore, &c.

4 Soon we pass this dreary desert,
 Soon we bid farewell to pain,
 Nevermore be sad and weary,
 Nevermore to sin again.
  Nevermore, &c.—*Bonar.*

BEAUTIFUL LAND ON HIGH.

W. U. BUTCHER.*

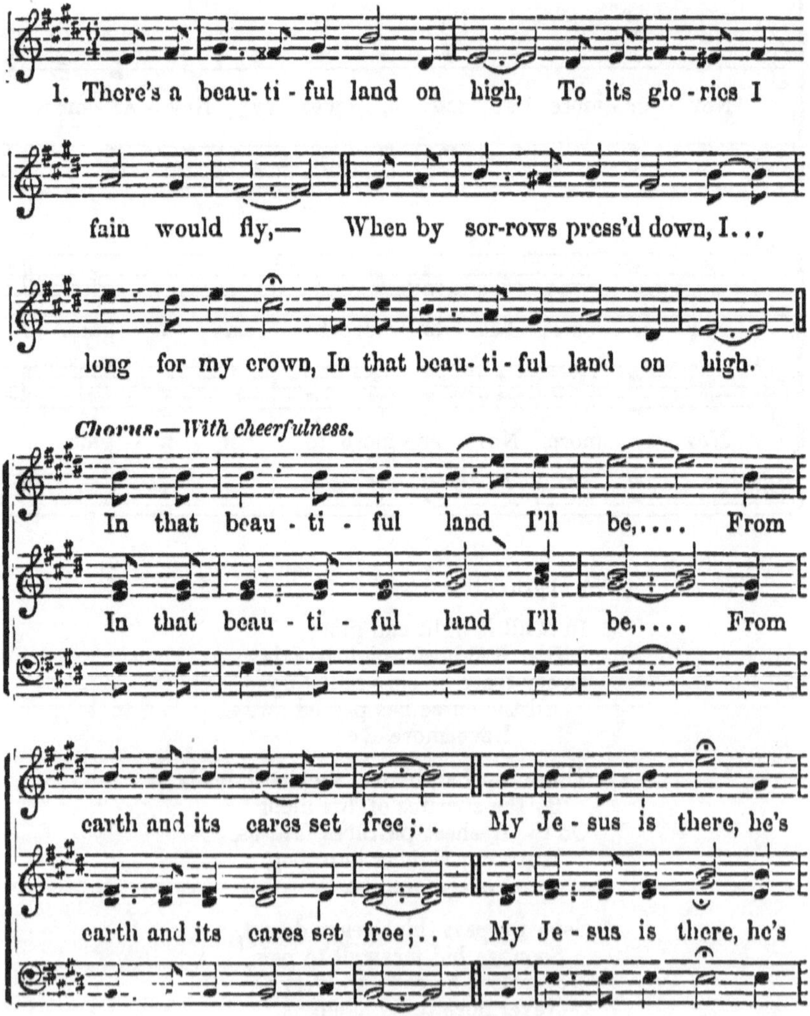

1. There's a beau- ti - ful land on high, To its glo - ries I
fain would fly,— When by sor-rows press'd down, I...
long for my crown, In that beau- ti - ful land on high.
Chorus.—With cheerfulness.
In that beau - ti - ful land I'll be,.... From
In that beau - ti - ful land I'll be,.... From
earth and its cares set free;.. My Je - sus is there, he's
earth and its cares set free;.. My Je - sus is there, he's

* From "Devotional Melodies."

No. 144.

2 There's a beautiful land on high,
   I shall enter it by-and-by;
There, with friends, hand in hand, I shall walk on the strand,
   In that beautiful land on high.
      Cho.—In that beautiful land, &c.

3 There's a beautiful land on high;
   Then why should I fear to die,
When death is the way to the realms of day,
   In that beautiful land on high?
      Cho.—In that beautiful land, &c.

4 There's a beautiful land on high,
   And my kindred its bliss enjoy;
Methinks I now see how they're waiting for me,
   In that beautiful land on high.
      Cho.—In that beautiful land, &c.

5 There's a beautiful land on high,
   And though here I oft weep and sigh,
My Jesus hath said that no tears shall be shed,
   In that beautiful land on high.
      Cho.—In that beautiful land, &c.

6 There's a beautiful land on high,
   Where we never shall say, "good-by!"
When over the river we're happy forever,
   In that beautiful land on high.
      Cho.—In that beautiful land, &c.—*J. Nicholson.*

WE'VE A HOME, OVER THERE.

T. C. O'KANE.

* From "Fresh Leaves."

No. 145.

2 O, think of the friends over there,
  Who before us the journey have trod,
  Of the songs that they breathe on the air,
  In their home in the palace of God.
    Over there, over there,
  O think of the friends over there.

3 My Savior is now over there,
  There my kindred and friends are at rest;
  Then away from my sorrow and care,
  Let me fly to the land of the blest.
    Over there, over there,
  My Savior is now over there.

4 I'll soon be at home over there,
  For the end of my journey I see;
  Many dear to my heart over there,
  Are watching and waiting for me.
    Over there, over there,
  I'll soon be at home over there.

CHILDREN OF THE HEAVENLY KING.

1. Chil-dren of the heaven-ly King, As we jour-ney

let us sing; Sing our worthy Sav-iour's praise, Glo-rious

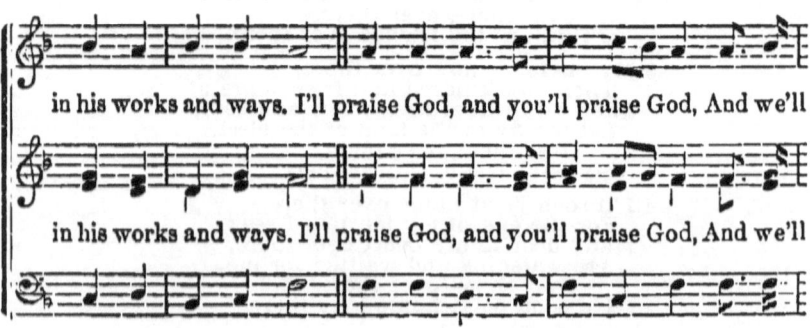

in his works and ways. I'll praise God, and you'll praise God, And we'll

No. 146.

2 We are traveling home to God,
In the way our fathers trod;
They are happy now, and we
Soon their happiness shall see.—I'll praise, &c.

3 O ye banished seed, be glad;
Christ our advocate is made;
Us to save our flesh assumes,—
Brother to our souls becomes.—I'll praise, &c.

4 Fear not, brethren, joyful stand
On the borders of our land;
Jesus Christ, our Father's Son,
Bids us undismayed go on.—I'll praise, &c.

5 Lord! obediently we'll go,
Gladly leaving all below:
Only thou our leader be,
And we still will follow thee.—I'll praise, &c.

JESUS IS HERE.

" Behold, I stand at the door and knock."

T. C. O'KANE.*

* From " *Singing Pilgrim.*'

Hallowed Songs, Revised. 207

Tho' Jesus bids them stay; Jesus is here, Jesus is here.

No. 147.

2 Oh, come this place within,
　　Jesus is here;
　He sees you full of sin,
　　Jesus is here;
　He knows you when you come,
　Poor, wretched, and undone,
　Seeking him and him alone;
　　Jesus is here.

3 Come, then, to Jesus now,
　　Jesus is here;
　All near him lowly bow,
　　Jesus is here;
　Oh, ye that feel your sin,
　And coming long have been,
　Now find your rest in him;
　　Jesus is here.

4 Oh, come to Jesus now,
　　Jesus is here;
　Old and young together bow,
　　Jesus is here;
　Oh, what a glorious thing,
　Sin's weary load to bring,
　And lose it while we sing;
　　Jesus is here.

CORONATION. C. M.

No. 148.   *General invitation to praise the Redeemer.*

 2 My gracious Master, and my God,
  Assist me to proclaim,—
 To spread, through all the earth abroad
  The honors of thy Name.

 3 Jesus!—the Name that charms our fears,
  That bids our sorrows cease:
 'Tis music in the sinner's ears,
  'Tis life, and health, and peace.

 4 Hear him, ye deaf; his praise, ye dumb,
  Your loosen'd tongues employ;
 Ye blind, behold your Saviour come;
  And leap, ye lame, for joy.—*C. Wesley.*

No. 149.   *Crown him Lord of all.*

1 ALL hail the power of Jesus' name!
 Let angels prostrate fall:
Bring forth the royal diadem,
 And crown him Lord of all.

2 Sinners, whose love can ne'er forget
 The wormwood and the gall;
Go, spread your trophies at his feet,
 And crown him Lord of all.

AZMON. C. M.

From GLASER.

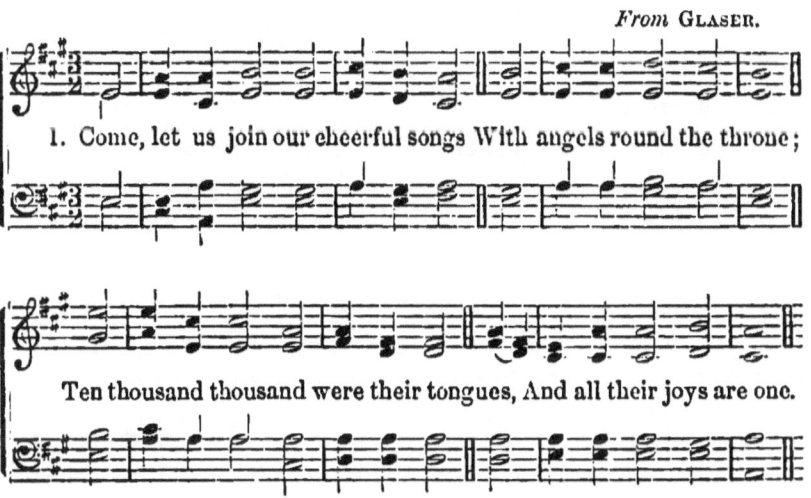

1. Come, let us join our cheerful songs With angels round the throne;
Ten thousand thousand were their tongues, And all their joys are one.

No. 150. *" Worthy the Lamb."*

2 "Worthy the Lamb that died," they cry,
"To be exalted thus:"
"Worthy the Lamb," our lips reply,
"For he was slain for us."

3 Jesus is worthy to receive
Honor and power divine;
And blessings, more than we can give,
Be, Lord, forever thine.

The whole creation join in one,
To bless the sacred name
Of him that sits upon the throne,
And to adore the Lamb.—*Watts.*

No. 149.—*Concluded.*

3 Let every kindred, every tribe,
On this terrestrial ball,
To him all majesty ascribe,
And crown him Lord of all.

4 Oh, that with yonder sacred throng
We at his feet may fall;
We'll join the everlasting song,
And crown him Lord of all.
Perronet.

NAOMI. C. M.

Dr. L. Mason.

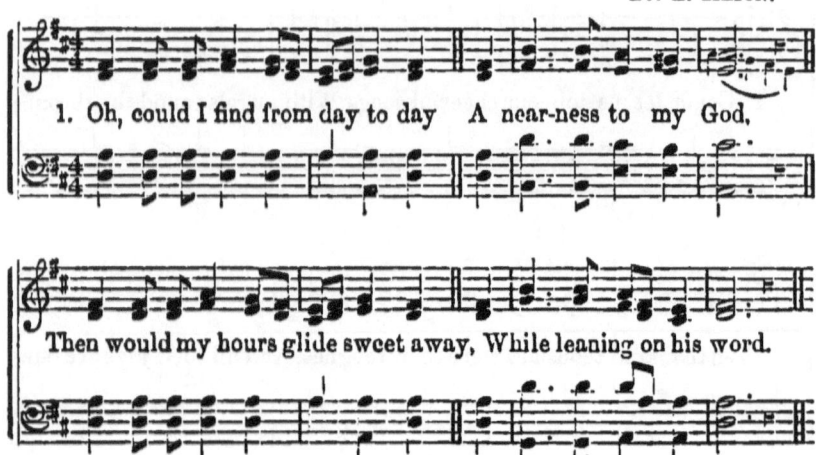

1. Oh, could I find from day to day A near-ness to my God,
Then would my hours glide sweet away, While leaning on his word.

No. 151. *Desire for holiness.*

2 Lord, I desire with thee to live
  Anew from day to day,
In joys the world can never give
  Nor ever take away.

3 Blest Jesus, come, and rule my heart,
  And make me wholly thine,
That I may never more depart,
  Nor grieve thy love divine.

4 Thus, till my last, expiring breath,
  Thy goodness I'll adore;
And when my frame dissolves in death
  My soul shall love thee more.—*Unknown.*

No. 152. *His quickening power.*

1 Come, Holy Spirit, heavenly Dove,
  With all thy quick'ning powers;
Kindle a flame of sacred love
  In these cold hearts of ours.

2 Look how we grovel here below,
  Fond of these earthly toys;
Our souls, how heavily they go,
  To reach eternal joys.

ORTONVILLE. C. M.

Dr. Thos. Hastings.

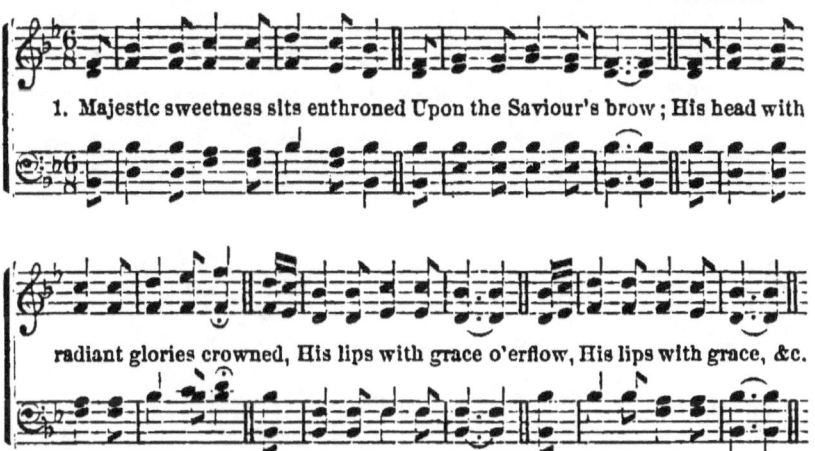

1. Majestic sweetness sits enthroned Upon the Saviour's brow; His head with radiant glories crowned, His lips with grace o'erflow, His lips with grace, &c.

No. 153.   *This is my friend.*

2 No mortal can with him compare,
Among the sons of men;
Fairer is he than all the fair
That fill the heavenly train.

3 He saw me plunged in deep distress,
He flew to my relief;
For me he bore the shameful cross,
And carried all my grief.

4 To him I own my life and breath,
And all the joys I have;
He makes me triumph over death,
He saves me from the grave.—*Stennett.*

No. 152.—Concluded.

3 In vain we tune our formal songs,—
In vain we strive to rise;
Hosannas languish on our tongues,
And our devotion dies.

4 Come, Holy Spirit, heavenly Dove,
With all thy quick'ning powers;
Come, shed abroad a Saviour's love,
And that shall kindle ours.—*Watts.*

AVON. C. M.

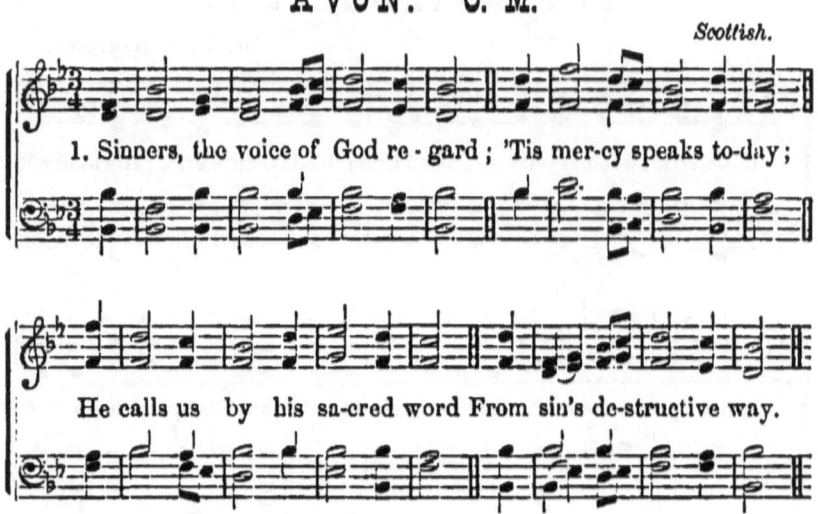

1. Sinners, the voice of God regard; 'Tis mercy speaks to-day; He calls us by his sacred word From sin's destructive way.

No. 154.   *No peace to the wicked.*

2 Like the rough sea that cannot rest
  You live, devoid of peace;
  A thousand stings within your breast
  Deprive your souls of ease.

3 Your way is dark, and leads to hell
  Why will you persevere!
  Can you in endless torments dwell,
  Shut up in black despair?

4 Why will you in the crooked ways
  Of sin and folly go?
  In pain you travel all your days,
  To reach eternal woe.—*Fawcett.*

No. 155.   *Sufficiency and freeness.*

Oh, what amazing words of grace
  Are in the gospel found!
Suited to every sinner's case,
  Who knows the joyful sound.

2 Poor, sinful, thirsty, fainting souls,
    Are freely welcome here;
  Salvation, like a river, rolls,
    Abundant, free, and clear.

SCOTT. C. M.

From " Dulcimer."

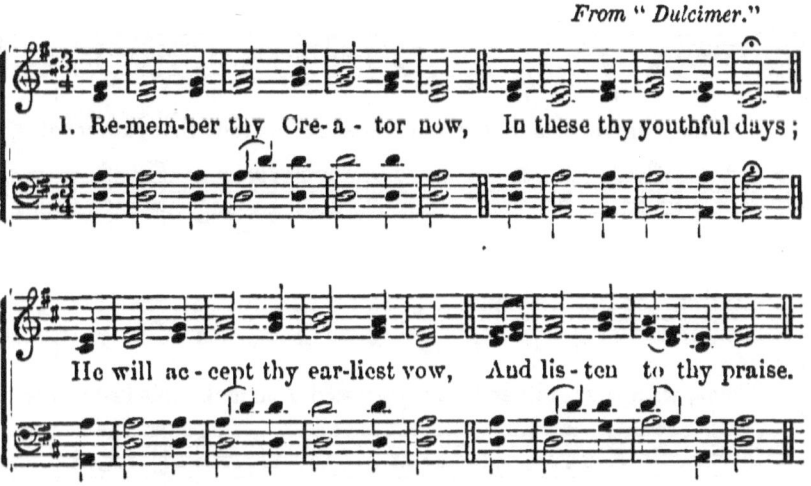

1. Re-mem-ber thy Cre-a-tor now, In these thy youthful days;
He will ac-cept thy ear-liest vow, And lis-ten to thy praise.

No. 156. *" Remember now thy Creator in the days of thy youth."*

    2 Remember thy Creator now,
       And seek him while he's near,
       For evil days will come, when thou
         Shalt find no comfort near.

    3 Remember thy Creator now ;
       His willing servant be :
       Then, when thy head in death shall bow,
         He will remember thee.

    4 Almighty God! our hearts incline
       Thy heavenly voice to hear;
       Let all our future days be thine,
         Devoted to thy fear.—*Unknown.*

No. 155.—Concluded.
                   [wounds;
3 Come, then, with all your wants and
   Your every burden bring:
   Here love, unchanging love, abounds—
   A deep, celestial spring.

4 Whoever will—O gracious word!—
   May of this stream partake;
   Come, thirsty souls, and bless the Lord;
   And drink, for Jesus' sake.—*Medley.*

RESOLUTION. C. M. Double. (Old.)

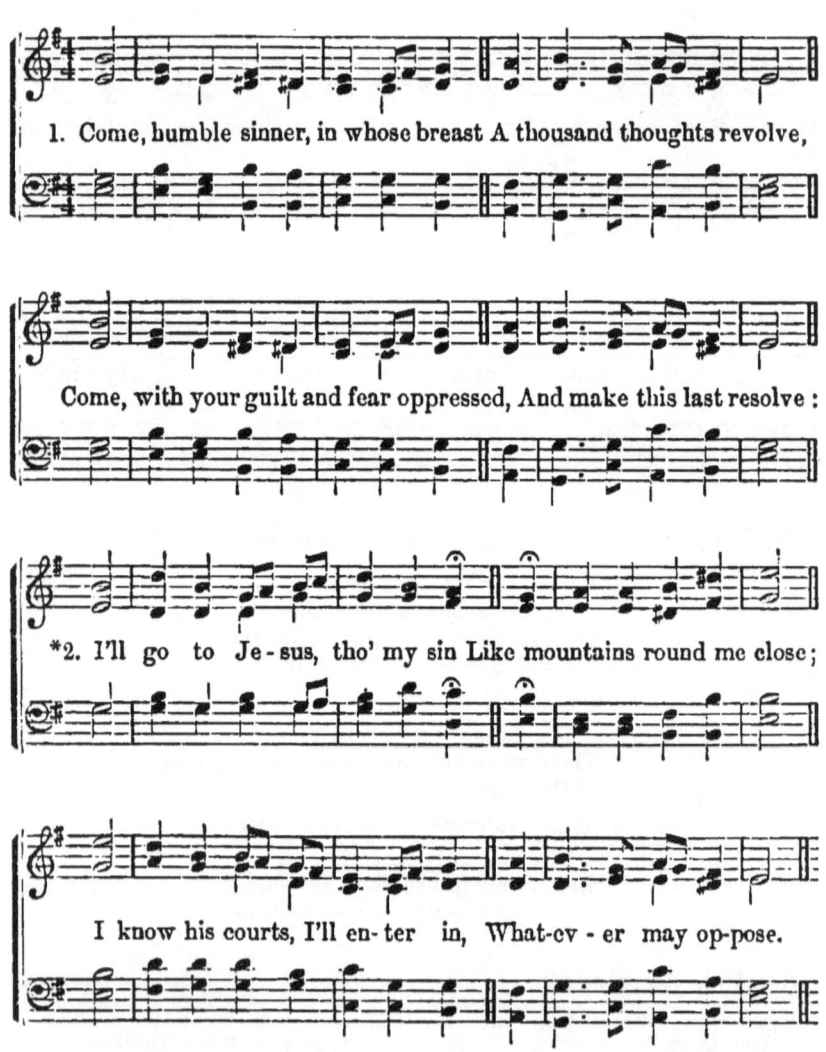

1. Come, humble sinner, in whose breast A thousand thoughts revolve,
Come, with your guilt and fear oppressed, And make this last resolve:

*2. I'll go to Je-sus, tho' my sin Like mountains round me close;
I know his courts, I'll en-ter in, What-ev-er may op-pose.

* *For the 5th verses of these Hymns repeat the last two braces of the music.*

No. 157. *The resolution.*

 3 Prostrate I'll lie before his throne,
  And there my guilt confess;
  I'll tell him, I'm a wretch undone
  Without his sov'reign grace.

 4 Perhaps he will admit my plea,
  Perhaps will hear my prayer;
  But, if I perish, I will pray
  And perish only there.

 5 I can but perish if I go—
  I am resolved to try;
  For if I stay away, I know
  I must forever die.—*Jones.*

OH, WHY SHOULD GLOOMY THOUGHTS ARISE.

No. 158. *Believe, and be at peace.*

 1 OH, why should gloomy thoughts arise,
  And darkness fill the mind?
  Why should that bosom heave with sighs
  And yet no refuge find?

 2 Hast thou not heard of Gilead's balm—
  The great Physician there,
  Who can thine every fear disarm,
  And save thee from despair?

 3 Still art thou overwhelm'd with grief,
  And fill'd with sore dismay?
  Still looking downward for relief,
  Without one cheering ray?

 3 Lift up thy streaming eyes to heaven;
  The great atonement see;
  And all thy sins shall be forgiven:—
  Believe, and thou art free.

 5 For thee the Saviour suffer'd shame,
  And shed his precious blood;
  Believe, believe in Jesus' name,
  And be at peace with God.—*T. Hastings.*

216   

I DO BELIEVE. C. M.

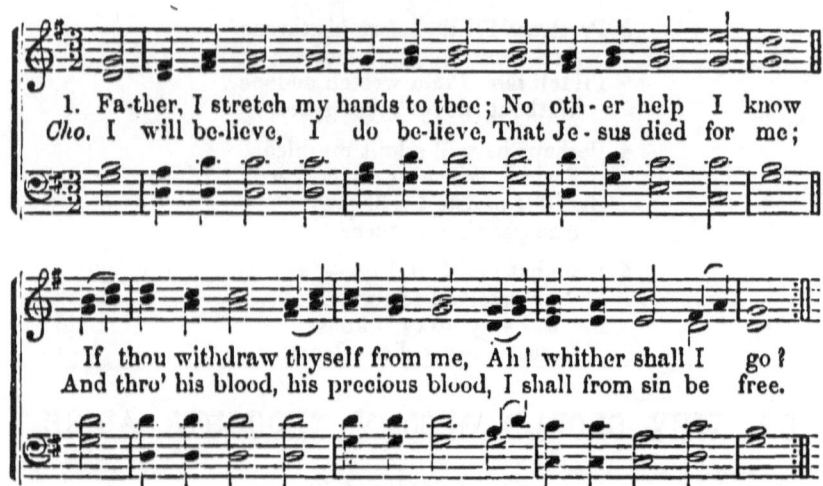

1. Fa-ther, I stretch my hands to thee; No oth-er help I know
Cho. I will be-lieve, I do be-lieve, That Je-sus died for me;
If thou withdraw thyself from me, Ah! whither shall I go?
And thro' his blood, his precious blood, I shall from sin be free.

No. 159.   *Unwearied earnestness.*

    2 What did thine only Son endure,
       Before I drew my breath!
      What pain, what labor, to secure
       My soul from endless death!—*Cho.*

    3 O Jesus, could I this believe,
       I now should feel thy power;
      And all my wants thou wouldst relieve,
       In this accepted hour.—*Cho.*

    4 Author of faith! to thee I lift
       My weary, longing eyes:
      Oh, let me now receive that gift,—
       My soul without it dies.—*Cho.*—*C. Wesley.*

No. 160.   *Lord, help my unbelief.*

1 How sad our state by nature is;
   Our sin, how deep its stains;
  And Satan binds our captive souls
   Fast in his slavish chains.

2 But there's a voice of sov'reign grace
   Sounds from the sacred word:—
  Ho! ye despairing sinners, come,
   And trust a faithful Lord.

FOUNTAIN. C. M.

Dr. LOWELL MASON.

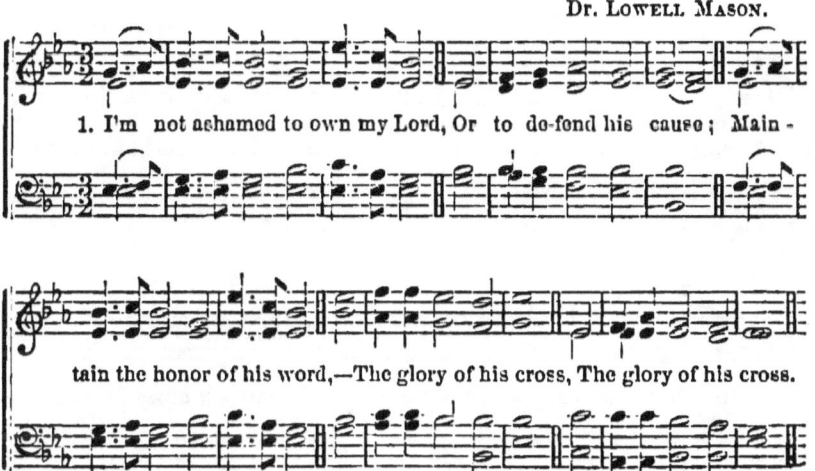

1. I'm not ashamed to own my Lord, Or to defend his cause; Maintain the honor of his word,—The glory of his cross, The glory of his cross.

No. 161. *Not ashamed of the Gospel.*

2 Jesus, my God!—I know his name;
His name is all my trust;
Nor will he put my soul to shame,
Nor let my hope be lost.

3 Firm as his throne his promise stands,
And he can well secure
What I've committed to his hands,
Till the decisive hour.

4 Then will he own my worthless name
Before his Father's face,
And in the new Jerusalem
Appoint my soul a place.—*Watts.*

No. 160.—*Concluded.*

3 My soul obeys the gracious call,
   And runs to this relief;
I would believe thy promise, Lord;
   Oh, help my unbelief!

4 To the blest fountain of thy blood,
   Incarnate God, I fly;
Here let me wash my guilty soul
   From crimes of deepest dye.
                      Watts.

CROSS AND CROWN. C. M.

Western Melody.

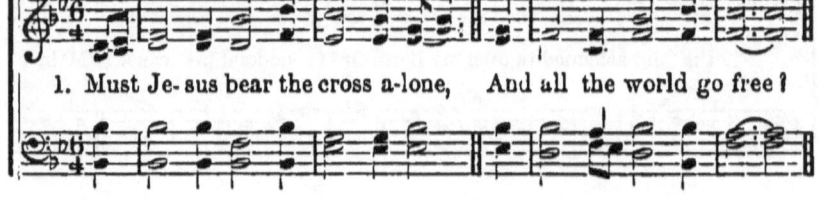

1. Must Je-sus bear the cross a-lone, And all the world go free?

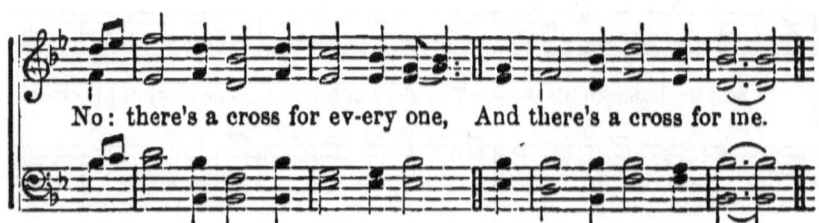

No: there's a cross for ev-ery one, And there's a cross for me.

No. 162. *The cross and the crown.*

1 Must Jesus bear the cross alone,
   And all the world go free?
   No: there's a cross for every one,
   And there's a cross for me.

2 How happy are the saints above
   Who once went sorrowing here;
   But now they taste unmingled love,
   And joy without a tear.

3 The consecrated cross I'll bear,
   Till death shall set us free,
   And then go home my crown to wear,—
   For there's a crown for me!—*G. N. Allen.*

No. 163. *His humiliation.*

1 And did the Holy and the Just,—
   The Sov'reign of the skies,—
   Stoop down to wretchedness and dust,
   That guilty man might rise?

2 Yes, the Redeemer left his throne,
   His radiant throne on high—
   Surprising mercy! love unknown!—
   To suffer, bleed, and die.

Hallowed Songs, Revised. 219

BELIEVER. C. M.

Arr. by H. P. MAIN.

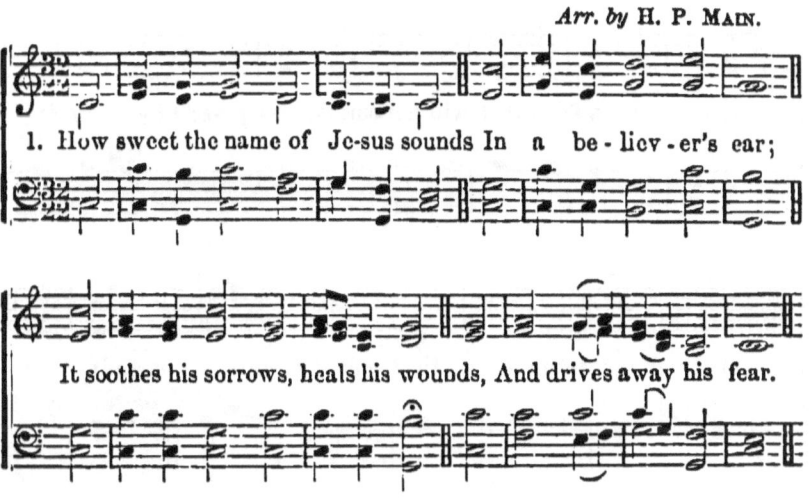

1. How sweet the name of Jesus sounds In a believer's ear;
It soothes his sorrows, heals his wounds, And drives away his fear.

No. 164. *The precious name.*

2 It makes the wounded spirit whole,
And calms the troubled breast;
'Tis manna to the hungry soul,
And to the weary, rest.

3 Dear Name, the rock on which I build,
My shield and hiding-place;
My never-falling treasure, fill'd
With boundless stores of grace

4 Jesus, my Shepherd, Saviour, Friend,
My Prophet, Priest, and King,
My Lord, my Life, my Way, my End,
Accept the praise I bring.—*Newton.*

No. 163.—*Concluded.*

3 To dwell with mis'ry here below,
The Saviour left the skies,
And sunk to wretchedness and woe,
That worthless man might rise.

4 He took the dying traitor's place,
And suffer'd in his stead;
For sinful man—O wondrous grace!—
For sinful man he bled.—*Steele.*

BALERMA. C. M.

Scottish.

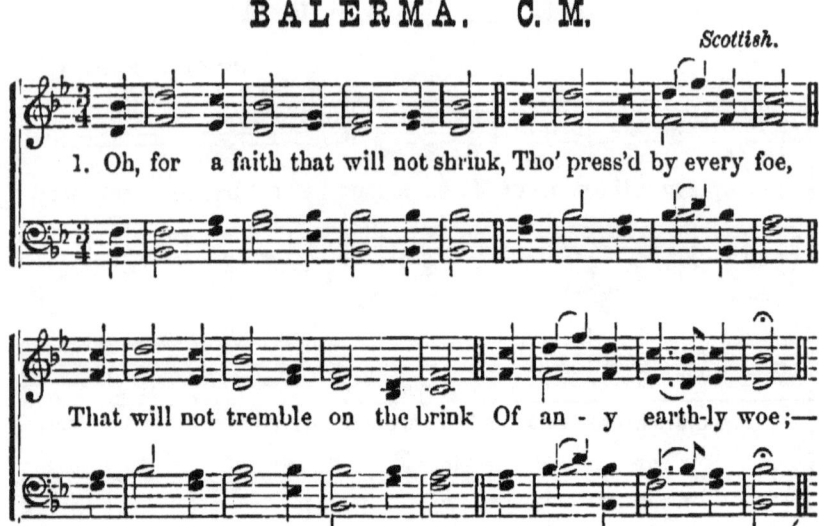

1. Oh, for a faith that will not shrink, Tho' press'd by every foe,
That will not tremble on the brink Of an-y earth-ly woe;—

No. 165.   *For victorious faith.*

2 That will not murmur or complain
   Beneath the chast'ning rod,
But, in the hour of grief or pain,
   Will lean upon its God;—

3 A faith that shines more bright and clear
   When tempests rage without;
That, when in danger, knows no fear,
   In darkness feels no doubt.

4 Lord, give us such a faith as this,
   And then, whate'er may come,
We'll taste, e'en here, the hallow'd bliss
   Of an eternal home.—*Bathurst.*

No. 166.   *His amazing love.*

1 PLUNGED in a gulf of dark despair,
   We wretched sinners lay,
Without one cheering beam of hope,
   Or spark of glimm'ring day.

2 With pitying eyes the Prince of peace
   Beheld our helpless grief;
He saw, and (oh, amazing love!)
   He flew to our relief.

ROSCOE. C. M.

From " Psaltery."

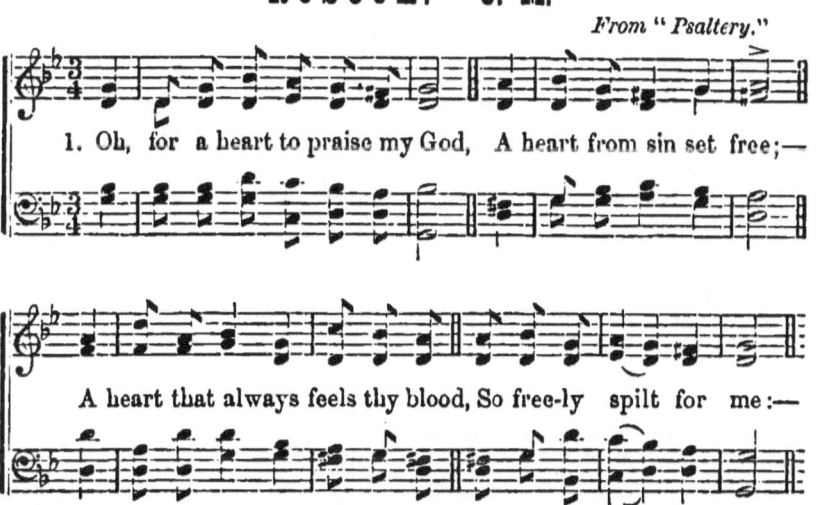

1. Oh, for a heart to praise my God, A heart from sin set free;—
A heart that always feels thy blood, So free-ly spilt for me:—

No. 167. *A perfect heart the Redeemer's throne.*

2 A heart resign'd, submissive, meek,
My great Redeemer's throne;
Where only Christ is heard to speak,—
Where Jesus reigns alone.

3 Oh, for a lowly, contrite heart,
Believing, true, and clean;
Which neither life nor death can part
From Him that dwells within:—

4 A heart in every thought renew'd,
And full of love divine;
Perfect, and right, and pure, and good,
A copy, Lord, of thine.—*C. Wesley.*

No. 166.—*Concluded.*

3 Down from the shining seats above,
   With joyful haste he fled;
Enter'd the grave in mortal flesh,
   And dwelt among the dead.

4 Oh, for this love let rocks and hills
   Their lasting silence break;
And all harmonious human tongues
   The Saviour's praises speak.
Watts.

WOODSTOCK. C. M.
D. DUTTON, Jr.

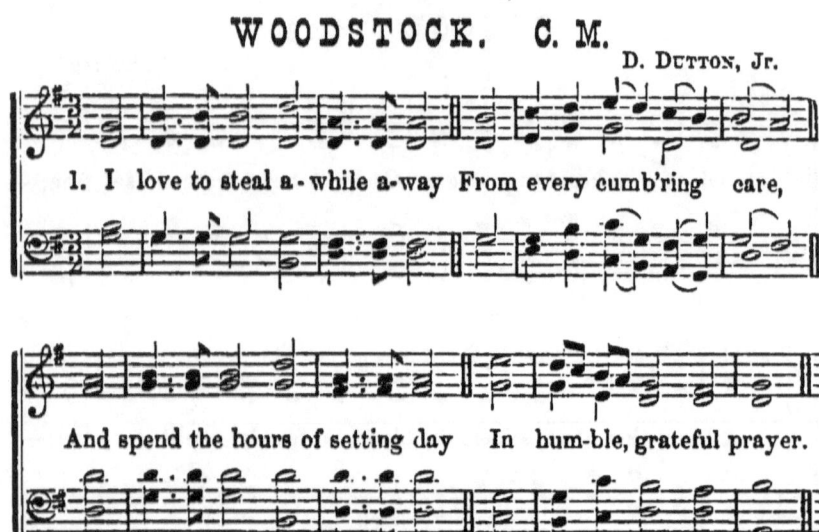

1. I love to steal a-while a-way From every cumb'ring care, And spend the hours of setting day In hum-ble, grateful prayer.

No. 168. *Evening.—Solitude.*

    2 I love in solitude to shed
        The penitential tear,
    And all his promises to plead
        Where none but God can hear.

    3 I love to think on mercies past,
        And future good implore,—
    And all my cares and sorrows cast
        On him whom I adore.

    4 I love by faith to take a view
        Of brighter scenes in heaven;
    The prospect doth my strength renew,
        While here by tempests driven.—*Mrs. Brown.*

No. 169. *Comfort in God.*

1 DEAR Refuge of my weary soul,
    On thee, when sorrows rise,
On thee, when waves of trouble roll,
    My fainting hope relies.

2 To thee I tell each rising grief,
    For thou alone canst heal;
Thy word can bring a sweet relief
    For every pain I feel.

SILOAM. C. M.

I. B. WOODBURY.

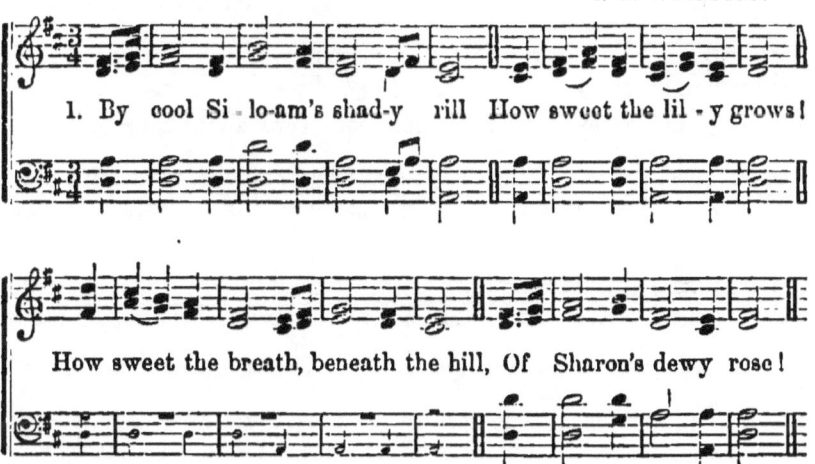

1. By cool Si - lo-am's shad-y rill How sweet the lil - y grows!
How sweet the breath, beneath the hill, Of Sharon's dewy rose!

No. 170. *The Christian child.*

2 Lo! such the child whose early feet
　The paths of peace have trod—
　Whose secret heart, with influence sweet,
　Is upward drawn to God.

3 By cool Siloam's shady rill
　The lily must decay;
　The rose that blooms beneath the hill
　Must shortly fade away.

4 And soon, too soon, the wintry hour
　Of man's maturer age
　Will shake the soul with sorrow's power,
　And stormy passion's rage.—*Heber.*

No. 169.—*Concluded.*

3 But, oh, when gloomy doubts prevail,
　I fear to call thee mine;
　The springs of comfort seem to fail,
　And all my hopes decline.

4 Yet, gracious God, where shall I flee?
　Thou art my only trust;
　And still my soul would cleave to thee,
　Though prostrate in the dust.
　　　　　　　　Steele.

EVAN. C. M.

Dr. Lowell Mason.*

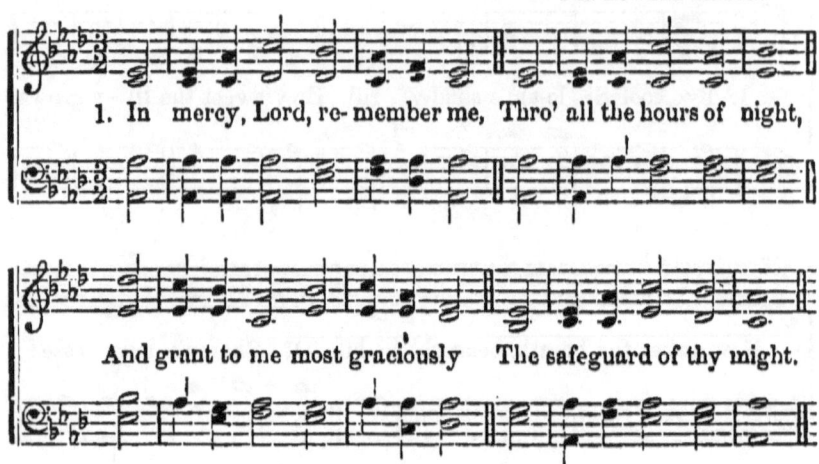

1. In mercy, Lord, re-member me, Thro' all the hours of night, And grant to me most graciously The safeguard of thy might.

No. 171.   *Evening: cheerful confidence.*

2 With cheerful heart I close mine eyes
Since thou wilt not remove:
O, in the morning let me rise,
Rejoicing in thy love.

3 Or, if this night should prove my last,
And end my transient days;
Lord, take me to thy promised rest,
Where I may sing thy praise.—*Moravian.*

Doxology.   To Father, Son, and Holy Ghost,   C. M.
Who sweetly all agree
To save a world of sinners lost,
Eternal glory be.

No. 172.   *Suffer the little children to come unto me.*

1 See, Israel's gentle Shepherd stands, | 2 Permit them to approach, he cries,
With all-engaging charms; | Nor scorn their humble name;
Hark, how he calls the tender lambs, | For 'twas to bless such souls as these
And folds them in his arms. | The Lord of angels came.

* *By permission of* Mason Brothers.

Hallowed Songs, Revised. 225

WARWICK. C. M.
STANLEY.

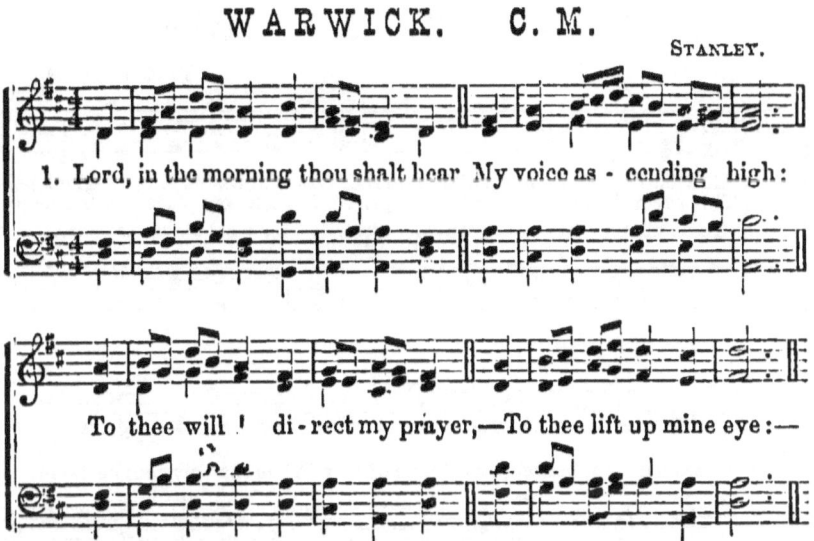

1. Lord, in the morning thou shalt hear My voice as-cending high: To thee will I di-rect my prayer,—To thee lift up mine eye:—

No. 173. *Sunday morning: preparing for public worship.*

2 Up to the hills where Christ is gone,
To plead for all his saints;
Presenting, at the Father's throne,
Our songs and our complaints.

3 Now to thy house will I resort,
To taste thy mercies there;
I will frequent thy holy court,
And worship in thy fear.

4 O may thy Spirit guide my feet
In ways of righteousness;
Make every path of duty straight,
And plain before my face.— *Watts.*

No. 172.—*Concluded.*

3 We bring them, Lord, in thankful bands,
And yield them up to thee;
Joyful that we ourselves are thine,
Thine let our offspring be.

4 Ye little flock! with pleasure hear,—
Ye children! seek his face;
And fly, with transports, to receive
The blessings of his grace.
Doddridge.

THORNTON. C. M. Double.

T. E. PERKINS.

1. How hap-py ev-ery child of grace, Who knows his sins for-given!
This earth, he cries, is not my place; I seek my place in heaven.
D. C. To dwell for-ev-er with the blest, E-ter-nal joys to share.

Cho. O heaven, dear heaven, sweet land of rest, When shall my soul be there,

No. 174.   *The full assurance of hope.*

2 A country far from mortal sight,
  Yet, oh, by faith I see :
  The land of rest, the saints' delight,—
  The heaven prepared for me.—*Cho.*

3 Oh, what a blessed hope is ours!
  While here on earth we stay,
  We more than taste the heavenly powers,
  And ante-date that day :—*Cho.*

4 We feel the resurrection near,—
  Our life in Christ conceal'd,—
  And with his glorious presence here
  Our earthen vessels fill'd.—*Cho.*—*C. Wesley.*

No. 175.   *Entire purification.*

1 FOREVER here my rest shall be,
  Close to thy bleeding side ;
  This all my hope, and all my plea,—
  For me the Saviour died

2 My dying Saviour, and my God,
  Fountain for guilt and sin,
  Sprinkle me ever with thy blood,
  And cleanse and keep me clean.

Hallowed Songs, Revised. 227

CHINA. C. M.
SWAN.

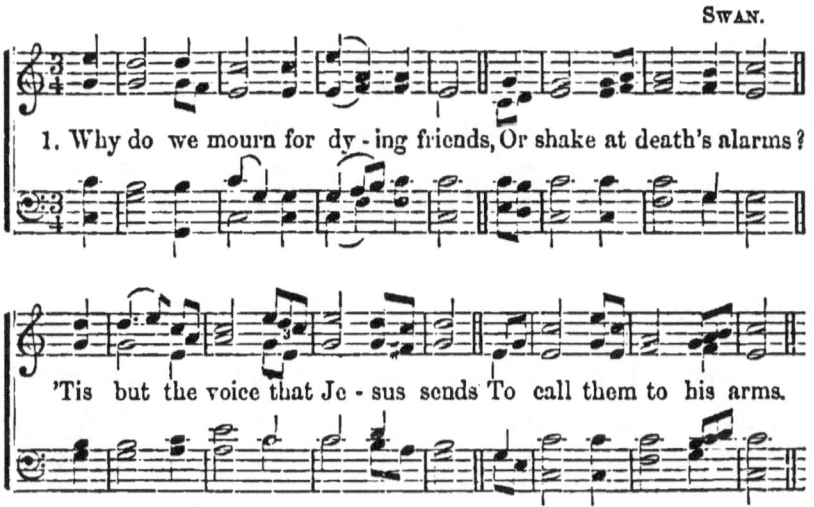

1. Why do we mourn for dy-ing friends, Or shake at death's alarms?
'Tis but the voice that Je-sus sends To call them to his arms.

No. 176. *Certainty of the Resurrection dispels the gloom of the grave.*

2 Are we not tending upward too,
  As fast as time can move?
Nor should we wish the hours more slow,
  To keep us from our love.

3 Why should we tremble to convey
  Their bodies to the tomb?
There once the flesh of Jesus lay,
  And left a long perfume.

4 The graves of all his saints he blest,
  And soften'd every bed:
Where should the dying members rest,
  But with their dying Head?—*Watts.*

No. 175.—*Concluded.*

3 Wash me, and make me thus thine own;
  Wash me, and mine thou art:
Wash me, but not my feet alone,—
  My hands, my head, my heart.

4 The' atonement of thy blood apply
  Till faith to sight improve;
Till hope in full fruition die,
  And all my soul be love.—*C. Wesley.*

ARLINGTON. C. M.

Dr. ARNE.

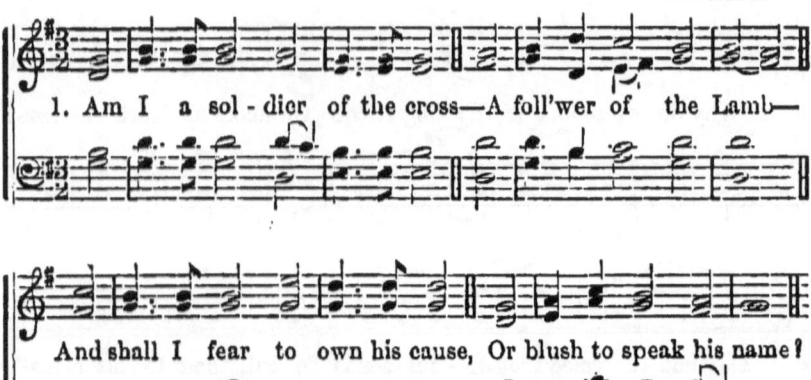

1. Am I a sol-dier of the cross—A foll'wer of the Lamb—
And shall I fear to own his cause, Or blush to speak his name?

No. 177.   *Faith sees the final triumph.*

2 Must I be carried to the skies
　On flowery beds of ease;
　While others fought to win the prize,
　And sail'd through bloody seas?

3 Are there no foes to face?
　Must I not stem the flood?
　Is this vile world a friend to grace,
　To help me on to God?

4 Since I must fight if I would reign,
　Increase my courage, Lord;
　I'll bear the toil, endure the pain,
　Supported by thy word.—*Watts.*

No. 178.   *The Promised Land.*

1 On Jordan's stormy banks I stand,
　And cast a wishful eye
　To Canaan's fair and happy land,
　Where my possessions lie.

2 Oh, the transporting, rapturous scene,
　That rises on my sight!
　Sweet fields array'd in living green,
　And rivers of delight.

Hallowed Songs, Revised.

STEPHENS. C. M.

JONES.

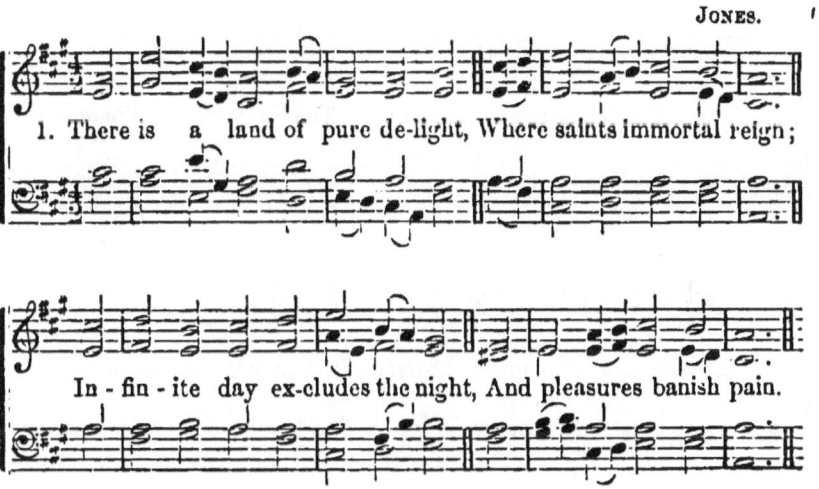

1. There is a land of pure de-light, Where saints immortal reign;
In-fin-ite day ex-cludes the night, And pleasures banish pain.

No. 179.   *The heavenly Canaan.*

2 There everlasting spring abides,
  And never-with'ring flowers:
  Death, like a narrow sea, divides
  This heavenly land from ours.

3 Sweet fields beyond the swelling flood
  Stand dressed in living green:
  So to the Jews old Canaan stood,
  While Jordan rolled between.

4 Could we but climb where Moses stood,
  And view the landscape o'er,
  Not Jordan's stream, nor death's cold flood,
  Should fright us from the shore.—*Watts.*

No. 178.—*Concluded.*

3 There generous fruits, that never fail,
   On trees immortal grow;
   There rock, and hill, and brook, and
   With milk and honey flow.   [vale,

4 O'er all those wide-extended plains
   Shines one eternal day:
   There God the Son forever reigns,
   And scatters night away.

DEDHAM. C. M.

From GARDNER.

1. Sweet was the time when first I felt
The Saviour's pard'ning blood
Applied to cleanse my soul from guilt,
And bring me home to God.

No. 180.   *Mourning departed joys.*

2 Soon as the morn the light reveal'd,
   His praises tuned my tongue;
And when the evening shades prevail'd,
   His love was all my song.

3 In prayer my soul drew near the Lord,
   And saw his glory shine;
And when I read his holy word,
   I call'd each promise mine.

4 But now, when evening shade prevails,
   My soul in darkness mourns;
And when the morn the light reveals,
   No light to me returns.—*Newton.*

No. 181.   "*Boast not thyself of to-morrow.*"

1 WHY should we boast of time to come,
   Though but a single day?
This hour may fix our final doom,
   Though strong, and young, and gay.

2 The present we should now redeem;
   This only is our own:
The past, alas! is all a dream;
   The future is unknown.

Hallowed Songs, Revised.

MELODY. C. M.

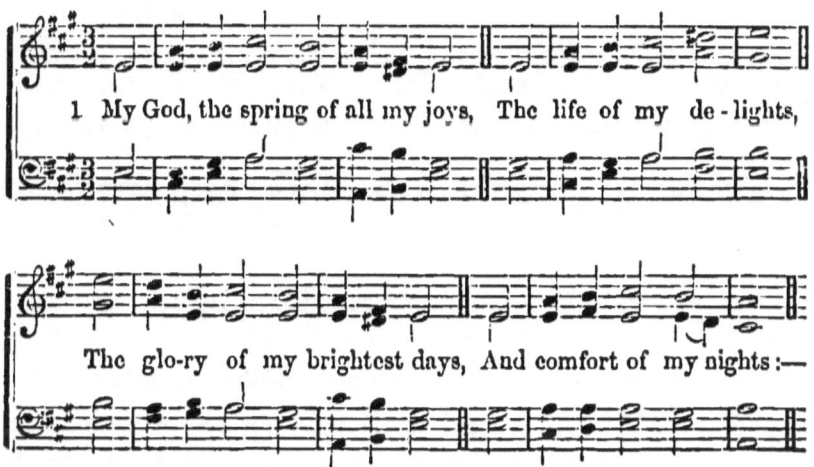

1 My God, the spring of all my joys, The life of my de-lights, The glo-ry of my brightest days, And comfort of my nights:—

No. 182. *Triumphant joy.*

2 In darkest shades, if thou appear,
My dawning is begun;
Thou art my soul's bright morning star,
And thou my rising sun.

3 The opening heavens around me shine
With beams of sacred bliss,
If Jesus shows his mercy mine,
And whispers I am his.

4 My soul would leave this heavy clay
At that transporting word,
Run up with joy the shining way,
To see and praise my Lord.—*Watts.*

No. 181.—*Concluded.*

3 Oh, think what vast concerns depend
Upon a moment's space,
When life and all its cares shall end
In vengeance or in grace!

4 Oh, for that power which melts the
And lifts the soul on high, [heart,
Where sin, and grief, and death depart,
And pleasures never die.
M. Wilkes.

BROWN. C. M.

WM. B. BRADBURY.

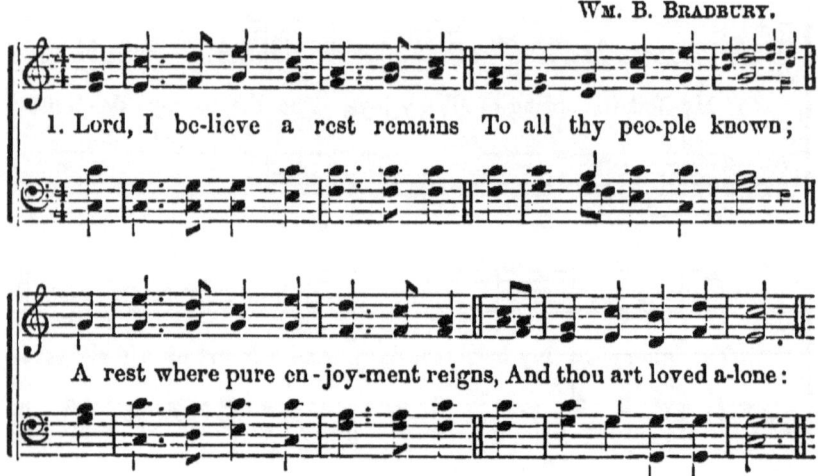

1. Lord, I believe a rest remains To all thy people known;
A rest where pure enjoyment reigns, And thou art loved alone:

No. 183. *The believer's rest.*

2 A rest where all our soul's desire
    Is fix'd on things above;
    Where fear, and sin, and grief expire,
    Cast out by perfect love.

3 Oh, that I now the rest might know,
    Believe, and enter in:
    Now, Saviour, now the power bestow,
    And let me cease from sin.

4 Remove this hardness from my heart,
    This unbelief remove;
    To me the rest of faith impart,—
    The Sabbath of thy love.—*C. Wesley.*

No. 184. *Death, gain to the faithful.*

1 WHY should our tears in sorrow flow
    When God recalls his own,
    And bids them leave a world of woe
    For an immortal crown?

2 Is not e'en death a gain to those
    Whose life to God was given?
    Gladly to earth their eyes they close,
    To open them in heaven.

Hallowed Songs, Revised. 233

PETERBORO'. C. M.

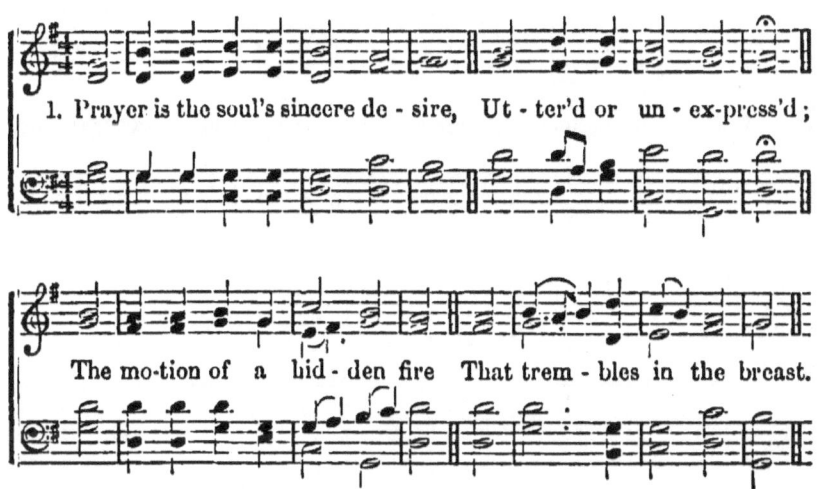

1. Prayer is the soul's sincere de - sire, Ut - ter'd or un - ex-press'd;
The mo-tion of a hid - den fire That trem - bles in the breast.

No. 185. *What is prayer?*

2 Prayer is the burden of a sigh,—
  The falling of a tear,—
  The upward glancing of an eye,
  When none but God is near.

3 Prayer is the simplest form of speech
  That infant lips can try;
  Prayer, the sublimest strains that reach
  The Majesty on high.

4 Prayer is the Christian's native breath,
  The Christian's native air;
  His watchword at the gates of death,—
  He enters heaven with prayer.—*Montgomery.*

No. 184.—*Concluded.*

3 Their toils are past, their work is done,
  And they are fully blest;
  They fought the fight, the vict'ry won,
  And enter'd into rest.

4 Then let our sorrows cease to flow;
  God has recall'd his own;
  But let our hearts, in every woe,
  Still say,—Thy will be done.
  Conder's Coll.

SILVERDALE. C. M.

T. E. PERKINS.

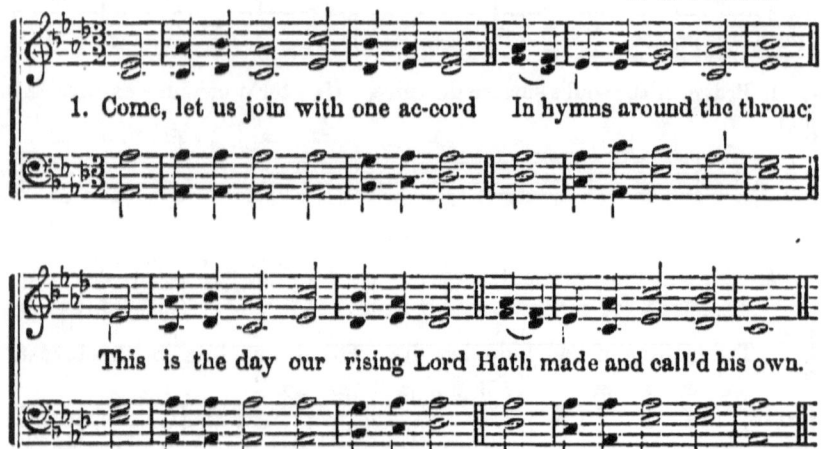

1. Come, let us join with one ac-cord In hymns around the throne;

This is the day our rising Lord Hath made and call'd his own.

No. 186. *The type of everlasting rest.*

2 This is the day which God hath blest,
  The brightest of the seven,
Type of that everlasting rest
  The saints enjoy in heaven.

3 Then let us in his name sing on,
  And hasten to that day
When our Redeemer shall come down,
  And shadows pass away.

4 Not one, but all our days below,
  Let us in hymns employ;
And, in our Lord rejoicing, go
  To his eternal joy.—*C. Wesley.*

No. 187. *The dreadful sentence.*

1 That awful day will surely come,
  Th' appointed hour makes haste,
When I must stand before my Judge,
  And pass the solemn test.

2 Jesus, thou source of all my joys,
  Thou ruler of my heart,
How could I bear to hear thy voice
  Pronounce the word,—Depart!

MEAR. C. M.

Williams' *Coll.*

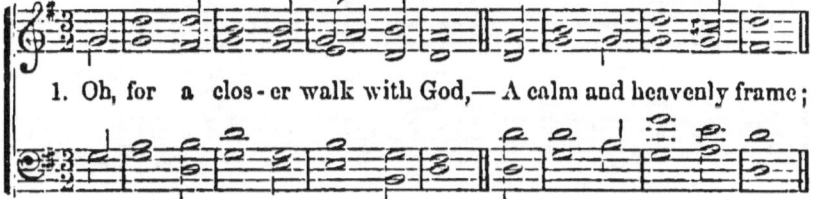

1. Oh, for a clos-er walk with God,—A calm and heavenly frame;

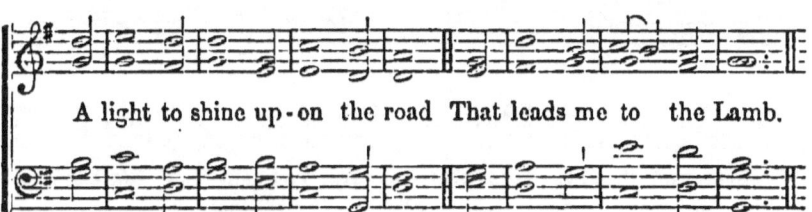

A light to shine up-on the road That leads me to the Lamb.

No. 188. *Lamenting the absence of the Spirit.*

2 Where is the blessedness I knew,
  When first I saw the Lord?
  Where is the soul-refreshing view
  Of Jesus and his word?

3 What peaceful hours I once enjoy'd!
  How sweet their mem'ry still!
  But they have left an aching void
  The world can never fill.

4 Return, O holy Dove, return,
  Sweet messenger of rest:
  I hate the sins that made thee mourn,
  And drove thee from my breast.—*Cowper.*

No. 187.—*Concluded.*

3 What, to be banish'd from my Lord,
  And yet forbid to die;
  To linger in eternal pain,
  And death forever fly?—

4 O wretched state of deep despair,
  To see my God remove,
  And fix my doleful station where
  I must not taste his love.—*Watts.*

ST. MARTIN'S. C. M.
WM. TANSUR.

No. 189.   *The Spirit's enlightening influences.*

    2 Come, Holy Ghost, for moved by thee
       The prophets wrote and spoke:
       Unlock the truth, thyself the key;
       Unseal the sacred book.

    3 Expand thy wings, Celestial Dove;
       Brood o'er our nature's night;
       On our disorder'd spirits move,
       And let there now be light.

    4 God, through himself, we then shall know,
       If thou within us shine;
       And sound, with all thy saints below,
       The depths of love divine.—*C. Wesley.*

Hallowed Songs, Revised. 237

DUKE STREET. L. M.
JOHN HATTON.

1. From all that dwell be-low the skies, Let the Cre-a-tor's praise arise;
Let the Re-deemer's name be sung, Thro' every land, by ev-ery tongue.

No. 190. *The creation invited to praise God.*

2 Eternal are thy mercies, Lord ;
Eternal truth attends thy word :
Thy praise shall sound from shore to shore,
Till sun shall rise and set no more.

3 Your lofty themes, ye mortals, bring ;
In songs of praise divinely sing ;
The great salvation loud proclaim,
And shout for joy the Saviour's name.

4 In every land begin the song;
To every land the strains belong;
In cheerful sounds all voices raise,
And fill the world with loudest praise.— *Watts.*

DOXOLOGY. L. M.

PRAISE God, from whom all blessings flow ;
Praise him, all creatures here below ;
Praise him above, ye heavenly host ;
Praise Father, Son, and Holy Ghost.

UPTON. L. M.

Dr. LOWELL MASON. *By permission.*

1. Bless, O my soul! the living God; Call home thy thoughts that rove abroad: Let all the powers within me join In work and worship so divine.

No. 192. *"Bless the Lord, O my soul."*

2 Bless, O my soul! the God of grace;
His favors claim thy highest praise;
Why should the wonders he hath wrought
Be lost in silence, and forgot?

3 'Tis he, my soul, that sent his Son
To die for crimes which thou hast done;
He owns the ransom, and forgives
The hourly follies of our lives.

4 Let every land his power confess;
Let all the earth adore his grace:
My heart and tongue with rapture join,
In work and worship so divine.—*Watts.*

No. 193. *Jesus reigns.*

1 Come, let us tune our loftiest song,
And raise to Christ our joyful strain;
Worship and thanks to him belong,
Who reigns, and shall forever reign.

2 His sovereign power our bodies made;
Our souls are his immortal breath;
And when his creatures sinn'd he bled,
To save us from eternal death.

WARD. L. M.

Arranged by Dr. MASON.

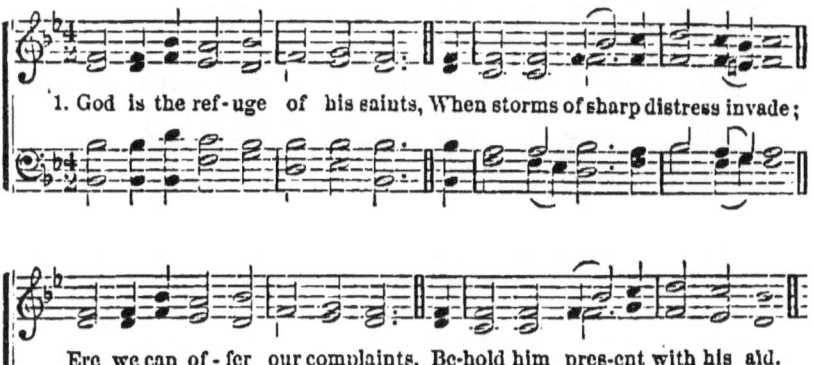

1. God is the ref-uge of his saints, When storms of sharp distress invade; Ere we can of-fer our complaints, Be-hold him pres-ent with his aid.

No. 194.   *God the refuge and portion of his people.*

2 Loud may the troubled ocean roar;
  In sacred peace our souls abide,
While every nation, every shore,
  Trembles and dreads the swelling tide

3 There is a stream whose gentle flow
  Supplies the city of our God;
Life, love, and joy still gliding through,
  And watering our divine abode.

4 That sacred stream, thy holy word,
  Supports our faith, our fear controls;
Sweet peace thy promises afford,
  And give new strength to fainting souls.— *Watts.*

No. 193.—*Concluded.*

3 Burn every breast with Jesus' love;
  Bound ev'ry heart with rapt'rous joy;
And saints on earth, with saints above,
  Your voices in his praise employ.

4 Extol the Lamb with loftiest song,
  Ascend for him our cheerful strain;
Worship and thanks to him belong,
  Who reigns, and shall forever reign.
    West.

OLD HUNDRED. L. M.

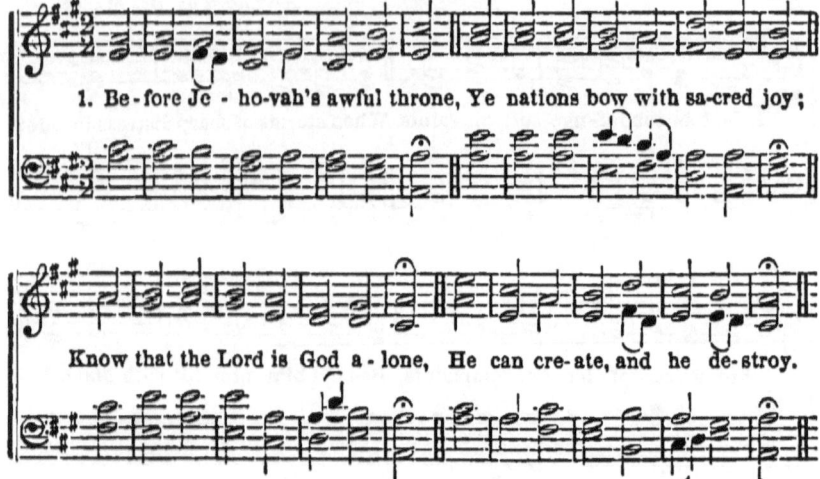

1. Be-fore Je-ho-vah's awful throne, Ye nations bow with sa-cred joy;
Know that the Lord is God a-lone, He can cre-ate, and he de-stroy.

No. 195. *Grateful adoration.*

2 His sov'reign power, without our aid,
   Made us of clay, and form'd us men;
 And when like wand'ring sheep we stray'd,
   He brought us to his fold again.

3 We'll crowd thy gates with thankful songs,
   High as the heavens our voices raise;
 And earth, with her ten thousand tongues,
   Shall fill thy courts with sounding praise.

4 Wide as the world is thy command:
   Vast as eternity thy love;
 Firm as a rock thy truth shall stand,
   When rolling years shall cease to move.—*Watts.*

No. 196. *"My heart is fixed; O God, my heart is fixed."*

1 My heart is fix'd on thee, my God;
   I rest my hope on thee alone;
 I'll spread thy sacred truths abroad,—
   To all mankind thy love make known.

2 Awake, my tongue; awake, my lyre:
   With morning's earliest dawn arise;
 To songs of joy my soul inspire,
   And swell your music to the skies.

Hallowed Songs, Revised. 241

SESSIONS. L. M.
EMERSON.

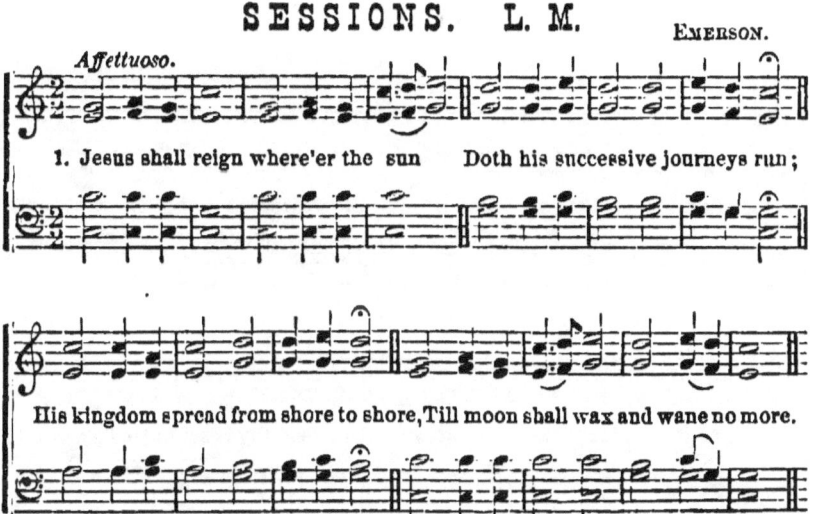

1. Jesus shall reign where'er the sun Doth his successive journeys run; His kingdom spread from shore to shore, Till moon shall wax and wane no more.

No. 197. *Christ's universal and everlasting kingdom.*

2 From north to south the princes meet,
To pay their homage at his feet;
While western empires own their Lord,
And savage tribes attend his word.

3 To him shall endless prayer be made,
And endless praises crown his head;
His Name like sweet perfume shall rise
With every morning sacrifice.

4 People and realms of every tongue
Dwell on his love with sweetest song,
And infant voices shall proclaim
Their early blessings on his Name.—*Watts.*

No. 196.—*Concluded.*

3 With those who in thy grace abound,
To thee I'll raise my thankful voice;
Till every land, the earth around,
Shall hear, and in thy Name rejoice.

4 Eternal God, celestial King,
Exalted be thy glorious Name;
Let hosts in heaven thy praises sing,
And saints on earth thy love proclaim.
Wrangham.

HAMBURG. L. M.

Arr. by Dr. L. MASON.

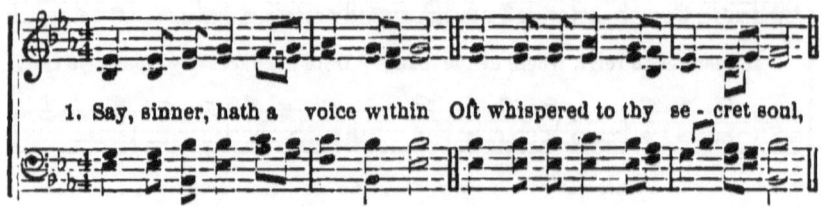

1. Say, sinner, hath a voice within Oft whispered to thy se-cret soul,

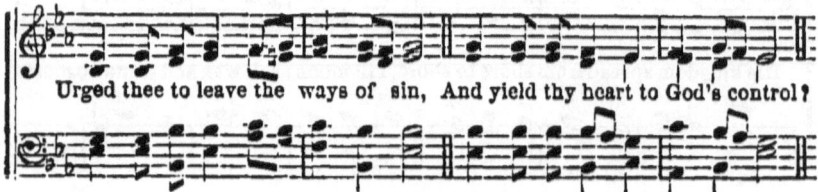

Urged thee to leave the ways of sin, And yield thy heart to God's control?

No. 198.   *The voice within.*

2 Sinner, it was a heav'nly voice,
   It was the Saviour's gracious call;
   It bade thee make the better choice,
   And haste to seek in Christ thine all.

3 Spurn not the call to life and light;
   Regard in time the warning kind;
   That call thou may'st not always slight,
   And yet the gate of mercy find.

4 Sinner, perhaps this very day
   Thy last accepted time may be;
   Oh, shouldst thou grieve him now away,
   Then hope may never beam on thee.—*Hyde.*

No. 199.   *" There remaineth a rest for the people of God."*

1 COME, O thou greater than our heart,
And make thy faithful mercies known;
The mind which was in thee impart:
Thy constant mind in us be shown.

2 Oh, let us by thy cross abide,
Thee, only thee, resolve to know,
The Lamb for sinners crucified,
A world to save from endless woe.

HARTEL. C. M.

Dr. L. MASON.

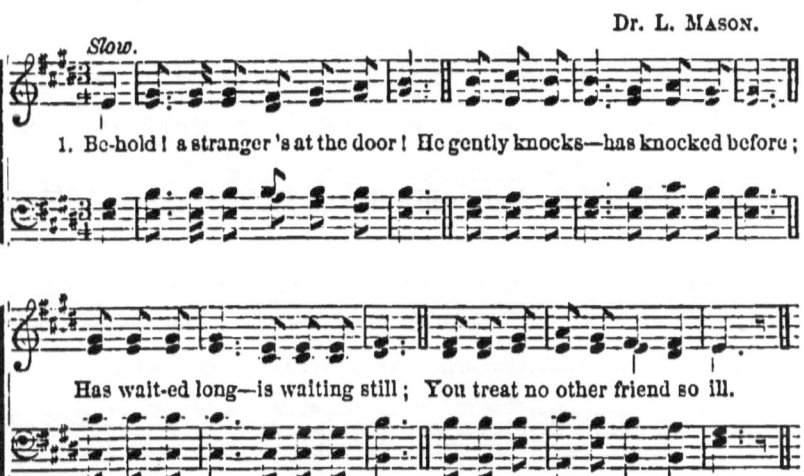

1. Be-hold! a stranger's at the door! He gently knocks—has knocked before;
Has wait-ed long—is waiting still; You treat no other friend so ill.

No. 200. *The waiting Saviour.*

2 But will he prove a friend indeed?
He will!—the very friend you need!
The Man of Nazareth!—'tis he,
With garments dyed at Calvary.

3 Oh! lovely attitude!—he stands
With melting hearts, and laden hands!
Oh! matchless kindness!—and he shows
This matchless kindness to his foes.

4 Admit him, ere his anger burn—
His feet departed ne'er return;
Admit him, or the hours at hand
When at his door denied you'll stand!—*Grigg.*

No. 199.—*Concluded.*

3 Take us into thy people's rest,
And we from our own works shall cease;
With thy meek Spirit arm our breast,
And keep our minds in perfect peace.

4 Jesus, for this we calmly wait;
Oh, let our eyes behold thee near!
Hasten to make our heaven complete;
Appear, our glorious God, appear.
C. Wesley.

UXBRIDGE. L. M.

Dr. L. Mason.

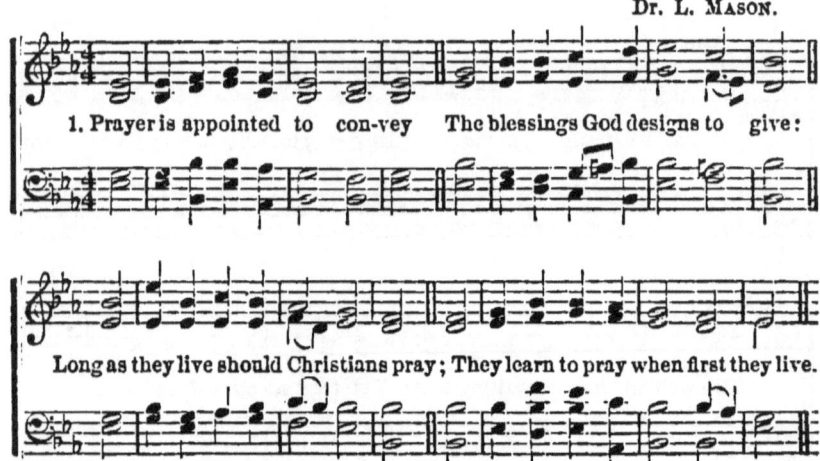

1. Prayer is appointed to convey
The blessings God designs to give:
Long as they live should Christians pray;
They learn to pray when first they live.

No. 201. *Design of prayer.*

2 If pain afflict, or wrongs oppress;
   If cares distract, or fear dismay;
If guilt deject; if sin distress;
   In every case, still watch and pray.

3 'Tis prayer supports the soul that's weak:
   Though thought be broken, language lame;
Pray, if thou canst or canst not speak;
   But pray with faith in Jesus' name.

4 Depend on him; thou canst not fail:
   Make all thy wants and wishes known;
Fear not; his merits must prevail:
   Ask but in faith, it shall be done.—*Hart.*

No. 202. *Blessings of prayer.*

1 What various hindrances we meet
   In coming to a mercy-seat;
Yet who that knows its worth of prayer,
   But wishes to be often there?

2 Prayer makes the darkened cloud withdraw;
Prayer climbs the ladder Jacob saw;
Gives exercise to faith and love;
Brings every blessing from above.

ILLINOIS. L. M.

Western Tune.

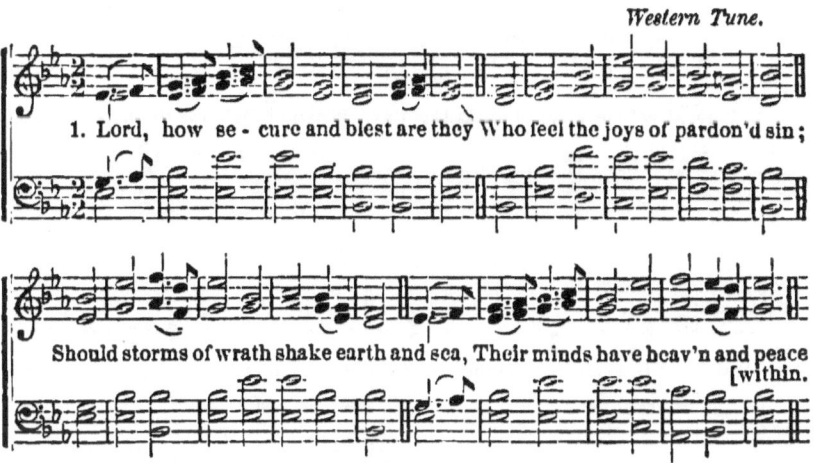

1. Lord, how se-cure and blest are they Who feel the joys of pardon'd sin;
Should storms of wrath shake earth and sea, Their minds have heav'n and peace [within.

No. 203. *The bliss of assurance.*

2 The day glides sweetly o'er their heads,
Made up of innocence and love;
And soft and silent as the shades,
Their nightly minutes gently move.

3 Quick as their thoughts, their joys come on,
But fly not half so swift away:
Their souls are ever bright as noon,
And calm as summer evenings be.

4 How oft they look to the heavenly hills,
Where groves of living pleasure grow;
And longing hopes, and cheerful smiles,
Sit undisturb'd upon their brow.— *Watts.*

No. 202.—*Concluded.*

3 Restraining prayer, we cease to fight:
Prayer keeps the Christian's armor bright;
And Satan trembles when he sees
The weakest saint upon his knees.
Cowper.

DOXOLOGY. L. M.

To God the Father, God the Son,
And God the Spirit, Trhee in One,
Be honor, praise, and glory given,
By all on earth, and all in heaven.

CAPTIVITY. L. M.

WM. B. BRADBURY.

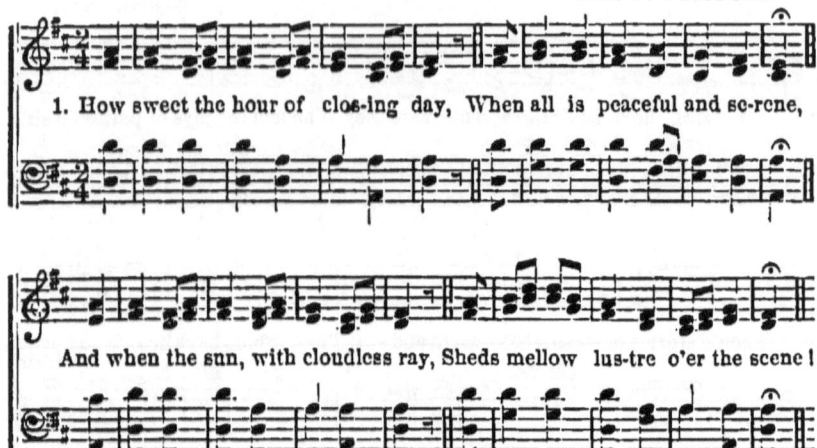

1. How sweet the hour of clos-ing day, When all is peaceful and se-rene,
And when the sun, with cloudless ray, Sheds mellow lus-tre o'er the scene!

No. 204. *The Christian's parting hour.*

2 Such is the Christian's parting hour;
  So peacefully he sinks to rest;
  When faith, endued from heaven with power,
  Sustains and cheers his languid breast.

3 Mark but that radiance of his eye,
  That smile upon his wasted cheek;
  They tell us of his glory nigh,
  In language that no tongue can speak.

4 A beam from heaven is sent to cheer
  The pilgrim on his gloomy road;
  And angels are attending near,
  To bear him to their bright abode.—*Bathurst.*

No. 205. *Earthly things vain and transitory.*

1 How vain is all beneath the skies!
How transient every earthly bliss!
How slender all the fondest ties
That bind us to a world like this!

2 The evening cloud, the morning dew,
The with'ring grass, the fading flower,
Of earthly hopes are emblems true—
The glory of a passing hour.

ZEPHYR. L. M.

Wm. B. Bradbury.

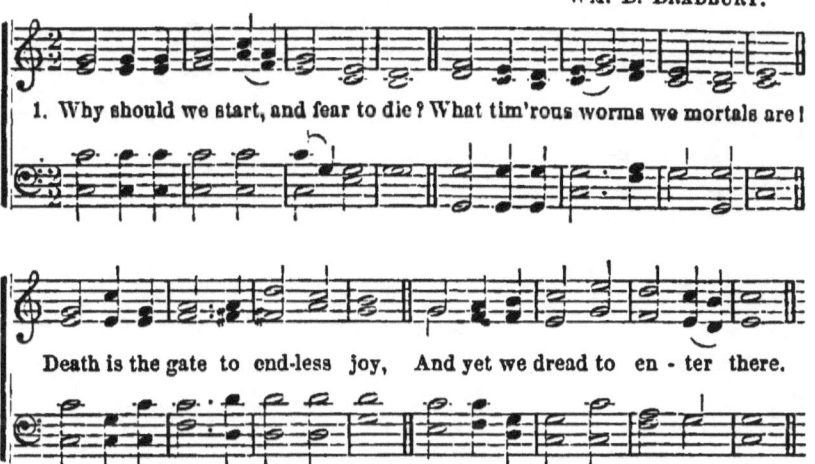

1. Why should we start, and fear to die? What tim'rous worms we mortals are! Death is the gate to end-less joy, And yet we dread to en-ter there.

No. 206.   *Christ's presence makes death easy.*

2 The pains, the groans, the dying strife,
  Fright our approaching souls away;
  And we shrink back again to life,
  Fond of our prison and our clay.

3 Oh, would my Lord his servant meet,
  My soul would stretch her wings in haste,
  Fly fearless through death's iron gate,
  Nor feel the terrors as she pass'd.

4 Jesus can make a dying bed
  Feel soft as downy pillows are,
  While on his breast I lean my head,
  And breathe my life out sweetly there.— *Watts.*

No. 205.—*Concluded.*

3 But tho' earth's fairest blossoms die,
  And all beneath the skies is vain,
  There is a brighter world on high,
  Beyond the reach of care and pain.

4 Then let the hope of joys to come
  Dispel our cares, and chase our fears:
  If God be ours, we're trav'ling home,
  Tho' passing through a vale of tears.
        Pratt's Coll.

RETREAT. L. M.
Dr. T. Hastings.

1. From ev-ery stormy wind that blows, From ev-ery swelling tide of woes,
There is a calm, a sure re-treat; 'Tis found be-neath the mer-cy-seat.

No. 207.   *The mercy-seat.*

2 There is a place, where Jesus sheds
The oil of gladness on our heads;
A place than all besides more sweet,—
It is the blood-bought mercy-seat.

3 There is a scene, where spirits blend,
Where friend holds fellowship with friend;
Though sunder'd far, by faith they meet,
Around one common mercy-seat.

4 There, there on eagles' wings we soar,
And sin and sense molest no more;
And heaven comes down our souls to greet,
While glory crowns the mercy-seat.—*Stowell.*

No. 208.   *Evening: Trusting in God.*

1 GLORY to thee, my God, this night,
For all the blessings of the light:
Keep me, oh, keep me, King of kings,
Beneath the shadow of thy wings.

2 Forgive me, Lord, for thy dear Son,
The ill which I this day have done;
That with the world, myself, and thee,
I, ere I sleep, at peace may be.

Hallowed Songs, Revised. 249

BE STILL, MY HEART.
S. J. Vail.

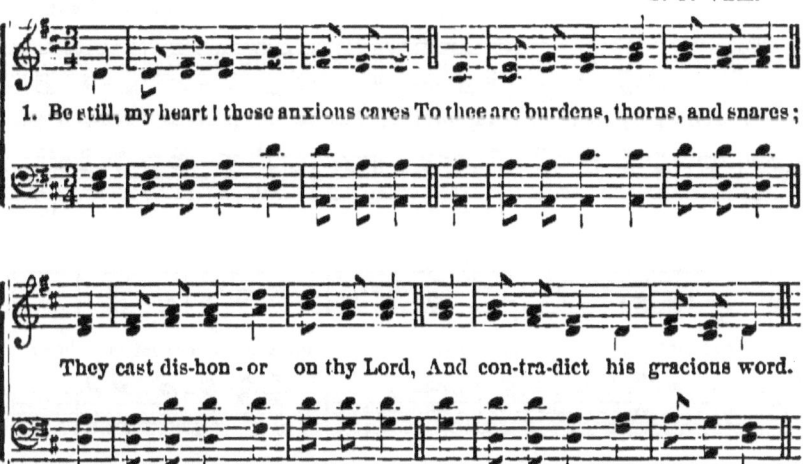

1. Be still, my heart! these anxious cares To thee are burdens, thorns, and snares;
They cast dis-hon-or on thy Lord, And con-tra-dict his gracious word.

No. 209.

2 Brought safely by his hand thus far,
Why wilt thou now give place to fear?
How canst thou want if he provide,
Or lose thy way with such a guide.

3 Did ever trouble yet befall,
And he refuse to hear thy call?
And has he not his promise pass'd
That thou shalt overcome at last.

4 He who has helped thee hitherto,
Will help thee all thy journey through,
And give thee daily cause to raise
New Ebenezers to his praise.

No. 208.—*Concluded.*

3 Teach me to live, that I may dread
The grave as little as my bed;
Teach me to die, that so I may
Rise glorious at the judgment-day.

4 Lord, let my soul forever share
The bliss of thy paternal care:
'Tis heaven on earth,'tis heaven above,
To see thy face, and sing thy love.

WINDHAM. L. M.

DANIEL READ.

1. Show pit-y, Lord, O Lord, forgive; Let a re-pent-ing reb-el live. Are not thy mercies large and free? May not a sin-ner trust in thee?

No. 210.   *Condemned, but pleading the promis*

2 My crimes are great, but don't surpass
The power and glory of thy grace;
Great God, thy nature hath no bound,—
So let thy pard'ning love be found.

3 Oh, wash my soul from every sin,
And make my guilty conscience clean;
Here on my heart the burden lies,
And past offences pain my eyes.

4 Yet save a trembling sinner, Lord,
Whose hope, still hov'ring round thy word,
Would light on some sweet promise there,—
Some sure support against despair.—*Watts.*

No. 211.   *The dreadful day.*

1 THE day of wrath, that dreadful day,
When heaven and earth shall pass away,
What power shall be the sinner's stay?
How shall he meet that dreadful day—

2 When, shriv'lling like a parched scroll,
The flaming heavens together roll;
And, louder yet, and yet more dread,
Swells the high trump that wakes the dead?

Hallowed Songs, Revised. 251

FOREST. L. M.

Chapin.

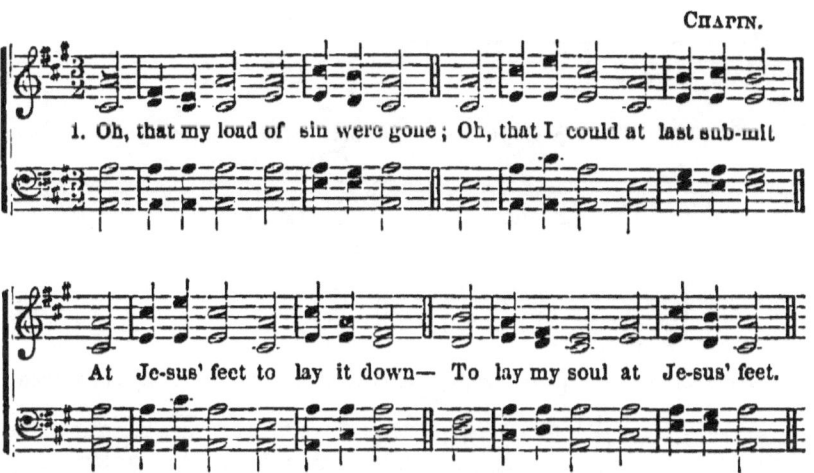

1. Oh, that my load of sin were gone; Oh, that I could at last sub-mit
At Jesus' feet to lay it down— To lay my soul at Jesus' feet.

No. 212. *The light yoke and easy burden.*

2 Rest for my soul I long to find;
 Saviour of all, if mine thou art,
 Give me thy meek and lowly mind,
 And stamp thine image on my heart.

3 Break off the yoke of inbred sin,
 And fully set my spirit free:
 I cannot rest till pure within,—
 Till I am wholly lost in thee.

4 Fain would I learn of thee, my God;
 Thy light and easy burden prove;
 The cross all stained with hallowed blood
 The labor of thy dying love.—*C. Wesley.*

No. 211.—*Concluded.*

3 Oh, on that day, that wrathful day,
 When man to judgment wakes from clay,
 Be thou, O Christ, the sinner's stay,
 Tho' heaven and earth shall pass away.
 W. Scott.

Doxology. L. M.

Praise to the Father, with the Son,
And Holy Spirit. Three in One;
As ever was in ages past,
And shall be so while ages last.

WELLS. L. M.

Israel Holdroyd.

1. While life prolongs its precious light, Mer-cy is found, and peace is given;
But soon, ah! soon, approaching night Shall blot out ev-ery hope of heaven.

No. 213. *The accepted time.*

2 While God invites, how blest the day!
  How sweet the gospel's charming sound!
  Come, sinners, haste, oh! haste away,
  While yet a pard'ning God is found.

3 Soon, borne on time's most rapid wing,
  Shall death command you to the grave,—
  Before his bar your spirits bring,
  And none be found to hear or save.

4 In that lone land of deep despair,
  No Sabbath's heavenly light shall rise,—
  No God regard your bitter prayer,
  No Saviour calls you to the skies.—*Dwight.*

No. 214. *All-sufficiency of His grace.*

1 Ho! every one that thirsts, draw nigh:
'Tis God invites the fallen race:
Mercy and free salvation buy,—
Buy wine, and milk, and gospel grace.

2 Come to the living waters, come!
Sinners, obey your Maker's call;
Return, ye weary wand'rers, home,
And find his grace is free for all.

Hallowed Songs, Revised. 253

OLIVE'S BROW. L. M.

Wm. B. Bradbury.

No. 215.   *The conflict.*

2 'Tis midnight; and, from all removed,
  The Saviour wrestles lone with fears;
  Ev'n that disciple whom he loved
  Heeds not his Master's grief and tears.

3 'Tis midnight; and, for others' guilt,
  The Man of Sorrows weeps in blood;
  Yet he, who hath in anguish knelt.
  Is not forsaken by his God.

4 'Tis midnight; and, from ether-plains
  Is borne the song that angels know:
  Unheard by mortals are the strains
  That sweetly soothe the Saviour's woe.—*Tappan.*

No. 214.—*Concluded.*

3 See from the Rock a fountain rise;
  For you in healing streams it rolls;
  Money ye need not bring, nor price,
  Ye lab'ring, burden'd, sin-sick souls.

4 Nothing ye in exchange shall give;
  Leave all you have, and are, behind;
  Frankly the gift of God receive;
  Pardon and peace in Jesus find.
  J. Wesley.

HEBRON. L. M.

Dr. L. Mason.

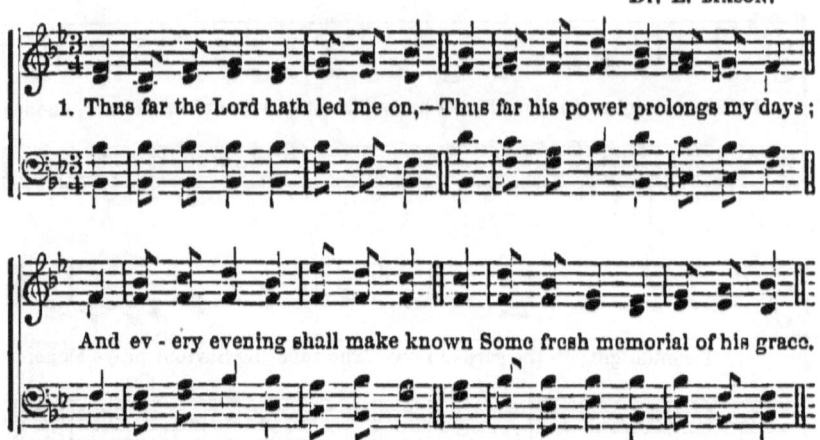

1. Thus far the Lord hath led me on,—Thus far his power prolongs my days;
And ev-ery evening shall make known Some fresh memorial of his grace.

No. 216. *Evening: memorials of his grace.*

2 Much of my time has run to waste,
   And I, perhaps, am near my home:
But he forgives my follies past,
   And gives me strength for days to come.

3 I lay my body down to sleep:
   Peace is the pillow for my head;
While well-appointed angels keep
   Their watchful stations round my bed.

4 Thus, when the night of death shall come
   My flesh shall rest beneath the ground,
And wait thy voice to rouse my tomb,
   With sweet salvation in the sound.— *Watts.*

No. 217. *Jesus everywhere present*

1 JESUS, where'er thy people meet,
   There they behold thy mercy-seat;
Where'er they seek thee, thou art found,
And every place is hallow'd ground.

2 For thou, within no walls confined,
   Dost dwell with those of humble mind;
Such ever bring thee where they come,
And, going, take thee to their home.

MIGDOL. L. M.

1. Soon may the last glad song arise, Thro' all the mil-lions of the skies— That song of triumph which records That all the earth is now the Lord's.

No. 218. *The song of triumph.*

2 Let thrones, and powers, and kingdoms, be
Obedient, mighty God, to thee;
And every land, and stream, and main,
Now wave the sceptre of thy reign.

3 Oh, let that glorious anthem swell;
Let host to host the triumph tell,
'Till not one rebel heart remains,
But over all the Saviour reigns —*Pratt's Coll.*

Dox. L. M. PRAISE God, from whom all blessings flow;
Praise him, all creatures here below;
Praise him above, ye heavenly host;
Praise Father, Son, and Holy Ghost.

No. 217.—*Concluded.*

3 Great Shepherd of thy chosen few,
Thy former mercies here renew;
Here, to our waiting hearts proclaim
The sweetness of thy saving name.
Cowper.

DOXOLOGY. L. M.
PRAISE to the Father, with the Son,
And Holy Spirit, Three in One;
As ever was in ages past,
And shall be so while ages last.

ROCKINGHAM. L. M.

Dr. LOWELL MASON.

1. Far from my thoughts, vain world, be gone, Let my re-lig-ious hours a-lone; Fain would mine eyes my Saviour see; I wait a vis-it, Lord, from thee.

No. 219. *In the sanctuary.*

2 Oh, warm my heart with holy fire,
And kindle there a pure desire:
Come, sacred Spirit, from above,
And fill my soul with heavenly love.

3 Blest Saviour, what delicious fare!
How sweet thine entertainments are!
Never did angels taste above
Redeeming grace and dying love.

4 Hail, great Immanuel, all divine!
In thee thy Father's glories shine;
Thy glorious name shall be adored,
And every tongue confess thee Lord.—*Watts.*

No. 220. *"The end of that man is peace."*

1 How blest the righteous when he dies!
When sinks a weary soul to rest!
How mildly beam the closing eyes!
How gently heaves th' expiring breast.

2 So fades a summer cloud away;
So sinks the gale when storms are o'er;
So gently shuts the eye of day;
So dies a wave along the shore.

Hallowed Songs, Revised. 257

FEDERAL STREET. L. M.

H. K. Oliver.

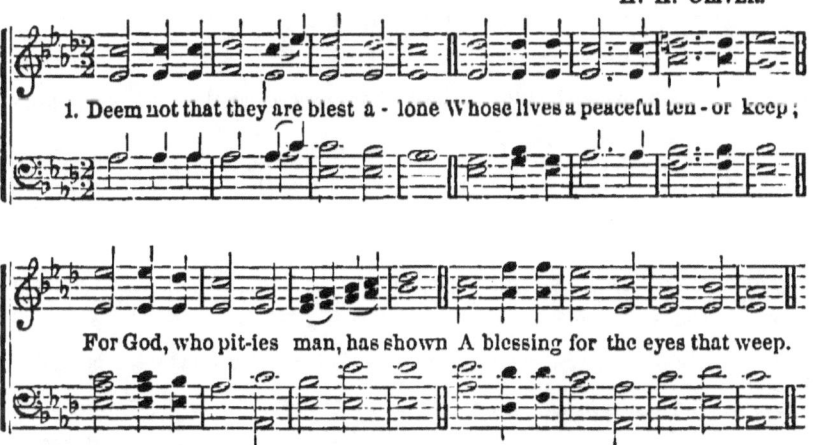

1. Deem not that they are blest a-lone Whose lives a peaceful ten-or keep;
For God, who pit-ies man, has shown A blessing for the eyes that weep.

No. 221.   *A blessing for those who mourn.*

2 The light of smiles shall fill again
The lids that overflow with tears;
And weary hours of woe and pain,
Are promises of happier years.

3 There is a day of sunny rest,
For every dark and troubled night;
Though grief may bide an evening guest
Yet joy shall come with early light.

4 Nor let the good man's trust depart,
Though life its common gifts deny,—
Though with a pierced and broken heart
And spurn'd of men, he goes to die.— *W. C. Bryant.*

No. 220.—*Concluded.*

3 A holy quiet reigns around,—
A calm which life nor death destroys;
And naught disturbs that peace profound
Which his unfetter'd soul enjoys.

4 Farewell, conflicting hopes and fears,
Where lights and shades alternate dwell!
How bright th' unchanging morn appears!
Farewell, inconstant world, farewell!
Barbauld.

LUTON. L. M.

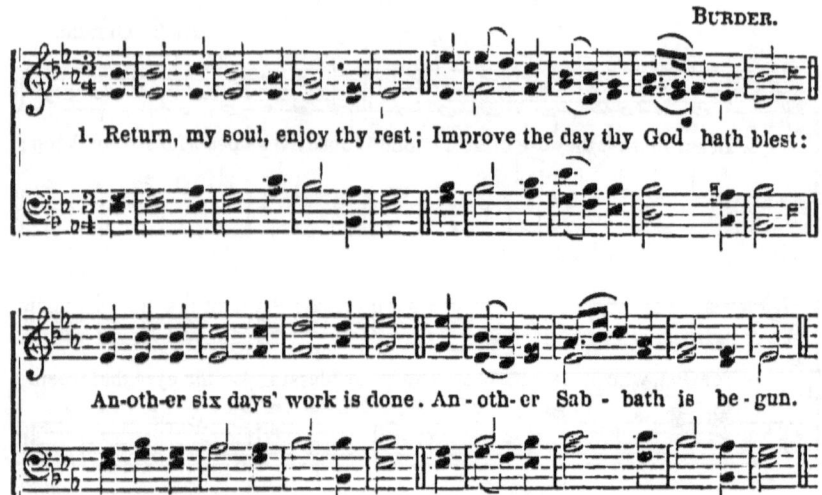

1. Return, my soul, enjoy thy rest; Improve the day thy God hath blest: An-oth-er six days' work is done. An-oth-er Sab-bath is be-gun.

No. 222. *Pledge of endless rest.*

2 Oh, that our thoughts and thanks may rise,
As grateful incense to the skies;
And draw from Christ that sweet repose,
Which none but he that feels it knows.

3 This heavenly calm within the breast,
Is the dear pledge of glorious rest,
Which for the Church of God remains,
The end of cares, the end of pains.

4 In holy duties, let the day,
In holy comforts pass away;
How sweet, a Sabbath thus to spend,
In hope of one that ne'er shall end.—*Montgomery.*

No. 223. *Triumphs of mercy.*

1 ARM of the Lord, awake, awake!
Put on thy strength—the nations shake,
And let the world, adoring, see
Triumphs of mercy wrought by thee.

2 Say to the heathen, from thy throne,
I am Jehovah—God alone;
Thy voice their idols shall confound,
And cast their altars to the ground.

ANVERN. L. M.

Dr. Lowell Mason.

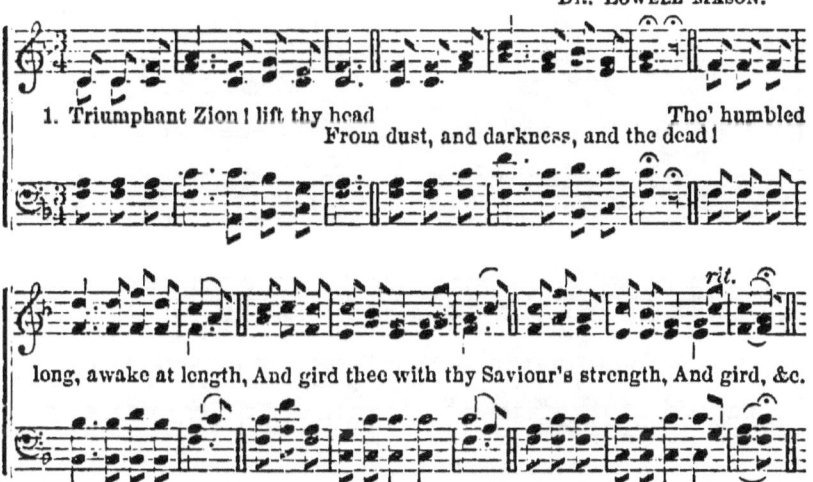

1. Triumphant Zion! lift thy head
From dust, and darkness, and the dead!
Tho' humbled long, awake at length,
And gird thee with thy Saviour's strength, And gird, &c.

No. 224.

Put all thy beauteous garments on,
And let thy excellence be known:
Decked in the robes of righteousness,
Thy glories shall the world confess.

3 No more shall foes unclean invade,
And fill thy hallowed walls with dread;
No more shall hell's insulting host
Their vict'ry and thy sorrows boast.

4 God, from on high, has heard thy prayer;
His hand thy ruin shall repair:
Nor will thy watchful monarch cease
To guard thee in eternal peace.

No. 223.—*Concluded.*

3 No more let creature blood be spilt—
Vain sacrifice for human guilt!
But to each conscience be applied
The blood that flow'd from Jesus' side.

4 Almighty God, thy grace proclaim,
In every land, of every name;
Let adverse powers before thee fall,
And crown the Saviour Lord of all.

Shrubsole.

GRATITUDE. L. M.

Bost.

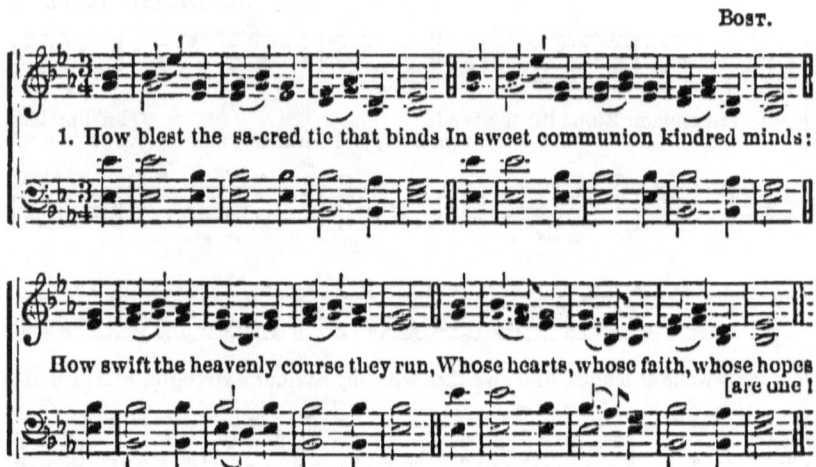

1. How blest the sa-cred tie that binds In sweet communion kindred minds;
How swift the heavenly course they run, Whose hearts, whose faith, whose hopes [are one!

No. 225. *Church union.*

2 To each the soul of each how dear!
  What tender love, and holy fear!
  How does the generous flame within
  Refine from earth, and cleanse from sin!

3 Their streaming eyes together flow
  For human guilt and human woe!
  Their ardent prayers together rise,
  Like mingling flames in sacrifice.

4 Nor shall the glowing flame expire,
  When dimly burns frail nature's fire;
  Then shall they meet in realms above—
  A heaven of joy—a heaven of love!—*Barbauld.*

No. 226. *Thirsting for the fullness of love.*

1 I THIRST, thou wounded'Lamb of God,
 To wash me in thy cleansing blood;
 To dwell within thy wounds; then pain
 Is sweet, and life or death is gain.

2 Take my poor heart, and let it be
 Forever closed to all but thee;
 Seal thou my breast, and let me wear
 That pledge of love forever there.

OLIVET. L. M.

I. B. WOODBURY.

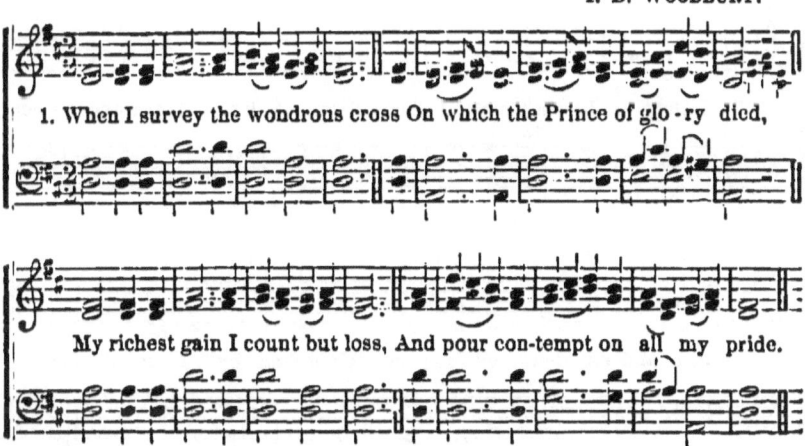

1. When I survey the wondrous cross On which the Prince of glo-ry died, My richest gain I count but loss, And pour con-tempt on all my pride.

No. 227.   *Glorying only in the cross.*

2 Forbid it, Lord, that I should boast,
    Save in the death of Christ, my God ;
All the vain things that charm me most,
    I sacrifice them to his blood.

3 See, from his head, his hands, his feet,
    Sorrow and love flow mingled down ;
Did e'er such love and sorrow meet,
    Or thorns compose so rich a crown?

4 Were the whole realms of nature mine,
    That were a present far too small ;
Love so amazing, so divine,
    Demands my soul, my life, my all.—*Watts.*

No. 226.—*Concluded.*

3 How blest are they who still abide
Close shelter'd in thy bleeding side!
Who thence their life and strength
    derive,
And by thee move, and in thee live.

4 What are our works but sin and death,
Till thou thy quick'ning Spirit breathe?
Thou giv'st the power thy grace to
    move ;
O wondrous grace! O boundless love!
    J. Wesley.

REST. L. M.

1. A-sleep in Je-sus! blessed sleep! From which none ever wake to weep;

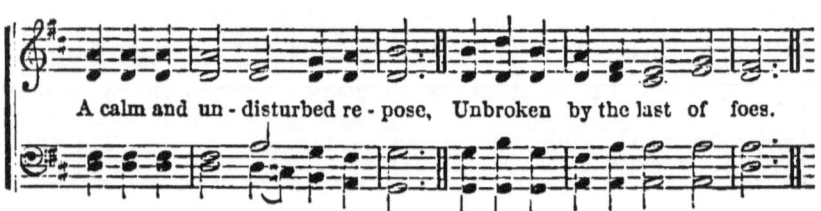

A calm and un-disturbed re-pose, Unbroken by the last of foes.

No. 228. *Asleep in Jesus.*

2 Asleep in Jesus! oh, how sweet
To be for such a slumber meet!
With holy confidence to sing,
That death hath lost its venomed sting!

3 Asleep in Jesus! peaceful rest!
Whose waking is supremely blest;
No fear, no woe, shall dim that hour,
Which manifests the Saviour's power.

4 Asleep in Jesus! oh, for me
May such a blissful refuge be!
Securely shall my ashes lie,
And wait the summons from on high.—*Mrs. Mackey*

No. 229. *They are not lost, but gone before."*

1 Dear is the spot where Christians sleep,
And sweet the strains their spirits pour;
Oh, why should we in anguish weep?
They are not lost, but gone before.

2 Secure from every mortal care,
By sin and sorrow vexed no more,
Eternal happiness they share
Who are not lost, but gone before.

SHEPHERD. L. M.

PHILIP PHILLIPS.

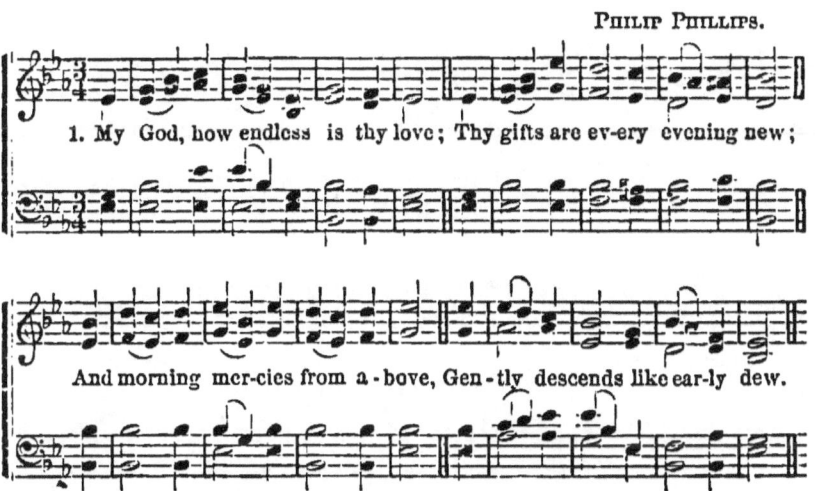

1. My God, how endless is thy love; Thy gifts are ev-ery evening new;
And morning mer-cies from a-bove, Gen-tly descends like ear-ly dew.

No. 230.   *Morning and evening mercies.*

2 Thou spread'st the curtains of the night,
  Great Guardian of my sleeping hours;
  Thy sov'reign word restores the light,
  And quickens all my drowsy powers.

3 I yield myself to thy command;
  To thee devote my nights and days;
  Perpetual blessings from thy hand
  *Demand perpetual songs of praise.— *Watts.*

Dox. L. M. PRAISE God, from whom all blessings flow;
  Praise him, all creatures here below;
  Praise him above, ye heavenly host;
  Praise Father, Son, and Holy Ghost.

No. 229.—*Concluded.*

3 To Zion's peaceful courts above
In faith triumphant may we soar,
Embracing, in the arms of love,
The friends not lost, but gone before.

4 To Jordan's bank whene'er we come,
And hear the swelling waters roar;
Jesus! convey us safely home,
To friends not lost, but gone before.

PARK STREET. L. M.

VENUA.

1. Stand up, my soul, shake off thy fears, And gird the gospel armor on; March to the gates of endless joy, Where Jesus, thy great Captain's, gone.

No. 231. *The march.*

2 Hell and thy sins resist thy course;
But hell and sin are vanquished foes;
Thy Saviour nailed them to the cross,
And sung the triumph when he rose.

3 Then let my soul march boldly on,—
Press forward to the heavenly gate;
Their peace and joy eternal reign,
And glittering robes for conquerors wait.

4 There shall I wear a starry crown,
And triumph in almighty grace;
While all the armies of the skies
Join in my glorious Leader's praise.— *Watts.*

No. 232. *National blessings.*

1 GREAT God of nations, now to thee
Our hymn of gratitude we raise;
With humble heart, and bending knee,
We offer thee our song of praise.

2 Thy Name we bless, almighty God,
For all the kindness thou hast shown
To this fair land the pilgrims trod,—
This land we fondly call our own.

WARE. L. M.

Geo. Kingsley.

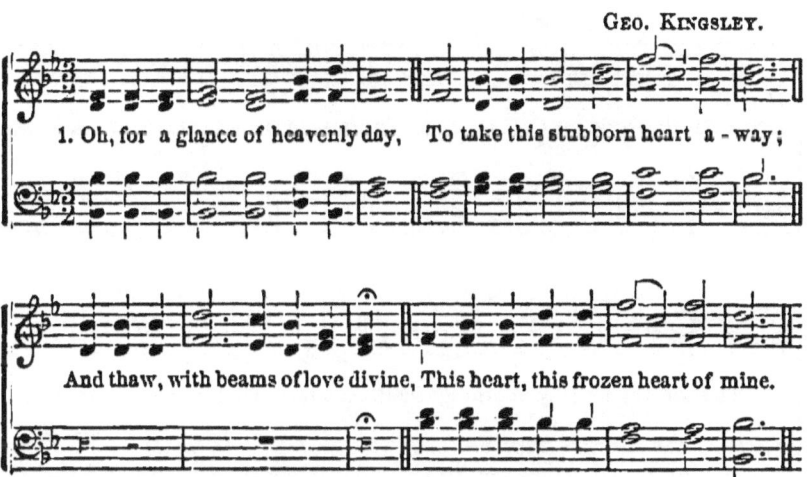

1. Oh, for a glance of heavenly day, To take this stubborn heart a-way;
And thaw, with beams of love divine, This heart, this frozen heart of mine.

No. 233.
The stubborn heart.

2 The rocks can rend; the earth can quake;
The seas can roar; the mountains shake:
Of feeling, all things show some sign,
But this unfeeling heart of mine.

3 To hear the sorrows thou hast felt,
O Lord, an adamant would melt:
But I can read each moving line,
And nothing moves this heart of mine.

4 But power divine can do the deed:
And, Lord, that power I greatly need:
Thy Spirit can from dross refine,
And melt and change this heart of mine.—*Hart.*

No. 232.—*Concluded.*

3 Here freedom spreads her banner wide,
And casts her soft and hallow'd ray;
Here thou our fathers' steps didst guide
In safety through their dang'rous way.

4 We praise thee that the gospel's light
Thro' all our land its radiance sheds;
Dispels the shades of error's night,
And heavenly blessings round us spreads.   *The Psalmodist.*

Hallowed Songs, Revised.

PORTUGAL. L. M.
T. THORLEY.

1. Sweet is the work, my God, my King, To praise thy name, give thanks, and sing;

To show thy love by morning light, And talk of all thy truth by night.

No. 234. *The joys of the Sabbath.*

2 Sweet is the day of sacred rest
No mortal cares shall seize my breast;
Oh, may my heart in tune be found,
Like David's harp of solemn sound.

3 When grace has purified my heart,
Then I shall share a glorious part:
And fresh supplies of joy be shed,
Like holy oil to cheer my head.

4 Then shall I see, and hear, and know
All I desired or wished below;
And every power find sweet employ
In that eternal world of joy.—*Watts.*

No. 235. *Not ashamed of Jesus.*

1 JESUS, and shall it ever be,
A mortal man ashamed of thee!
Ashamed of thee, whom angels praise,—
Whose glories shine thro' endless days.

2 Ashamed of Jesus!—that dear Friend,
On whom my hopes of heaven depend;
No!—when I blush, be this my shame,—
That I no more revere his Name.

Hallowed Songs, Revised. 267

BOWRING. L. M.
I. B. WOODBURY.

1. Stay, thou in-sult-ed Spir-it, stay, Tho' I have done thee such despite;
Nor cast the sin-ner quite a-way, Nor take thine ev-er-last-ing flight.

No. 236. *Deprecating the withdrawal of the Spirit.*

    2 Though I have steel'd my stubborn heart,
       And shaken off my guilty fears;
       And vex'd, and urged thee to depart,
       For many long rebellious years:

    3 Though I have most unfaithful been,
       Of all who e'er thy grace received;
       Ten thousand times thy goodness seen;
       Ten thousand times thy goodness grieved:

    4 Yet, oh! the chief of sinners spare,
       In honor of my great High Priest;
       For in thy righteous anger swear
       To' exclude me from thy people's rest.—*C. Wesley.*

No. 235.—*Concluded.*

3 Ashamed of Jesus!—yes, I may,
  When I've no guilt to wash away;
  No tear to wipe, no good to crave,
  No fears to quell, no soul to save.

4 Till then—nor is my boasting vain—
  Till then, I boast a Saviour slain;
  And, oh, may this my glory be,—
  That Christ is not ashamed of me.
                      Grigg.

JUDAH. L. M.

A. DOTY.*

1. Awake, Jerusalem, awake,—No longer in thy sins lie down;
The garment of salvation take; Thy beauty and thy strength put on.

No. 237. *" Put on thy beautiful garments, O Jerusalem."*

2 Shake off the dust that blinds thy sight,
   And hides the promise from thine eyes;
Arise, and struggle into light;
   The great Deliv'rer calls,—Arise!

3 Shake off the bands of sad despair;
   Zion, assert thy liberty;
Look up, thy broken heart prepare,
   And God shall set the captive free.

4 Vessels of mercy, sons of grace,
   Be purged from every sinful stain;
Be like our Lord, his word embrace,
   Nor bear his hallow'd name in vain.—*C. Wesley.*

DOXOLOGY. L. M.

PRAISE God, from whom all blessings flow;
Praise him, all creatures here below;
Praise him above, ye heavenly host;
Praise Father, Son, and Holy Ghost.

* *From " New Hymn and Tune Book."*

SUN OF MY SOUL. L. M.*

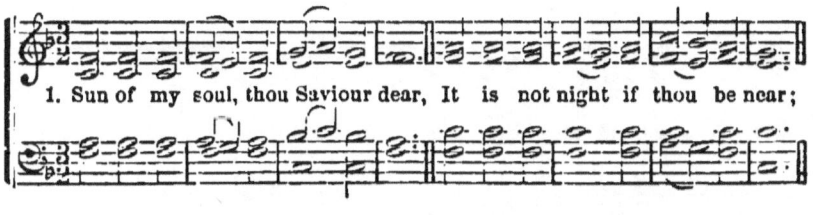

1. Sun of my soul, thou Saviour dear, It is not night if thou be near;

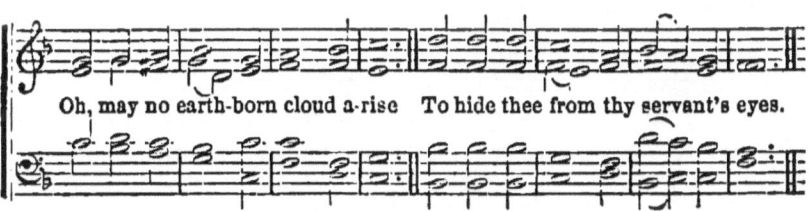

Oh, may no earth-born cloud a-rise To hide thee from thy servant's eyes.

No. 238.   "*Thou art my trust from my youth.*"

2 Abide with me from morn till eve,
For without thee I cannot live;
Abide with me when night is nigh,
For without thee I dare not die.

3 If some poor wandering child of thine
Have spurned to-day the voice divine—
Now, Lord, the gracious work begin;
Let him no more lie down in sin.

4 Watch by the sick; enrich the poor
With blessings from thy boundless store;
Be every mourner's sleep to-night,
Like infant's slumbers, pure and light.

5 Come near and bless us when we wake,
Ere through the world our way we take,
Till in the ocean of thy love
We lose ourselves in heaven above.

* From the "*New Standard Singer.*" Sent to Mr. Phillips from Constantinople by our earnest Missionary, Rev. A. G. LONG.

ST. THOMAS. S. M.

HANDEL.

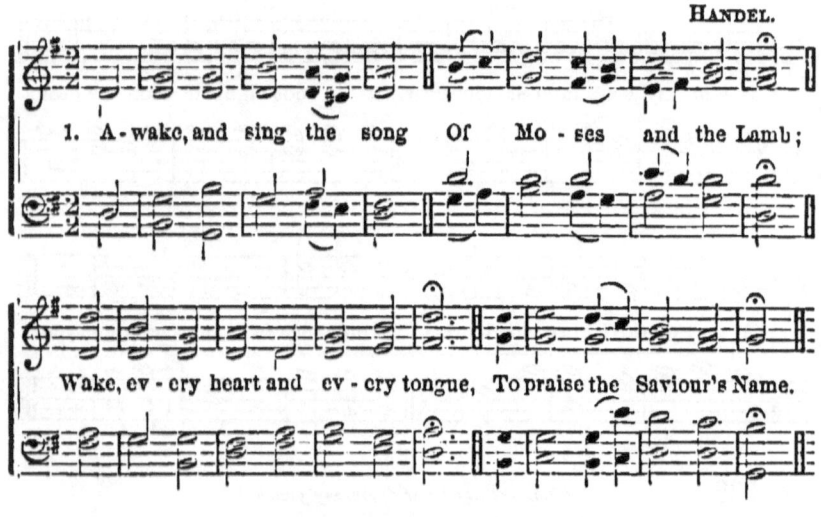

1. A-wake, and sing the song Of Mo-ses and the Lamb;
Wake, ev-ery heart and ev-ery tongue, To praise the Saviour's Name.

No. 239. *The Song of Moses and the Lamb.*

2 Sing of his dying love;
 Sing of his rising power;
 Sing how he intercedes above
 For those whose sins he bore.

3 Ye pilgrims, on the road
 To Zion's city, sing;
 Rejoice ye in the Lamb of God,—
 In Christ, the eternal King.

4 There shall each raptured tongue
 His endless praise proclaim;
 And sweeter voices tune the song
 Of Moses and the Lamb.—*Hammond.*

No. 240. *The universal King.*

1 Come, sound his praise abroad,
 And hymns of glory sing:
 Jehovah is the sov'reign God,
 The universal King.

2 He formed the deeps unknown;
 He gave the seas their bound;
 The wat'ry worlds are all his own,
 And all the solid ground.

Hallowed Songs, Revised. 271

SILVER STREET. S. M.

I. SMITH.

1. My soul, re-peat his praise, Whose mer-cies are so great, Whose an-ger is so slow to.... rise, So read-y to a-bate.

No. 241. *Mercy of God.*

2 His power subdues our sins;
And his forgiving love,
Far as the east is from the west,
Doth all our guilt remove.

3 High as the heavens are raised
Above the ground we tread,
So far the riches of his grace
Our highest thoughts exceed.— *Watts.*

Dox. S. M. To God, the Father, Son,
And Spirit, One in Three,
Be glory, as it was, is now,
And shall forever be.

No. 240.—*Concluded.*

3 Come, worship at his throne,
Come, bow before the Lord;
We are his works, and not our own,
He formed us by his word.

4 To-day attend his voice,
Nor dare provoke his rod;
Come, like the people of his choice,
And own your gracious God.
Watts.

KENTUCKY. S. M.

1. A charge to keep I have, A God to glo-ri-fy;
A nev-er-dy-ing soul to save, And fit it for the sky.

No. 242. *For diligence and watchfulness.*

2 To serve the present age,
   My calling to fulfill,—
Oh, may it all my powers engage,
   To do my Master's will.

3 Arm me with jealous care,
   As in thy sight to live;
And oh, thy servant, Lord, prepare,
   A strict account to give.

4 Help me to watch and pray,
   And on thyself rely,
Assured, if I my trust betray,
   I shall forever die.—*C. Wesley.*

No. 243. *The spirit of prayer.*

1 THE praying spirit breathe!
   The watching power impart;
From all entanglements beneath
   Call off my peaceful heart;

2 My feeble mind sustain,
   By worldly thoughts oppress'd;
Appear, and bid me turn again
   To my eternal rest.

Hallowed Songs, Revised. 273

AYLESBURY. S. M.

Moderato. HARVEY CAMP.

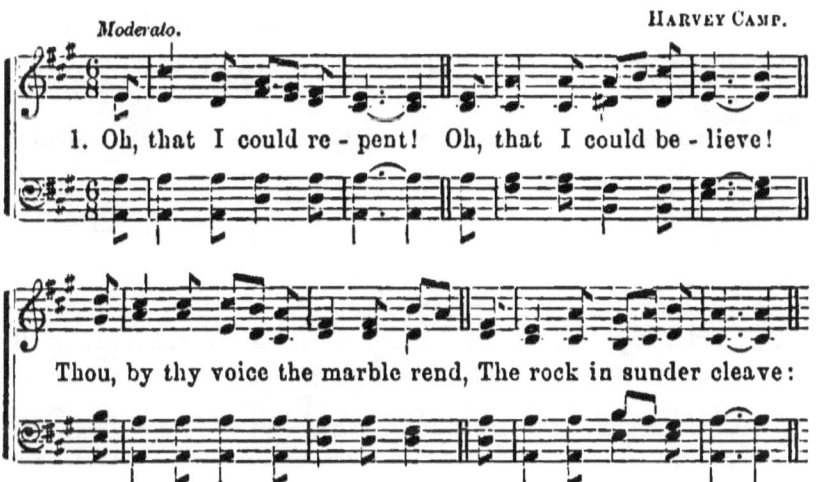

1. Oh, that I could re - pent! Oh, that I could be - lieve!
Thou, by thy voice the marble rend, The rock in sunder cleave:

No. 244. *Hardness of heart lamented.*

2 Thou, by thy two-edged sword,
   My soul and spirit part;
Strike with the hammer of thy word,
   And break my stubborn heart.

3 Saviour, and Prince of peace!
   The double grace bestow;
Unloose the bands of wickedness
   And let the captive go:

4 Grant me my sins to feel,
   And then the load remove:
Wound, and pour in, my wounds to heal,
   The balm of pard'ning love.—*C. Wesley.*

No. 243.—*Concluded.*

3 Swift to my rescue come;
   Thine own this moment seize;
Gather my wand'ring spirit home,
   And keep in perfect peace:

4 Suffer'd no more to rove
   O'er all the earth abroad.
Arrest the pris'ner of thy love,
   And shut me up in God.—*C. Wesley.*

OLMUTZ. S. M.

Arr. by Dr. L. Mason.

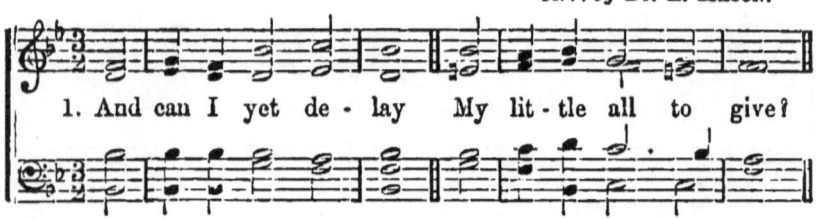

No. 245.   *Embracing the all-sufficient portion.*

2 Nay, but I yield, I yield;
   I can hold out no more:
  I sink, by dying love compell'd,
   And own thee conqueror.

3 Though late, I all forsake;
   My friends, my all, resign:
  Gracious Redeemer, take, oh, take,
   And seal me ever thine.

4 Come, and possess me whole,
   Nor hence again remove;
  Settle and fix my wav'ring soul
   With all thy weight of love.—*C. Wesley.*

No. 246.   *Sow beside all waters.*

1 Sow in the morn thy seed;
   At eve hold not thy hand;
  To doubt and fear give thou no heed,—
   Broad-cast it o'er the land.

2 Thou know'st not which shall thrive,
   The late or early sown;
  Grace keeps the precious germ alive
   When and wherever strown:

Hallowed Songs, Revised. 275

HUNTINGTON. S. M.

T. E. PERKINS.

1. Far from these scenes of night, Un-bounded glo-ries rise,
And realms of joy and pure de-light, Un-known to mor-tal eyes.

No. 247. *The goodly land.*

2 Fair land!—could mortal eyes
But half its charms explore,
How would our spirits long to rise,
And dwell on earth no more!

3 No cloud those regions know,—
Realms ever bright and fair;
For sin, the source of mortal woe,
Can never enter there.

4 Oh, may the prospect fire
Our hearts with ardent love,
Till wings of faith, and strong desire,
Bear every thought above.—*Steele.*

No. 246.—*Concluded.*

2 And duly shall appear,
In verdure, beauty, strength,
The tender blade, the stalk, the ear,
And the full corn at length.

4 Thou canst not toil in vain:
Cold, heat, and moist, and dry,
Shall foster and mature the grain
For garners in the sky.
Montgomery.

GOLDEN HILL. S. M.

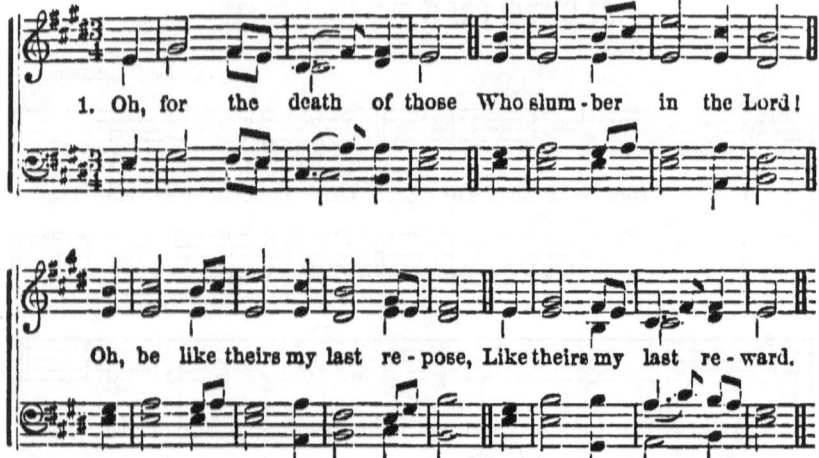

1. Oh, for the death of those Who slum-ber in the Lord! Oh, be like theirs my last re-pose, Like theirs my last re-ward.

No. 248. *" Let me die the death of the righteous."*

2 Their bodies in the ground,
   In silent hope, may lie,
Till the last trumpet's joyful sound
   Shall call them to the sky.

3 Their ransom'd spirits soar
   On wings of faith and love,
To meet the Saviour they adore,
   And reign with him above.

4 Oh, for the death of those
   Who slumber in the Lord!
Oh, be like theirs my last repose,
   Like theirs my last reward.—*Church Psalmody.*

No. 249. *For a revival.*

1 O LORD, thy work revive
   In Zion's gloomy hour,
And let our dying graces live
   By thy restoring power.

2 Oh, let thy chosen few
   Awake to earnest prayer;
Their covenant again renew,
   And walk in filial fear.

LUTHER. S. M.

Dr. THOS. HASTINGS.

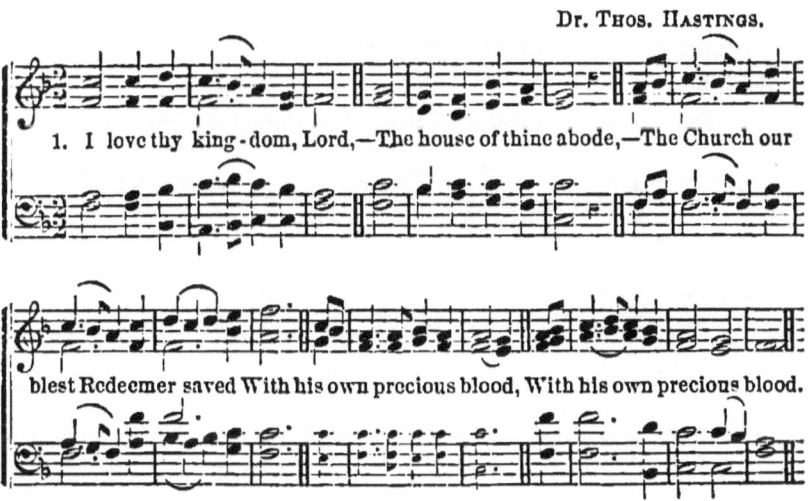

1. I love thy king-dom, Lord,—The house of thine abode,—The Church our blest Redeemer saved With his own precious blood, With his own precious blood.

No. 250. *Love for Zion.*

2 I love thy Church, O God!
   Her walls before thee stand,
Dear as the apple of thine eye,
   And graven on thy hand.

3 For her my tears shall fall;
   For her my prayers ascend;
To her my care and toils be given,
   Till toils and cares shall end.

4 Sure as thy truth shall last,
   To Zion shall be given
The brightest glories earth can yield,
   And brighter bliss of heaven.—*Dwight.*

No. 249.—*Concluded.*

3 Thy Spirit then will speak
   Through lips of humble clay,
Till hearts of adamant shall break,—
   Till rebels shall obey.

4 Now lend thy gracious ear;
   Now listen to our cry:
Oh, come, and bring salvation near,
   Our souls on thee rely.
      Dr. Thos. Hastings.

BOYLSTON. S. M.

Dr. LOWELL MASON.

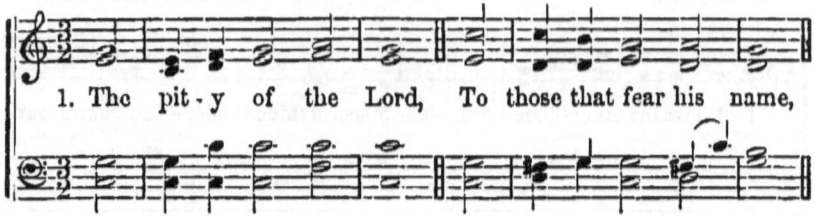

1. The pit-y of the Lord, To those that fear his name,

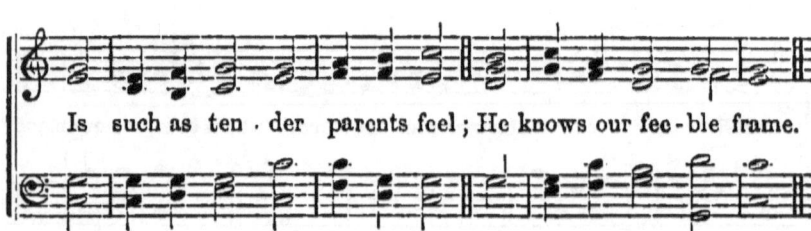

Is such as ten-der parents feel; He knows our fee-ble frame.

No. 251.   *Kindness to our frailty.*

2 He knows we are but dust,
　Scattered with every breath;
His anger, like a rising wind,
　Can send us swift to death.

3 Our days are as the grass,
　Or like the morning flower;
When blasting winds sweep o'er the field,
　It withers in an hour.

4 But thy compassions, Lord,
　To endless years endure;
And children's children ever find
　Thy word of promise sure.—*Watts.*

No. 252.   *The Redeemer's tears.*

1 DID Christ o'er sinners weep,
　And shall our cheeks be dry?
Let floods of penitential grief
　Burst forth from every eye.

2 The Son of God in tears
　The wond'ring angels see;
Be thou astonish'd, O my soul;
　He shed those tears for thee.

VESPER. S. M.

1. The day is past and gone, The evening shades ap-pear; Oh, may we all re-member well, The night of death draws near.

No. 253. *Evening hymn.*

2 We lay our garments by,
  Upon our beds to rest;
So death will soon disrobe us all
  Of what we here possess.

3 Lord, keep us safe this night,
  Secure from all our fears;
May angels guard us while we sleep,
  Till morning light appears.

4 And when we early rise,
  And view th' unwearied sun,
May we set out to win the prize,
  And after glory run.—*Unknown.*

No. 252.—*Concluded.*

3 He wept that we might weep;
  Each sin demands a tear;
In heaven alone no sin is found,
  And there's no weeping there.
    Beddomi.

DOXOLOGY.

To God, the Father, Son,
  And Spirit, One in Three,
Be glory, as it was, is now,
  And shall forever be.

DOVER. S. M.

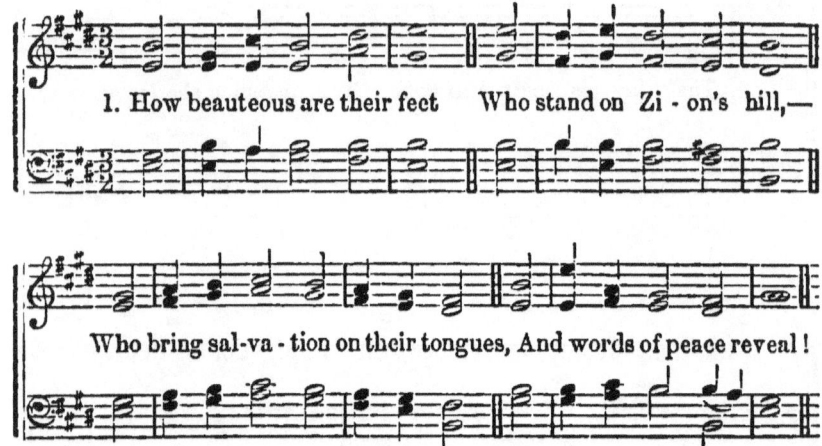

1. How beauteous are their feet Who stand on Zi-on's hill,—
Who bring sal-va-tion on their tongues, And words of peace reveal!

No. 254.   *The joyful sound.*

2 How charming is their voice,—
    So sweet the tidings are;
  Zion, behold thy Saviour King;
    He reigns and triumphs here.

3 How happy are our ears,
    That hear the joyful sound,
  Which kings and prophets waited for,
    And sought, but never found.

4 How blessed are our eyes,
    That see this heavenly light;
  Prophets and kings desired it long,
    But died without the sight.—*Watts.*

No. 255.   *The whole armor of God.*

1 SOLDIERS of Christ, arise,
    And put your armor on,
  Strong in the strength which God sup-
    Through his eternal Son;   [plies

2 Strong in the Lord of Hosts,
    And in his mighty power,
  Who in the strength of Jesus trusts,
    Is more than conqueror.

FARLAND. S. M.

E. HAMILTON.

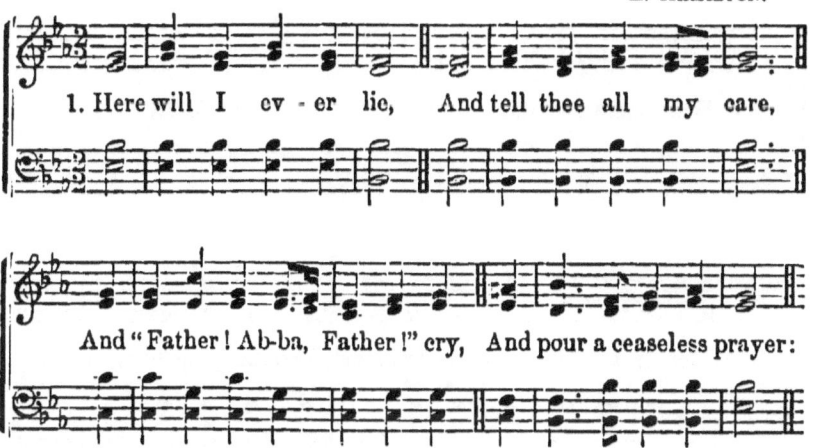

1. Here will I ev-er lie, And tell thee all my care, And "Father! Ab-ba, Father!" cry, And pour a ceaseless prayer:

No. 256.   *At the cross.*

1 HERE will I ever lie,
  And tell thee all my care,
  And "Father! Abba, Father!" cry
  And pour a ceaseless prayer:

2 Till thou my sins subdue,
  Till thou my sins destroy,
  My spirit after God renew,
  And fill with peace and joy.—*C. Wesley.*

Dox. S. M.   To God, the Father, Son,
  And Spirit, One in Three,
  Be glory, as it was, is now,
  And shall forever be.

No. 255.—*Concluded.*

3 Leave no unguarded place,—
  No weakness of the soul;
  Take every virtue, every grace
  And fortify the whole;

4 Indissolubly join'd,
  To battle all proceed;
  But arm yourselves with all the mind
  That was in Christ your Head.
    C. Wesley.

LISBON. S. M.

I. READ.

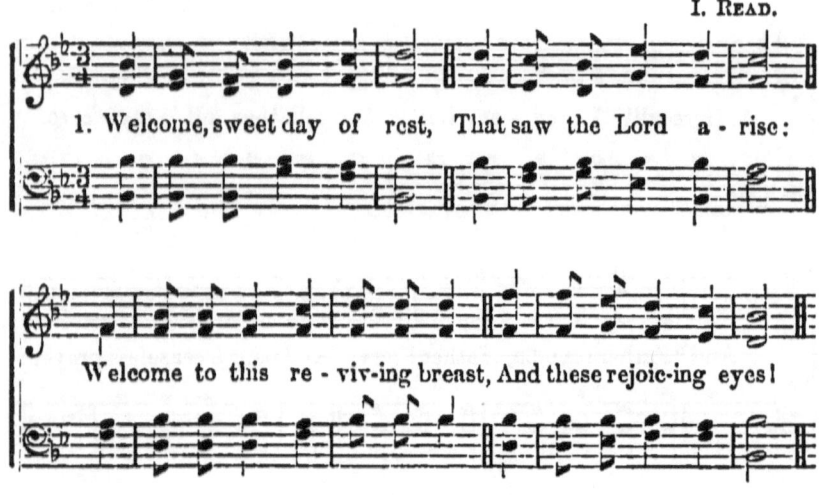

1. Welcome, sweet day of rest, That saw the Lord a-rise: Welcome to this re-viv-ing breast, And these rejoic-ing eyes!

No. 257.   *Delight in ordinances.*

2 The King himself comes near,
   And feasts his saints to-day;
 Here we may sit, and see him here,
   And love, and praise, and pray.

3 One day in such a place,
   Where thou, my God, art seen,
 Is sweeter than ten thousand days
   Of pleasurable sin.

4 My willing soul would stay
   In such a frame as this,
 And sit and sing herself away
   To everlasting bliss.—*Watts.*

No. 258.   *Gentleness of God's commands.*

1 How gentle God's commands!
   How kind his precepts are!
 Come, cast your burdens on the Lord,
   And trust his constant care.

2 Beneath his watchful eye
   His saints securely dwell;
 That hand which bears all nature up,
   Shall guard his children well.

Hallowed Songs, Revised. 283

SHAWMUT. S. M.

Arranged by Dr. L. MASON.

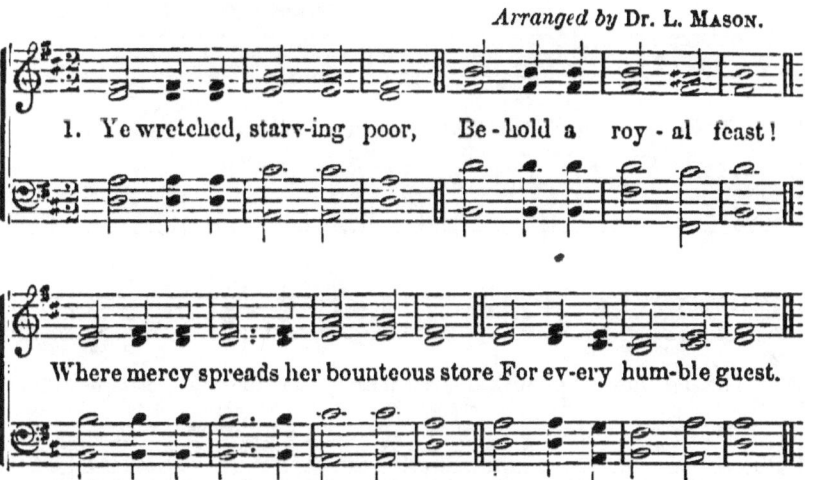

1. Ye wretched, starv-ing poor, Be-hold a roy-al feast! Where mercy spreads her bounteous store For ev-ery hum-ble guest.

No. 259. "*And yet there is room.*"

 2 See, Christ, with open arms,
   Invites, and bids you come;
 Oh, stay not back, though fear alarms;
   For yet there still is room.

 3 Oh, come, and with us taste
   The blessings of his love:
 While hope expects the sweet repast
   Of nobler joys above.

 4 There, with united voice,
   Before th' eternal throne,
 Ten thousand thousand souls rejoice,
   In ecstasies unknown.—*Steele.*

No. 258.—*Concluded.*

3 Why should this anxious load
   Press down your weary mind?
 Haste to your heavenly Father's throne,
   And sweet refreshment find.

4 His goodness stands approved,
   Unchanged from day to day:
 I'll drop my burden at his feet,
   And bear a song away.
        Doddridge.

DENNIS. S. M.

Arranged from H. G. NAGELI.

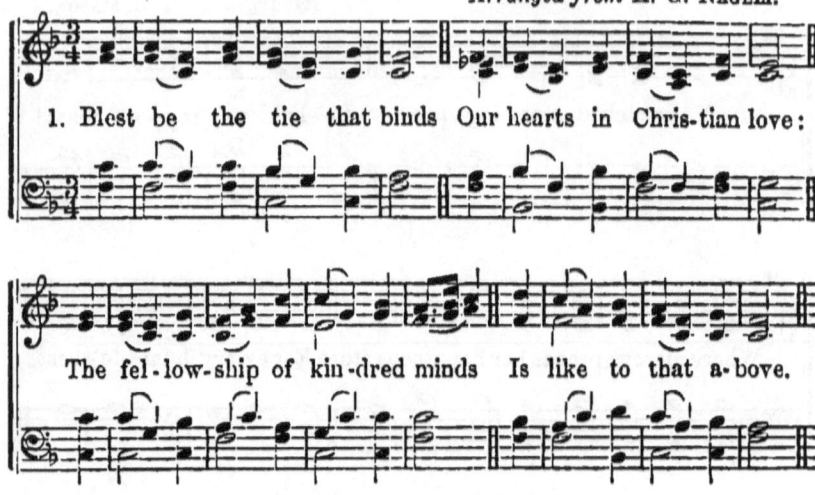

1. Blest be the tie that binds Our hearts in Christian love: The fellowship of kindred minds Is like to that above.

No. 260. *Sympathy and mutual love.*

2 Before our Father's throne
 We pour our ardent prayers;
Our fears, our hopes, our aims are one,—
 Our comforts and our cares.

3 We share our mutual woes:
 Our mutual burdens bear;
And often for each other flows
 The sympathizing tear.

4 When we asunder part,
 It gives us inward pain
But we shall still be join'd in heart,
 And hope to meet again.—*Fawcett.*

No. 261. *Meeting, after absence.*

1 AND are we yet alive,
 And see each other's face?
Glory and praise to Jesus give,
 For his redeeming grace.

2 Preserved by power divine
 To full salvation here,
Again in Jesus' praise we join,
 And in his sight appear.

Hallowed Songs, Revised. 285

DOWNIEVILLE. S. M.
E. L. M., *California.*

Slow and Gentle.

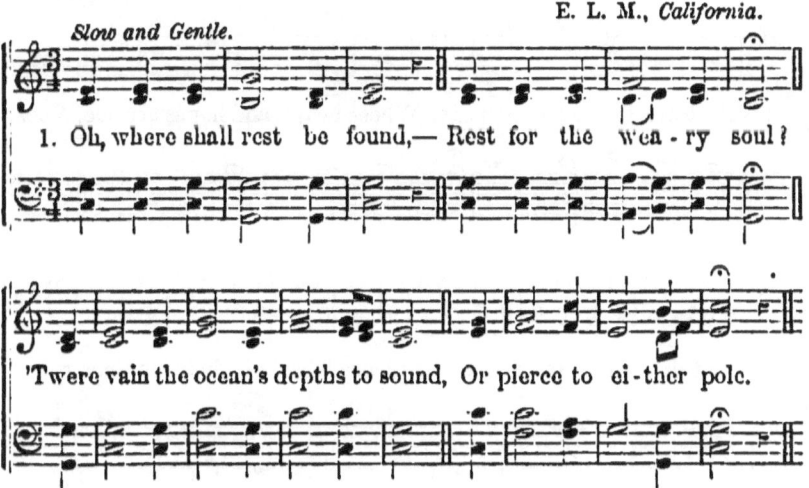

1. Oh, where shall rest be found,— Rest for the wea-ry soul?
'Twere vain the ocean's depths to sound, Or pierce to ei-ther pole.

No. 262. *The horrors of the second death.*

2 The world can never give
 The bliss for which we sigh;
 'Tis not the whole of life to live,
 Nor all of death to die.

3 Beyond this vale of tears
 There is a life above,
 Unmeasured by the flight of years;
 And all that life is love.

4 There is a death, whose pang
 Outlasts the fleeting breath:
 Oh, what eternal horrors hang
 Around the second death!—*Montgomery.*

No. 261.—*Concluded.*

3 What troubles have we seen!
 What conflicts have we past!
 Fightings without, and fears within,
 Since we assembled last!

4 But out of all the Lord
 Hath brought us by his love,
 And still he doth his help afford,
 And hides our life above.
 C. Wesley.

SHIRLAND. S. M.
STANLEY.

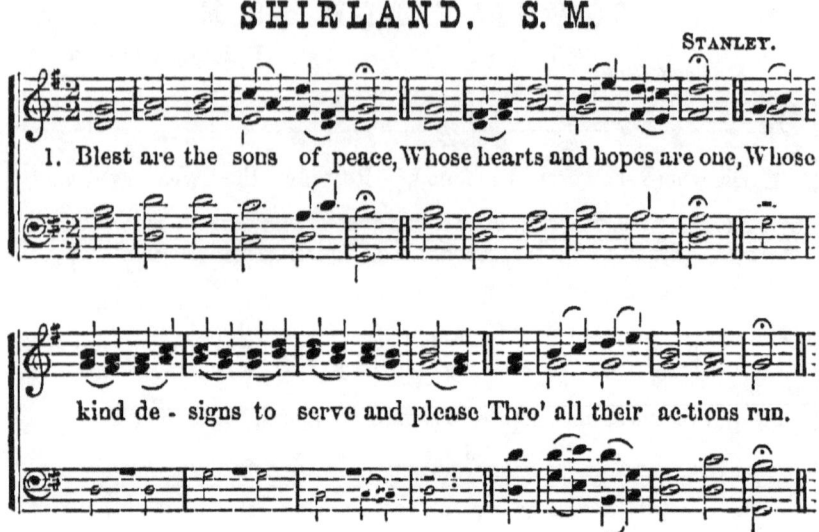

1. Blest are the sons of peace, Whose hearts and hopes are one, Whose kind de-signs to serve and please Thro' all their ac-tions run.

No. 263. *Sweet communion.*

    2 Blest is the pious house
      Where zeal and friendship meet;
      Their songs of praise, their mingled vows
      Make their communion sweet

    3 Thus on the heavenly hills
      The saints are blest above,
      Where joy like morning dew distils,
      And all the air is love.—*Watts.*

Dox. S. M. To God, the Father, Son,
      And Spirit, One in Three,
      Be glory, as it was, is now,
      And shall forever be.

No. 264. *Sanctifying Influence.*

1 Come, Holy Spirit, come;
  Let thy bright beams arise;
  Dispel the sorrow from our minds,
  The darkness from our eyes.

2 Convince us all of sin;
  Then lead to Jesus' blood,
  And to our wondering view reveal
  The mercies of our God.

Hallowed Songs, Revised. 287

LABAN. S. M.

Dr. Lowell Mason.

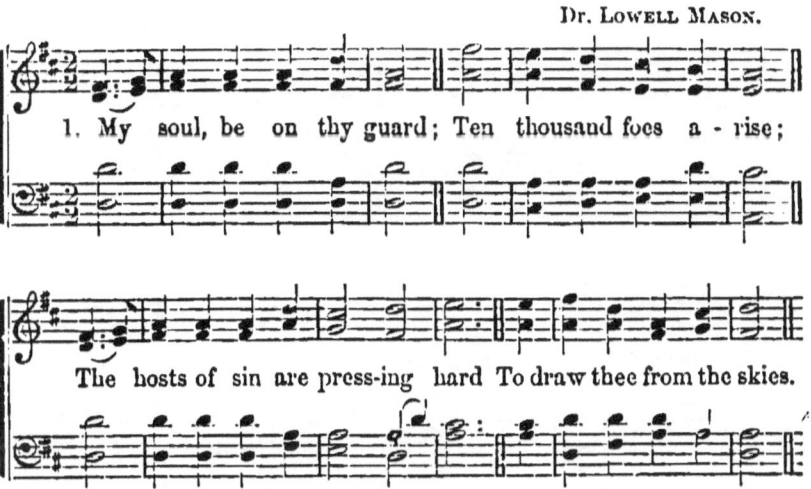

1. My soul, be on thy guard; Ten thousand foes a-rise;
The hosts of sin are pressing hard To draw thee from the skies.

No. 265.   *Perseverance.*

2 Oh, watch, and fight, and pray,
  The battle ne'er give o'er;
  Renew it boldly every day,
  And help divine implore.

3 Ne'er think the vict'ry won,
  Nor lay thine armor down:
  The work of faith will not be done,
  Till thou obtain the crown.

4 Then persevere till death
  Shall bring thee to thy God;
  He'll take thee, at thy parting breath,
  To his divine abode.—*Heath*

No. 264.—*Concluded.*

3 Revive our drooping faith,
  Our doubts and fears remove,
  And kindle in our breasts the flame
  Of never-dying love.

4 'Tis thine to cleanse the heart,
  To sanctify the soul,
  To pour fresh life in every part,
  And new create the whole.
      Hart.

PLEYEL'S HYMN. 7s.

J. PLEYEL.

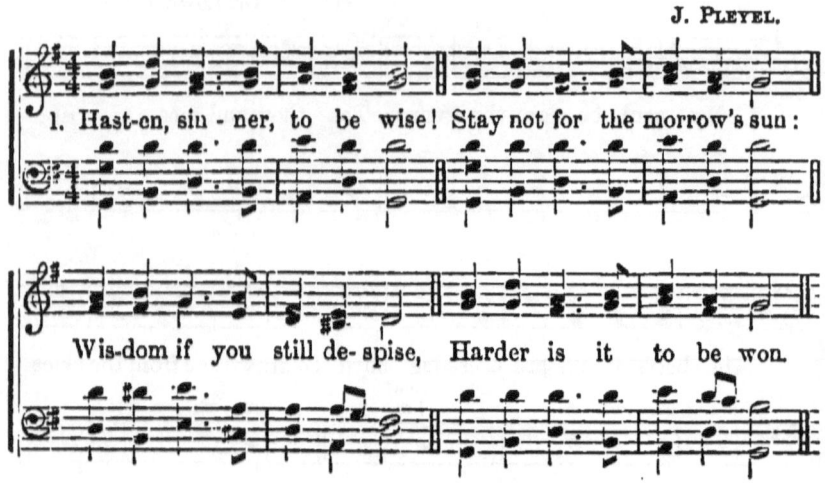

1. Hasten, sinner, to be wise! Stay not for the morrow's sun: Wisdom if you still despise, Harder is it to be won.

No. 266. *The danger of delay.*

2 Hasten, mercy to implore!
  Stay not for the morrow's sun,
Lest thy season should be o'er
  Ere this evening's stage be run.

3 Hasten, sinner, to return!
  Stay not for the morrow's sun,
Lest thy lamp should fail to burn
  Ere salvation's work is done.

4 Hasten, sinner, to be blest!
  Stay not for the morrow's sun,
Lest perdition thee arrest
  Ere the morrow is begun.—*T. Scott.*

DOXOLOGY. 7s.

SING we to our God above,
Praise eternal as his love;
Praise him, all ye heavenly host,—
Father, Son, and Holy Ghost.

EVENING SHADES.

D. A. JONES.

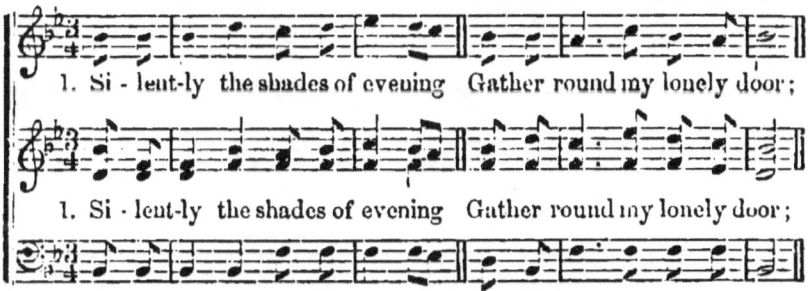

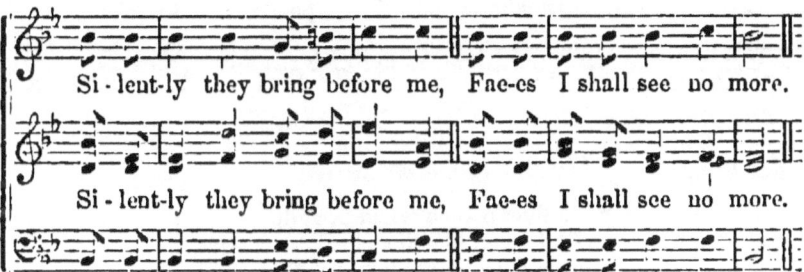

No. 267.   *The lost and unforgotten*

2 Oh, the lost, the unforgotten,
  Though the world be oft forgot;
  Oh, the shrouded and the lonely!
  In our hearts they perish not.

3 Living in the silent hours,
  Where our spirits only blend;
  They unlinked with earthly trouble
  We still hoping for its end.

4 How such holy mem'ries cluster,
  Like the stars when storms are past,
  Pointing up to that fair haven
  We may hope to gain at last.

LOVEST THOU ME. 7s.

1. Hark, my soul, it is the Lord! 'Tis thy Sav-iour, hear his word!
Jesus speaks, he speaks to thee, "Say, poor sinner, lovest thou me?"

No. 268. *Love to the Saviour.*

2 "I deliver'd thee when bound,
    And when bleeding, heal'd thy wound,
Sought thee wandering, set thee right,
    Turn'd thy darkness into light.

3 "Thou shall see my glory soon,
    When the work of faith is done;
Partner of my throne shalt be:
    Say, poor sinner, lovest thou me?"

4 Lord, it is my chief complaint
    That my love is still so faint,
Yet I love thee and adore,
    Oh, for grace to love thee more!—*Cowper.*

No. 269. *The sinner at the judgment.*

1 When thy mortal life is fled,
When the death-shades o'er thee spread,
When is finished thy career,
Sinner, where wilt thou appear?

2 When the world has passed away,
When draws near the judgment-day,
When the awful trump shall sound,
Say, oh, where wilt thou be found?

MARTYN. 7s.

S. B. MARSH.

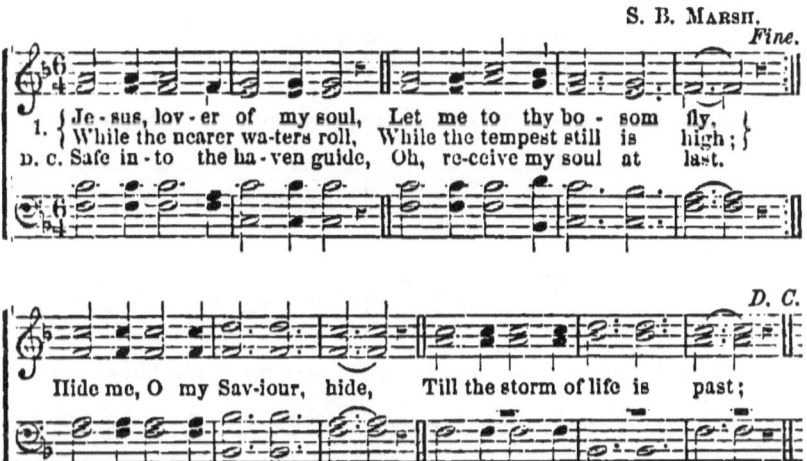

1. Jesus, lover of my soul, Let me to thy bosom fly,
   While the nearer waters roll, While the tempest still is high;
   D. C. Safe in-to the haven guide, Oh, receive my soul at last.

Hide me, O my Saviour, hide, Till the storm of life is past;

No. 270. *The only refuge.*

2 Other refuge have I none ;
  Hangs my helpless soul on thee :
  Leave, oh, leave me not alone ;
  Still support and comfort me :
  All my trust on thee is stay'd ;
  All my help from thee I bring ;
  Cover my defenceless head
  With the shadow of thy wing.

3 Thou, O Christ, art all I want :
  More than all in thee I find :
  Raise the fallen, cheer the faint,
  Heal the sick, and lead the blind ;

Just and holy is thy name ;
I am all unrighteousness ;
False, and full of sin I am ;
Thou art full of truth and grace.

4 Plenteous grace with thee I found—
  Grace to cover all my sin ;
  Let the healing streams abound ;
  Make and keep me pure within.
  Thou of life the fountain art ;
  Freely let me think of thee ;
  Spring thou up within my heart ;
  Rise to all eternity.—*C. Wesley.*

No. 269.—*Concluded.*

3 When the Judge descends in light,
  Clothed in majesty and might,
  When the wicked quail with fear,
  Where, oh, where wilt thou appear ?

4 While the Holy Ghost is nigh,
  Quickly to the Saviour fly ;
  Then shall peace thy spirit cheer ;
  Then in heaven shall thou appear.
  S. F. Smith.

HORTON. 7s.

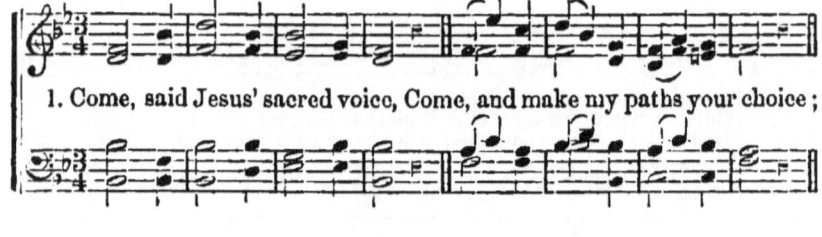

1. Come, said Jesus' sacred voice, Come, and make my paths your choice;

I will guide you to your home; Weary wanderer, hither come!

No. 271. *The Voice of Jesus.*

2 Thou who, homeless and forlorn,
Long hast borne the proud world's scorn,
Long hast roamed the barren waste
Weary wanderer, hither haste.

3 Ye who, tossed on beds of pain,
Seek for ease, but seek in vain;
Ye, by fiercer anguish torn,
In remorse for guilt who mourn:—

4 Hither come! for here is found
Balm that flows for every wound;
Peace that ever shall endure,
Rest eternal, sacred, sure.—*Mrs. Barbauld.*

No. 272. *Thanksgiving.*

1 SWELL the anthem, raise the song;
Praises to our God belong;
Saints and angels join to sing
Praises to the heavenly King.

2 Blessing from his liberal hand
Flow around this happy land:
Kept by him, no foes annoy;
Peace and freedom we enjoy.

NUREMBURG. 7s.

Arr. by Dr. L. MASON.

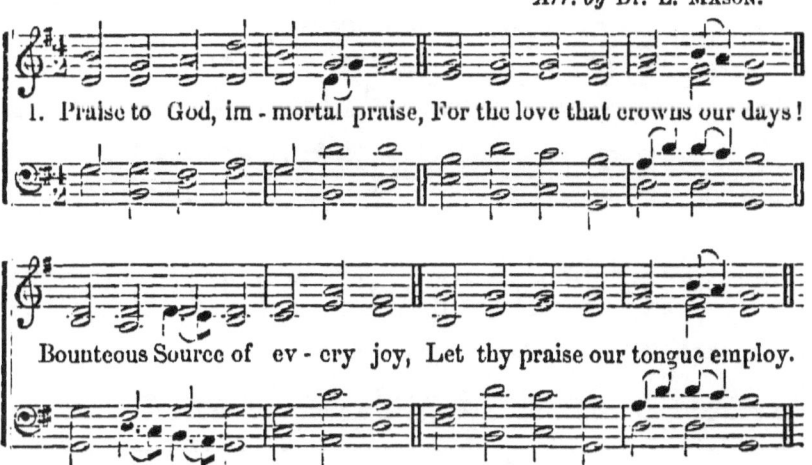

1. Praise to God, im-mortal praise, For the love that crowns our days! Bounteous Source of ev-ery joy, Let thy praise our tongue employ.

No. 273. *"Lord, thou hast been favorable unto thy land."*

2 For the blessings of the field,
For the stores the gardens yield;
For the joy which harvests bring,
Grateful praises now we sing.

3 Clouds that drop refreshing dews;
Suns that genial heat diffuse;
Flocks that whiten all the plain;
Yellow sheaves of ripened grain;

4 All that spring, with bounteous hand,
Scatters o'er the smiling land;
All that liberal autumn pours
From her overflowing stores.—*Mrs. Barbauld.*

No. 272.—*Concluded.*

3 Here, beneath a virtuous sway,
May we cheerfully obey,—
Never feel oppression's rod,—
Ever own and worship God.

4 Hark! the voice of nature sings
Praises to the King of kings;
Let us join the choral song,
And the grateful notes prolong.

HENDON. 7s.

MALAN.

1. Christ, the Lord, is risen to-day, Sons of men and angels say: Raise your joys and triumph high; Sing, ye heavens—and earth, reply; Sing, ye heavens—and, &c.

No. 274. *"If we suffer with Him we shall reign with Him."*

    2 Love's redeeming work is done,—
       Fought the fight, the battle won:
       Lo! the sun's eclipse is o'er;
       Lo! he sets in blood no more.

    3 Vain the stone, the watch, the seal,—
       Christ has burst the gates of hell;
       Death in vain forbids his rise;
       Christ has open'd Paradise.

    4 Lives again our glorious King;
       Where, O death, is now thy sting?
       Once he died our souls to save;
       Where's thy vict'ry, boasting grave?—*C. Wesley.*

No. 275. *The Sun of righteousness.*

1 HARK! the herald-angels sing,—
  Glory to the new-born King;
  Peace on earth, and mercy mild;
  God and sinners reconciled.

2 Joyful all ye nations rise,—
  Join the triumphs of the skies;
  With angelic hosts proclaim,—
  Christ is born in Bethlehem.

Hallowed Songs, Revised. 295

WILMOT. 7s.

From C. VON WEBER.

1. Morn-ing breaks upon the tomb; Je-sus scat-ters all its gloom:
Day of tri-umph thro' the skies, See the glorious Saviour rise!

No. 276. *Morning at the tom*

2 Christian! dry your flowing tears;
Chase those unbelieving fears:
Look on his deserted grave;
Doubt no more his power to save.

3 Ye, who are of death afraid,
Triumph in the scattered shade;
Drive your anxious cares away:
See the place where Jesus lay!

4 Lo! the rising sun appears,
Shedding radiance o'er the spheres;
Lo! returning beams of light
Chase the terrors of the night.—*Collyer.*

No. 275.—*Concluded.*

3 Christ, by highest heaven adored,—
Christ, the everlasting Lord;
Veil'd in flesh the Godhead see;
Hail, incarnate Deity!

4 Hail the heaven-born Prince of peace!
Hail the Sun of righteousness!
Light and life to all he brings,—
Risen with healing in his wings.
C. Wesley.

ALL TO CHRIST I OWE.

J. T. GRAPE. *Arranged.**

1. I hear the Sav-iour say, Thy strength indeed is small;
Child of weakness, watch and pray, Find in me thine all in all.

Chorus.

Je - sus paid it all, All to him I owe;
Sin had left a crim-son stain; He washed it white as snow.

No. 277.

2 Lord, now indeed I find
Thy faith, and thine alone,
Can change the leper's spots,
And melt the heart of stone.
Cho.—Jesus paid it all, &c.

* *From "Pilgrim Harp."*

Hallowed Songs, Revised.

2 For nothing good have I
  Whereby thy grace to claim—
  I'll wash my garment white
  In the blood of Calv'ry's Lamb.
    Cho.—Jesus paid it all, &c.

4 When from my dying bed
  My ransomed soul shall rise,
  Then " Jesus paid it all "
  Shall rend the vaulted skies.
    Cho—Jesus paid it all, &c.

5 And when before the throne
  I stand, in him complete,
  I'll lay my trophies down,
  All down, at Jesus' feet.
    Cho.—Jesus paid it all, &c.
                            Mrs. E. M. Hall.

THE SWEETEST NAME. 7s. Chorus.*

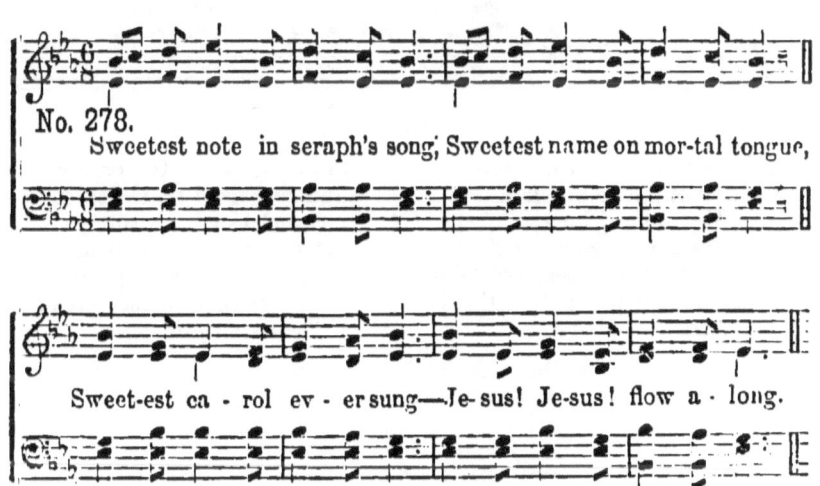

No. 278.
Sweetest note in seraph's song, Sweetest name on mortal tongue,
Sweet-est ca - rol ev - er sung—Je-sus! Je-sus! flow a - long.

* *May be sung after any appropriate hymn in 7s.*

AMERICA. 6s & 4s.

1. My coun-try, 'tis of thee, Sweet land of lib-er-ty, Of thee I sing: Land where my fathers died, Land of the pilgrim's pride, From ev-ery mountain side Let freedom ring.

No. 279.   *National hymn.*

2 My native country, thee—
Land of the noble, free—
Thy name I love;
I love thy rocks and rills,
Thy woods and templed hills;
My heart with rapture thrills,
Like that above.

3 Let music swell the breeze,
And ring from all the trees
Sweet freedom's song;
Let mortal tongues awake;
Let all that breathe partake;
Let rocks their silence break—
The sound prolong.

4 Our fathers' God, to thee,
Author of liberty,
To thee we sing:
Long may our land be bright
With freedom's holy light·
Protect us by thy might,
Great God, our King.—*S. F. Smith.*

GOD BLESS OUR SCHOOL.

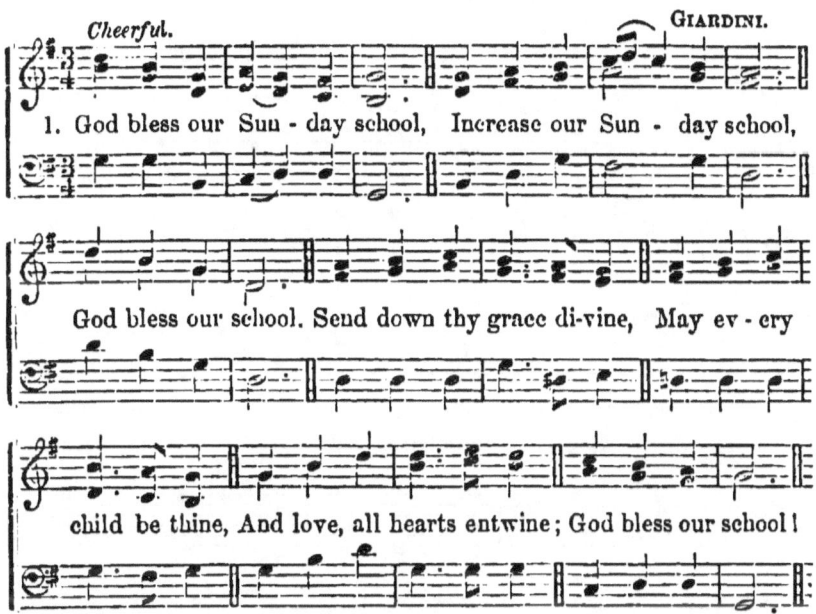

1. God bless our Sun-day school, Increase our Sun-day school, God bless our school. Send down thy grace di-vine, May ev-ery child be thine, And love, all hearts entwine; God bless our school!

No. 280. "*The knowledge of the holy is understanding.*"

2 All our dear teachers bless,
  And give them large success
    In winning souls:
  May they encouraged be,
  And oft around them see
  Their labors crown'd by thee;
    God bless our school.

3 So may our school increase
  In knowledge, love, and peace;
    God bless our school.
  And when death's arrows fly,
  And useful teachers die,
  Their places still supply;
    God bless our school.

GOD BLESS OUR NATIVE LAND.

No. 281. *God save the State.*

1 GOD bless our native land!
  Firm may she ever stand,
    Through storm and night;
  When the wild tempests rave,
  Ruler of winds and wave,
  Do thou our country save
    By thy great might.

2 For her our prayer shall rise
  To God, above the skies;
    On him we wait:
  Thou who art ever nigh,
  Guarding with watchful eye,
  To thee aloud we cry,
    God save the State!—*Dwight.*

HINTON. 11s.

Arranged by S. J. VAIL.

1. De-lay not, de-lay not, O sin-ner, draw near,
The wa-ters of life are now float-ing for thee;
D.S. Re-demp-tion is purchased, sal-va-tion is free.
No price is de-mand-ed, the Sav-iour is here,

No. 282.

2 Delay not, delay not, why longer abuse
   The love and compassion of Jesus thy God?
A fountain is opened, how canst thou refuse
   To wash and be cleaned in his pardoning blood?

2 Delay not, delay not, the Spirit of grace,
   Long grieved and resisted may take its sad flight,
And leave thee in darkness to finish thy race,
   To sink in the gloom of eternity's night.

DALSTON. S. P. M.

A. WILLIAMS.

1. How pleased and blest was I To hear the peo-ple cry, "Come, let us seek our God to - day!" Yes, with a cheerful zeal We haste to Zi-on's hill, And there our vows and hon-ors pay.

No. 283.

2 Zion, thrice happy place,
 Adorn'd with wondrous grace,
And walls of strength embrace thee
 In thee our tribes appear [round:
 To pray, to praise, to hear
The sacred gospel's joyful sound.

3 There David's greater Son
 Has fixed his royal throne;
He sits for grace and judgment there:
 He bids the saints be glad,
 He makes the sinners sad,
And humble souls rejoice with fear.

4 May peace attend thy gate,
 And joy within thee wait,
To bless the soul of every guest:
 The man that seeks thy peace,
 And wishes thine increase,
A thousand blessings on him rest!

ESTIS. 7s.

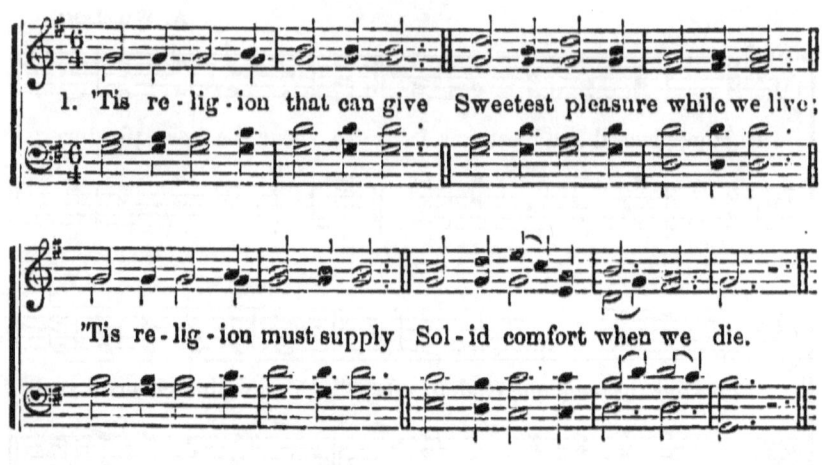

No. 284.   *What religion gives.*

2 After death its joys shall be
Lasting as eternity;
Be the living God our friend,
Then our bliss shall never end.—*Masters.*

DOXOLOGY. 7s.

SING we to our God above,
Praise eternal as his love;
Praise him, all ye heavenly host,—
Father, Son, and Holy Ghost.

THE CONVERT. 6s & 9s.

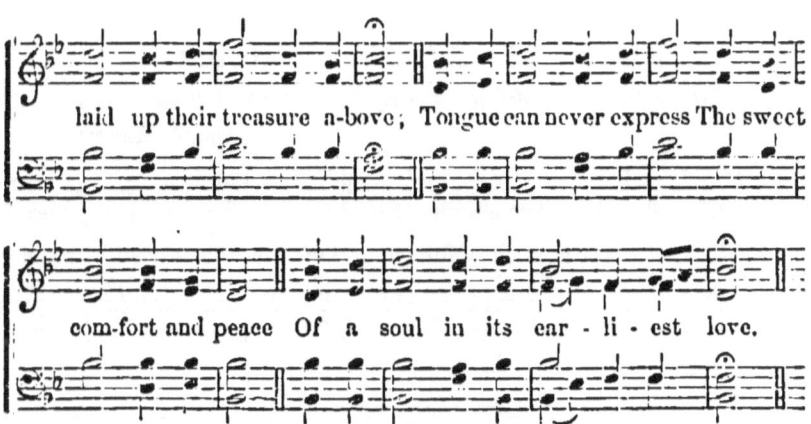

laid up their treasure a-bove; Tongue can never express The sweet com-fort and peace Of a soul in its ear - li - est love.

No. 285. *Joy of the young convert.*

2 That sweet comfort was mine,
When the favor divine
I received through the blood of the Lamb;
When my heart first believed,
What a joy I received,—
What a heaven in Jesus' name!

3 'Twas a heaven below
My Redeemer to know,
And the angels could do nothing more,
Then to fall at his feet,
And the story repeat,
And the Lover of sinners adore.

4 Jesus all the day long
Was my joy and my song:
Oh, that all his salvation might see;
He hath loved me, I cried,
He hath suffer'd, and died,
To redeem even rebels like me.

5 Oh, the rapturous height
Of that holy delight,
Which I felt in the life-giving blood;
Of my Saviour possess'd,
I was perfectly blest,
As if fill'd with the fullness of God.—*C. Wesley.*

ROCK OF AGES. 7s (6 lines).

"But the Lord is my defence, and my God is the rock of my refuge."

Dr. T. HASTINGS.

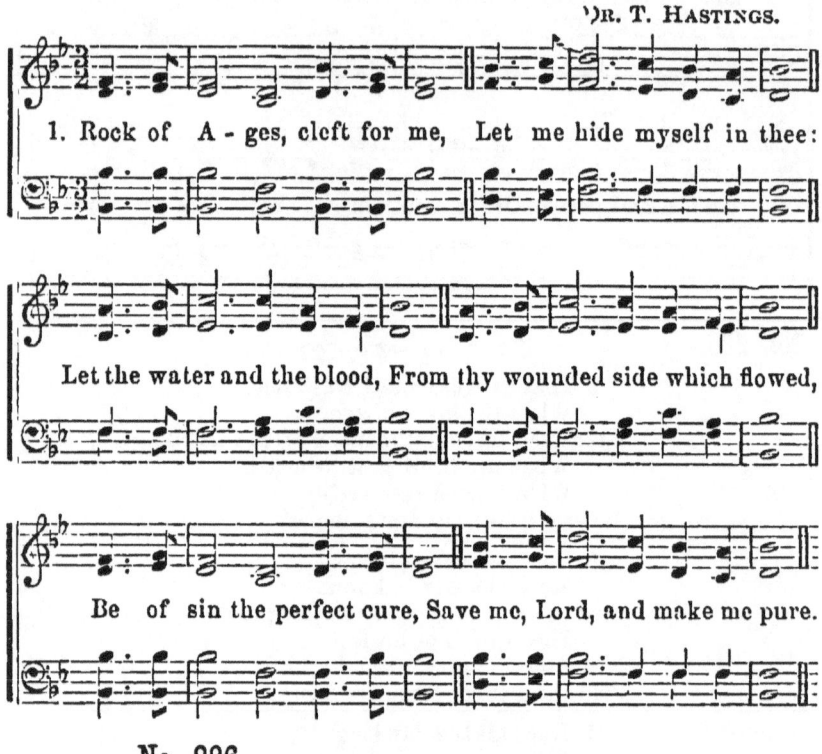

1. Rock of A-ges, cleft for me, Let me hide myself in thee:
Let the water and the blood, From thy wounded side which flowed,
Be of sin the perfect cure, Save me, Lord, and make me pure.

No. 286.

2 Should my tears forever flow,
Should my zeal no languor know,
This for sin could ne'er atone,
Thou must save, and thou alone;
In my hand no price I bring,
Simply to thy cross I cling.

3 While I draw this fleeting breath,
When mine eyelids close in death,
When I rise to worlds unknown,
And behold thee on thy throne,
Rock of Ages! cleft for me,
Let me hide myself in thee.

WILT THOU NOT VISIT ME?

WM. B. BRADBURY.

No. 287. *"Our soul waiteth for the Lord. He is our help and our shield."*

1 Wilt thou not visit me?
The plant beside me feels thy | gentle | dew;
  Each blade of grass I see,
From thy deep earth its quickening | moisture | drew.
  Wilt thou not visit me?

2 Wilt thou not visit me?
Thy morning calls on me with | cheering | tone;
  And every hill and tree
Lend but one voice, the voice of | thee a- | lone.
  Wilt thou not visit me?

3 Wilt thou not visit me? I need thy love
More than the flower the dew, or | grass the | rain;
  Come, like thy holy dove,
And let me in thy sight rejoice to | live a- | gain.
  Wilt thou not visit me?

4 Yes! thou wilt visit me:
Nor plant, nor tree, thine eye de- | lights so | well,
  As when from sin set free,
Man's spirit comes with thine in | peace to | dwell.
  Yes, thou wilt visit me.

THE LORD'S PRAYER.

(PITCH E.*) OUR Father which art in heaven, Hallowed be thy name. Thy kingdom come. Thy will be done on earth, as it is in heaven. Give us this day our daily bread. And forgive us our trespasses, as we forgive those who trespass against us. And lead us not into temptation, but deliver us from evil. For thine is the kingdom, and the power, and the glory, for ever.

A - men.

* *Let the words be deliberately, distinctly, and reverently pronounced by a single voice, or in unison, adding the Amen in harmony parts, as written.*

THAT BLESSED NAME.

A SONG FOR JESUS.

" Thou shalt call his Name JESUS: for he shall save his people from their sins."

F. C. GOUGH.

Hallowed Songs, Revised. 307

Full Chorus, to each verse.

Je-sus, Name all names a-bove; Name I cherish, honor, love;

Je - sus will forsake us nev - er; Je - sus will I love for - ev - er:

Ev- er, ev - er, ev - er, ev - er, Je - sus will I love for - ev - er

No. 288.

2 Healing streams are freely flowing,
   Crimson-tinged, from Calvary;
   Life and blessedness bestowing;—
   Jesus saves so willingly.

3 Millions living, millions dying,
   Prove the cleansing remedy;
   Life and death are testifying;—
   Jesus saves effectually.

4 With the Father interceding,
   Throned on high in majesty,
   There, for us, his merits pleading;—
   Jesus lives immortally.

5 Coming, in the day appointed,
   Crowned and throned victoriously,
   Over all, as King anointed,
   Jesus shall reign gloriously.

6 Publish now to every nation,
   Shout the tidings glad and free;
   Trumpet wide the proclamation:—
   Jesus saves eternally.—*D. Dana Buck, D.D.*

LOVE BEYOND DEGREE.

"This I did for thee.* What hast thou done for me?"

Slow and expressive.   PHILIP PHILLIPS.

1. I gave my life for thee, My pre-cious blood I shed, That thou might'st ransomed be, And quickened, quickened from the dead. I gave my life for thee, for thee; What hast thou given for me, for

* Motto placed under a print of Christ on the Cross, in the study of a German clergyman. It is said that Count Zinzendorf was first taught to love the Saviour by reading this motto.

Hallowed Songs, Revised.

me? What hast thou given for me, for me?

No. 289.

2 I spent long years for thee,
   In weariness and woe,
That one eternity
   Of joy thou mightest know.
I spent long years for thee, for thee;
|: Hast thou spent *one* for me, for me? :|

3 My Father's house of light,
   My rainbow-circled throne,
I left for earthly night,
   For wanderings sad and lone.
I left it all for thee, for thee;
|: Hast thou left *aught* for me, for me? :|

4 I suffered much for thee,
   More than thy tongue can tell,
Of bitterest agony,
   To rescue thee from hell.
I suffered much for thee, for thee;
|: What dost thou *bear* for me, for me? :|

5 And I have brought to thee,
   Down from my house above,
Salvation full and free,
   My pardon and my long.
Great gifts I brought to thee, to thee;
|: What hast thou *brought* to me, to me? :|

6 Oh, let thy life be given,
   Thy years for me be spent,
World fetters all be riven,
   And joy with suffering blent.
Give thou *thyself* to me, to me,
|: And I will welcome thee, *yes* thee! :|

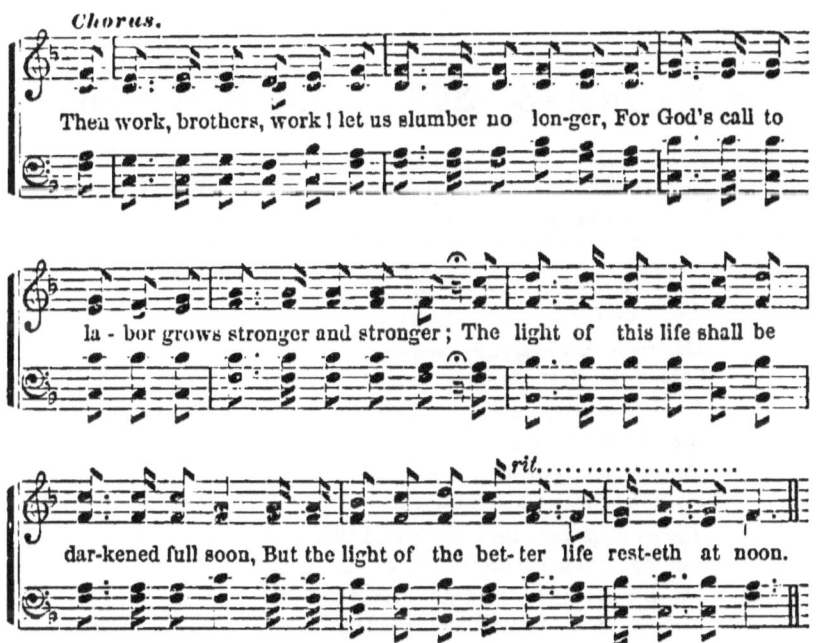

4 Work for the good that is nighest;
  Dream not of greatness afar ;
That glory is ever the highest,
  Which shines upon men as they are.
Work, though the world would defeat you;
  Heed not its slander and scorn ;
Nor weary till angels shall greet you
  With smiles through the gates of the morn.—*Cho.*

5 Offer thy life on the altar ;
  In the high purpose be strong ;
And if the tired spirit should falter,
  Then sweeten thy labor with song.
What, if the poor heart complaineth,
  Soon shall its waiting be o'er ;
For there, in the rest which remaineth,
  It shall grieve and be weary no more.—*Cho.*

Rev. W. MORLEY PUNSHON, A.M., *Jan.*, 1870.

Responsive Scripture Reading.

No. 291.   NINETY-SIXTH PSALM.

O sing unto the Lord a new song:
Sing unto the Lord, all the earth.

Sing unto the Lord, bless his name:
Shew forth his salvation from day to day.

Declare his glory among the heathen,
His wonders among all people.

For the Lord is great, and greatly to be praised:
He is to be feared above all gods.

For all the gods of the nations are idols:
But the Lord made the heavens.

Honor and majesty are before him:
Strength and beauty are in his sanctuary.

Give unto the Lord, O ye kindreds of people,
Give unto the Lord glory and strength.

Give unto the Lord the glory due unto his name:
Bring an offering, and come into his courts.

O worship the Lord in the beauty of holiness:
Fear before him, all the earth.

Say among the heathen that the Lord reigneth:
The world also shall be established that it shall not be moved:
He shall judge the people righteously.

Let the heavens rejoice,
And let the earth be glad:
Let the sea roar, and the fullness thereof.

Let the field be joyful, and all that is therein:
Then shall all the trees of the wood rejoice before the Lord;

For he cometh,
For he cometh to judge the earth:

He shall judge the world with righteousness,
And the people with his truth.

No. 292. THE TEN COMMANDMENTS.

And God spake all these words, saying:
FIRST COMMANDMENT.—Thou shalt have no other gods before me.
We know that an idol is nothing in the world, and that there is none other god but one.—1 Cor. 8 : 4.
SECOND COMMANDMENT.—Thou shalt not make unto thee any graven image, or any likeness *of anything* that *is* in heaven above, or that *is* in the earth beneath, or that *is* in the water under the earth: Thou shalt not bow down thyself to them, nor serve them; for I the Lord thy God am a jealous God, visiting the iniquity of the fathers upon the children unto the third and fourth *generation* of them that hate me; and shewing mercy unto thousands of them that love me and keep my commandments.
We ought not to think that the Godhead is like unto gold, or silver, or stone, graven by art and man's device.—Acts. 17 : 29.
THIRD COMMANDMENT.—Thou shalt not take the name of the Lord thy God in vain; for the Lord will not hold him guiltless that taketh his name in vain.
Let your yea, be yea; and your nay, nay; lest ye fall into condemnation.—James 5 : 12.
FOURTH COMMANDMENT.—Remember the sabbath-day to keep it holy. Six days shalt thou labor, and do all thy work: But the seventh day *is* the sabbath of the Lord thy God; *in it* thou shalt not do any work, thou, nor thy son, nor thy daughter, thy manservant, nor thy maidservant, nor thy cattle, nor the stranger that *is* within thy gates: For *in* six days the Lord made heaven and earth, the sea, and all that in them *is*, and rested the seventh day: wherefore the Lord blessed the sabbath-day and hallowed it.
The sabbath was made for man, and not man for the sabbath.—Mark 2 : 27.
FIFTH COMMANDMENT.—Honor thy father and thy mother: that thy days may be long upon the land which the Lord thy God giveth thee.
Children, obey your parents in all things: for this is well-pleasing unto the Lord.— Col. 3 : 20.
SIXTH COMMANDMENT.—Thou shalt not kill.
Whosoever hateth his brother is a murderer; and ye know that no murderer hath eternal life abiding in him.—1 John 3 : 15.
SEVENTH COMMANDMENT.—Thou shalt not commit adultery.
*Know ye not that ye are the temple of God? * * * If any man defile the temple of God, him shall God destroy.*—1 Cor. 3 ; 16, 17.
EIGHTH COMMANDMENT.—Thou shalt not steal.
Nor thieves, nor covetous, nor drunkards, nor revilers, nor extortioners, shall inherit the kingdom of God.—1 Cor 6 : 10.
NINTH COMMANDMENT—Thou shalt not bear false witness against thy neighbor.
Let no corrupt communication proceed out of your mouth.—Eph. 4 : 29.
TENTH COMMANDMENT.—Thou shalt not covet thy neighbor's house, thou shalt not covet thy neighbor's wife, nor his manservant, nor his maidservant, nor his ox, nor his ass, nor anything that *is* thy neighbor's.
How hard it is for them that trust in riches to enter into the kingdom of God!— Mark 10 : 24.

BEATITUDES.

No. 293.

Blessed are the poor in spirit:
For theirs is the kingdom of heaven.

Blessed are they that mourn:
For they shall be comforted.

Blessed are the meek:
For they shall inherit the earth.

Blessed are they that do hunger and thirst after righteousness:
For they shall be filled.

Blessed are the merciful:
For they shall obtain mercy

Blessed are the pure in heart:
For they shall see God.

Blessed are the peacemakers:
For they shall be called the children of God.

Blessed are they which are persecuted for righteousness' sake:
For theirs is the kingdom of heaven.

Blessed are they that dwell in thy house:
They will be still praising thee.

Blessed is he that considereth the poor:
The Lord will deliver him in time of trouble.

Blessed is the man that endureth temptation:
For when he is tried he shall receive the crown of life.

The blessing of the Lord it maketh rich, and he addeth no sorrow with it.

REVERENCE.

No. 294.

O come, let us worship and bow down: let us kneel before the Lord our maker. For he is our God; and we are the people of his pasture, and the sheep of his hand. —Ps. 95 : 6, 7.

God is a spirit: and they that worship him, must worship him in spirit and in truth.—Jno. 4 : 24.

The sacrifice of the wicked is an abomination to the Lord: but the prayer of the upright is his delight.—Prov. 15 : 8.

Return, we beseech thee, O God of host: look down from heaven, and behold, and visit this vine.—Ps. 80 : 14.

THANKSGIVING.
No. 295.

Praise ye the Lord. Sing unto the Lord a new song, and his praise in the congregation of saints.—Ps. 149 : 1.

Speaking to yourselves in psalms, and hymns, and spiritual songs, singing and making melody in your heart to the Lord.—Eph. 5 · 19.

I will sing of mercy and judgment: unto thee, O Lord, will I sing.—Ps. 101 : 1.
Rejoice in the Lord alway : and again I say, Rejoice.—Phil. 4 : 4.

Sing unto the Lord with the harp ; with the harp, and the voice of a psalm.—Ps. 98 : 5.
And I heard the voice of the harpers harping with their harps ; and they sung, as it were, a new song before the throne.—Rev. 14 : 2, 3.

I will sing of the mercies of the Lord forever : with my mouth will I make known thy faithfulness to all generations.—Ps. 89 : 1.
Praise him with the psaltery and harp ; Praise him with stringed instruments and organs. Let every thing that hath breath praise the Lord.

CONSOLING PROMISES OF CHRIST.
No. 296.

Where two or three are gathered together in my name, there am I in the midst of them.
Whatsoever ye shall ask the Father in my name, he will give it you: ask and ye shall receive, that your joy may be full.

He that endureth to the end shall be saved.
It is your father's good pleasure to give you the kingdom.

I go to prepare a place for you, that where I am ye may be also.
And I will give them eternal life, and they shall never perish, neither shall any man pluck them out of my hands.

Peace I will leave with you : my peace will give unto you.
They that seek me early shall find me.

Eye hath not seen, nor ear heard : neither have entered into the heart of man the things which God hath prepared for them that love him.

Index of Tunes.

	PAGE		PAGE		PAGE
ABIDING Rest	12	Christian Union	41	Go, and tell Jesus	196
Alas! and did my	14	Climbing up Zion's	124	God bless our native	299
Alleta	91	Cling to the Mighty		God bless our school	299
All to Christ I owe	296	One	118	God is Love	94
A light in the window	176	Cleansing Fountain	10	Golden Hill	276
America	298	Coronation	208	Going Home	93
Angels hovering	92	Come, Crown and	102	Gratitude	269
Anvern	259	Come, ye disconsolate	33	Greenville	49
Ariel	38	Come, ye sinners	35	Guide	7
Arise, my soul	31	Congregational Chorus	98	Guide us, Saviour	162
Arlington	223	Consecration Hymn	56	Guide us, Shepherd	28
Autumn	39	Consoling Promise	315		
Avon	212	Cross and Crown	218	HAMBURG	242
Aylesbury	273	Conquest	192	Hamden	74
Azmon	209			Happy Day	79
		DALSTON	301	Happy Zion	48
BALERMA	220	De Fleury	60	Hartel	243
Battling for the Lord	160	Dedham	230	Harwell	81
Bartimeus	17	Dennis	254	Hebron	254
Beatitudes	314	Dover	250	He leadeth me	178
Beautiful Cross	42	Downieville	285	Hendon	291
Beautiful Zion	77	Duane St	55	Hinton	300
Beautiful Land on	200	Duke St	237	Horton	292
Beautiful Land	186			Home of the Soul	114
Believer	219	ELTHAM	82	Homeward	69
Be still, my heart	249	Enon's Isle	59	Huntington	275
Blessed Bible	155	Estis	302		
Bless us to-night	22	Eternal Life	11	I DO believe	216
Boylston	278	Evan	224	Illinois	245
Bowring	267	Even me	15	I love to tell the story	181
Brown	232	Evening Shades	289	I'm a pilgrim	64
Bright Home	154	Evening Shadows	148	I'm kneeling at the	136
				Invitation	31
CALLING us away	152	FARLAND	281	Ives	68
Captivity	246	Federal St	257	I will sing for	110
Children of the	201	Forest	251		
China	227	Forever with the	199	JESUS is here	203
Christ at the Wheel	62	Fountain	217	Jesus is mine	45
Christ on the Mount	183	Frederick	71	Jesus loves me	46

Hallowed Songs, Revised. 317

	PAGE		PAGE		PAGE
Jesus paid it all	16	O say, shall we	121	The Heavenly Land	51
Jesus waits for thee	9	Outside the gate	130	The House upon	142
Joyfully	172			The Land of Beulah	171
Judah	268	PARK St	254	The Living Well	104
		Penitence	36	The Lord's Prayer	305
Keep on praying	149	Peterboro'	233	The old, old Story	144
Kentucky	272	Pleyel's Hymn	288	The Pilgrim invited	18
		Portland	190	The River of Life	13
LABAN	287	Portugal	256	The Shining Way	89
Lebanon	37	Pilgrim's Mission	310	The Sweetest Name	297
Lenox	30			The Valley of Blessing	132
Let me go	112	Rally round the Cross	156	The World is my	116
Love beyond degree	308	Rest	262	The Water of Life	133
Lisbon	282	Rest for the weary	166	There is an hour	43
Looking Home	73	Resolution	214	There is joy for	65
Love ones gone before	44	Responsive Scripture	312	Thornton	226
Lord, revive us	95	Retreat	248	Title clear	150
Lovest thou me	230	Reverence	314	'Tis blessed to give	134
Loving-Kindness	75	Rockingham	256	To-day the Saviour	187
Love Divine	88	Roscoe	221		
Luther	277	Rock of Ages	304	UNITY	66
Luton	258	SAFE within the vail	80	Upton	238
Lyons	63	Scott	213	Uxbridge	244
		Sessions	241		
MACEDONIAN Cry	24	Shall we gather	108	VESPER	279
Martyn	291	Shall we meet	78		
Mary Magdalene	57	Shawmut	283	WAITING by the River	21
Mear	235	Shepherd	263	Ward	229
Migdol	255	Shining Shore	72	Ware	265
Melody	231	Shirland	286	Warwick	225
Merdin	70	Sicilian Hymn	40	Watch and pray	182
Meribah	26	Siloam	222	Watchman	53
Missionary Hymn	51	Silver St	271	Webb	52
More like Jesus	97	Silverdale	234	Weep for the Fallen	146
Mount Vernon	67	Soldiers of the Cross	180	Wells	252
		Stand up for Jesus	84	We've a home over	202
NAOMI	210	Stephens	229	We shall sleep	126
Nearer, my God	29	St. Martin's	236	What are you going	168
Nearer my home	170	St. Thomas	270	Who's like Jesus	96
Nettleton	27	Sun of my soul	269	Why not to-night	8
Never sin more	198	Sweet Hour of Prayer	25	Willow-dale	90
New Haven	23	Sweet Land of Rest	87	Will you go	86
Ninety-sixth Psalm	312	Sweet Rest	76	Wilmot	295
No Sorrow there	54			Wilt thou not visit	305
Nuremburg	293	TALMAR	85	Windham	250
		Ten Commandments	313	With me abide	20
OAK	61	Thanksgiving	315	Woodland	58
Oh! how I love	19	That blessed Name	306	Woodstock	222
Oh! why should	215	That will be joyful	164	Woodworth	32
Old Hundredth	240	The Convert	302	Work, for the night	139
Olive's Brow	253	The Future Rest	106	Working for the	123
Olivet	261	The Farther Shore	83		
Olmutz	274	The Golden Shore	194	Zephyr	247
Ortonville	211			Zion	47

Index of Hymns.

	PAGE		PAGE
A BEAUTIFUL land	186	Come, Holy Spirit, come	236
Abide with me	20	Come, Holy Spirit, heavenly	210
A charge to keep	272	Come, humble sinner	214
A crown of glory	170	Come, let us tune	233
Ah! this heart	73	Come, let us join with one	231
Alas! and did my	14	Come, said Jesus'	242
All hail the power	208	Come, sound his praise	270
Am I a soldier	228	Come, O thou	212
And are we yet	234	Come, thou fount	27
And can I yet	274	Come unto Jesus	188
And did the Holy	218	Come, ye sinners	85
And God spake	313	Come, ye disconsolate	23
And may I still	54		
Arise, my soul	31	*DEAR brother	310
Arm of the Lord	258	Dear comrade	193
Asleep in Jesus	262	Dear is the spot	232
As God has kindly	134	Dear refuge	223
Awake, and sing	270	Deem not that they	257
Awake, Jerusalem	268	Depth of mercy	91
Awake, my soul	75	Delay not	300
Away with our sorrow	190	Did Christ o'er sinners	278
		Disciples of Jesus	116
BEAUTIFUL cross	42		
Beautiful Zion	77		
Before Jehovah's	240	EARTH's stormy night	90
Behold a stranger	243		
Be still, my heart	249	FADE, fade each	45
Blessed bible	158	Far from these scenes	255
Blessed are the poor	314	Far from my thoughts	256
Bless, O my soul	238	Father, I stretch	216
Blest are the sons	236	Father of love	22
Blest be the tie	234	Forever here my	236
Blow ye the trumpet	30	Forever with the Lord	100
Bright home of	154	From all that dwell	237
Burst, ye emerald	70	From every stormy	248
By cool Siloam's	223	From Greenland's	51
CENTRE of my hopes	91	GIVE me the wings	152
Churches below	41	Glory to thee. my	248
Children of the	204	God bless our native	299
Christ, the Lord	294	God bless our schools	299
Cling to the mighty	118	God has said	162
Come, come to Jesus	9	God is the refuge	239
Come, brethren	76	Go and tell Jesus	196
Come, let us join	209	Great God of	264
Come, Holy Ghost	236	Guide me, O thou	71

*Listen, the Master beseecheth...... 310

Hallowed Songs, Revised. 319

	PAGE		PAGE
HAIL! my ever blessed	81	Jesus, my all	55
Hark! my soul	290	Jesus shall reign	2,1
Hark, the gospel	156	Jesus the water	133
Hark, the herald	294	Jesus, where'er	254
Hark, what means	40	Joyfully, joyfully	172
Hasten, Lord	82	Just as I am	32
Hasten, sinner	288		
Hear, O sinner	34	LAND ahead	80
He leadeth me	178	Lord, dismiss us	4J
Here will I ever	281	Lord, how secure	24.
Holy Spirit, faithful	7	Lord, I believe	232
Ho! every one	252	Lord, I hear	15
How beauteous are	280	Lord, in the morning	225
How blest the righteous	256	Love divine	83
How blest the sacred	260	Let me go	112
How gentle God's	282	Listen to the gentle	85
How happy every	226	Long my spirit	140
How pleased and	301		
How pleasant thus	161	MAJESTIC sweetness	211
How sad our state	216	More like Jesus	97
How sweet the hour	216	Morning breaks upon	295
How sweet the name	219	Must Jesus bear	218
How tedious and	60	My body, soul	56
How vain is all	2.6	My country, 'tis of	208
		My days are gliding	72
I AM waiting	21	My faith looks up	23
I gave my life	308	My God, how endless	263
I have entered	132	My God, the spring	251
I hear the Saviour	296	My heavenly home	93
I love to steal awhile	222	My heart is fixed	240
I love thy kingdom	277	My latest sun	174
I love to think	50	My soul, be on	287
I'm a pilgrim	64	My soul, repeat	271
I'm but a stranger	61		
I'm kneeling	136	NAUGHT of merit	16
I'm not ashamed	217	Nearer, my God	29
I'm trying to	124		
I'm working for	128	O COME, let us worship	314
I now have found	12	Of him who did	96
In mercy, Lord	224	O happy day	79
I stood outside	130	Oh! come to Jesus	205
In the christian's	166	Oh! could I find	210
In the cross	17	Oh! could I speak	38
I thirst, thou	260	Oh, do not let	8
I love to tell the story	184	Oh, for a closer	235
I was a wandering	37	Oh, for a faith	220
I will sing	110	Oh, for a glance	265
I will sing you a	114	Oh, for a heart	221
I would not live	71	Oh, for a thousand	263
		Oh, for the death	276
JESUS, and shall	266	Oh, how happy are	302
Jesus, I my	39	Oh, how I love Jesus	19
Jesus, let thy	36	Oh, how sweet when	41
Jesus, light of	306	Oh, if my house	112
Jesus, lover of	291	Oh, let not your	65
Jesus loves me	46	Oh, that I could	273

	PAGE		PAGE
Oh, that my load	251	The morning light	52
Oh, there is a river	13	The pearly gate	89
Oh, what amazing	214	The pity of the Lord	273
Oh, what are you	168	The praying spirit	232
Oh, when shall	59	There are angels	92
Oh, where shall rest	285	There is a fountain	10
Oh, why should gloomy	215	There is an hour	43, 58
O Lord, thy work	276	There is a land	229
Only waiting till	148	There's a beautiful	204
On Jordan's stormy	228	There's a light	176
On the cross	104	These are the crowns	104
On the mountain top	47	Think of a home over there	202
O sing unto the Lord	312	This is not my place	198
Our Father, which	303	Though troubles assail	63
Out on an ocean	69	Thus far the Lord	254
		'Tis midnight	253
PILGRIM, burdened	18	'Tis religion	302
Plunged in a gulf	220	To-day the Saviour	187
Praise God	237	To the hall of the	57
Praise to God	293	Triumphant Zion	259
Praise ye the Lord	315		
Prayer is appointed	244		
Prayer is the soul's	233	WATCHMAN, tell me	53
		We are out	194
REMEMBER thy	213	Weep for the fallen	146
Return, my soul	258	Welcome, sweet	282
Rock of Ages	304	We're traveling home	86
		We shall meet	106
SAVIOUR, like	28	We shall sleep	126
Saviour, visit	95	We've listed in	160
Say, sinner, hath	242	What various	244
See, Israel's gentle	224	When I can read	150
Shall we gather	108	When I survey	261
Shall we meet	78	When on the ocean	62
Show pity, Lord	250	When shall we meet	66
Silently the shades	289	When thou, my righteous	26
Sinner, the voice	212	When thy mortal	200
Sister, thou wast	67	When we pass	83
Softly on the breath	182	When two or three	315
Soldiers of Christ	280	Where do you	121
Soon may the last	255	While life prolongs	232
Sow in the morn	274	Who are these	68
Stand up for Jesus	84	Why do we mourn	227
Stand up, my soul	264	Why should our tears	232
Stay, thou insulted	267	Why should we boast	230
Sun of my soul	209	Why should we start	247
Swell the anthem	292	Wilt thou not visit	305
Sweetest note in	297	Work, for the night	120
Sweet hour of prayer	25	Wouldst thou be	11
Sweet is the work	266		
Sweet land of rest	87		
Sweet was the time	230	YES, let our	98
		Yes, my native	24
TELL me the old, old	144	Ye soldiers of	180
That awful day	234	Ye wretched, starving	23
The day is past	279		
The day of wrath	250	ZION stands with	49

www.ingramcontent.com/pod-product-compliance
Lightning Source LLC
Chambersburg PA
CBHW022019240426
43667CB00042B/957